CADOGAN

Dana Facaros & Michael Pauls

W9-AUI-136

Rome
Padua Assisi

Cadogan Guides
West End House, 11 Hills Place, London W1R 1AH
becky.kendall@morrispub.co.uk

The Globe Pequot Press
6 Business Park Road, PO Box 833, Old Saybrook,
Connecticut 06475–0833

Copyright © Dana Facaros and Michael Pauls 1999
Updated by Dana Facaros, Michael Pauls and Jon Eldan
Illustrations © Horatio Monteverde 1996

Book and cover design by Animage

Cover photographs © front: John Ferro Sims
                             back:

Maps © Cadogan Guides, drawn by Map Creation Ltd

Editorial Director: Vicki Ingle
Series Editor: Linda McQueen

Editor: Catherine Charles
Proofreading: Patrick Alexander
Specialist reader: Emma Winkley
Indexing: Isobel McLean
Production: Book Production Services

A catalogue record for this book is available from the British Library

ISBN 1-86011-952-2

The author and publishers have made every effort to ensure the accuracy of the
information in this book at the time of going to press. However they cannot accept
any responsibility for any loss, injury or inconvenience resulting from the use of
information contained in this guide.

Printed and bound in Great Britain by The Cromwell Press Ltd.

About the Authors

Dana Facaros and Michael Pauls are professional travel writers, and have now written over 30 Cadogan Guides. For three years they and their two children, Jackson and Lily, lived in a tiny Italian hilltop village, and they reckon they could whip 98 per cent of the world's non-Italian population in Italian Trivial Pursuit (except for the sport questions). They now live in Ireland.

About the Updaters

Jon Eldan studied history and baked bread in Berkeley, California before travelling to Europe in 1994, where he met Carla Lionello (a pastry chef from Venice) in a restaurant kitchen. They live in Rome and travel together.

Please help us to keep this guide up to date

We have done our best to ensure that the information in this guide is correct at the time of going to press. But places and facilities are constantly changing, and standards and prices in hotels and restaurants fluctuate. We would be delighted to receive any comments concerning existing entries or omissions, as well as suggestions for new features. Authors of the most helpful letters may be offered a copy of the Cadogan Guide of their choice.

Contents

Art and Architecture 49–56

Rome 57–142

Padua 143–66

Assisi 167–88

Other Pilgrim Destinations Around Italy 189–204

Language 205–210

Further Reading 211

Maps and Plans

The very first guidebooks, works of the Middle Ages, were written for pilgrims. Books such as the 12th-century *Mirabilia Urbis Romae*, the 'Wonders of the City of Rome', catalogued the ruins of antiquity along with the tombs of the Christian martyrs, adding in a good helping of well-cooked legends and snippets of classical history. The *Mirabilia*, full of folktales and wide-eyed medieval wonder, does its best to entertain, but some guidebook writers of the age expected a lot more from their readers than we do now. When the *Mirabilia* was still in the scriptorium, the Crusaders had

Introduction

just reconquered the Holy Land, and a Frenchman named Jacques de Vitry was writing a guidebook called the Jerusalem History, in which he complained about some of his fellow Christians in Palestine: 'Light-hearted and inquisitive persons go on pilgrimages not out of devotion, but out of mere curiosity and love of novelty. All they want to do is investigate the absurd, exaggerated stories they have heard...'

In the year 1336, an Italian traveller—none other than the poet Petrarch—turned up in a Provençal village looking for a guide to take him up to the summit of Mont Ventoux. The villagers were certainly amused at this rare soul, a foreigner who had come to climb a mountain just for the fun of it. As Petrarch told the story, sitting above the clouds on his mountaintop, he remembered that it was ten years to the day that he had left his native town to go wandering. He carried Augustine's *Confessions* with him that day, and he chanced to open it and fell upon the passage: '...and men go forth, and admire lofty mountains and broad seas, and roaring torrents, and the course of the stars, and forget their own selves while doing so.' An uncomfortable thought, for a medieval Christian and poet. Petrarch climbed down, and the next day he started off back home to Italy.

Of all the pilgrims who walked the roads of Europe in those days, not many may have stopped to climb a mountain, but very few, most likely, were so pious that they would not spare a moment for a glance at the Colosseum or the Pantheon or the other wonders of the ancient world. The Age of Faith had its spiritual ideals, but it was also an age of rapidly expanding minds, of new growth and new ideas, one where the sacred and the secular loved to intertwine, just as they do in the scriptural episodes and scenes of worldly life and fantasy juxtaposed in stone on the portals of the great cathedrals.

In this guidebook, prepared for pilgrims and travellers in the Great Jubilee year of 2000, we hope we may recapture some of this spirit. Pope John Paul II has expressed his wish that this Jubilee year will be celebrated by every Catholic, in every parish around the globe. Nevertheless, in the Holy Year of 2000 the eyes of the Catholic world will be on Italy, and the number of visitors expected is estimated between 20 and 30 million. Throughout the year, events are planned for every city and village in the nation, though naturally the most important will be in Rome. Along with the Vatican, the Roman authorities have been working feverishly to get things ready for the Holy Year. Many of the great monuments have been cleaned and repaired, including St John Lateran, the Pantheon, the Forum, Bernini's Triton Fountain, the Palazzo Quirinale and the Vittoriano. Places that have been closed to the public for years have been restored and reopened: Nero's Domus Aurea, and the collections of the Palazzo Borghese and the Palazzo Altemps. Similar efforts have been under way at Padua and Assisi, at San Giovanni Rotondo in Puglia, and in the other pilgrimage sites all over Italy. Good luck, then, and a safe and happy voyage to all. May all find exactly what they are looking for.

The Via Francigena

In Spain, for the pilgrimage to Santiago de Compostela, they have an elaborate and growing network of hostels and assistance for pilgrims. There certainly is a need for it; the crowds of pilgrims, mostly happy young folk, tramping or bicycling across northern Spain with their hats and cockle-shell badges, make a surprising and gratifying sight. Nothing like this exists anywhere else in western Europe, but anyone who might be travelling to Italy along the old Roman or medieval routes might take some time along the way to consider what the journey was like for people long ago. In Italy, the path for pilgrims coming down from the north carried the ancient name *Via Francigena*, the 'way of the Franks' (that pious nation did send especially large numbers in Charlemagne's day, but to a medieval Italian foreigners were all barbarians anyhow, and they might as well all have been Franks). Another name was the *Via Romea*—a *romeo* was a pilgrim bound for Rome.

In Britain pilgrims would collect at **Canterbury**, crossing over from Dover to Calais and following the main route across France, passing through Rheims, Besançon and Lausanne, and reaching Italy through the **St Bernard Pass**. From there, the Via Francigena did not always follow a precise route; some roads were better at certain times of the year, and side routes might attract pilgrims in times of strife, or where some charitable order had opened a new hospice. Generally, the path went through **Aosta**, **Vercelli**, **Pavia**, **Piacenza** and

Parma, crossing the Apennines by various routes and entering Tuscany near **Lucca**. That was the hard part—think of the travails of the old pilgrims as you pass over their routes on the A15, that remarkable motorway that seems to be made entirely of bridges and tunnels. In Tuscany the travelling was easy and the hospices many and well-endowed. In no time at all you would be through **Siena** and on your way to **Rome**.

One of the earliest accounts of the trip is the travel diary of an Archbishop of Canterbury, named Sigeric, in the year 994. Sigeric doesn't have much to say about the places he passed through, but then he seems to have been a man with his mind firmly fixed on business: 50 days to Rome (no doubt on horseback), 50 days back—and only three days in the city to receive his investiture from the pope and see the sights.

In the Middle Ages pilgrims did not commonly enter Rome by the main route, the Via Flaminia, where later popes would create their grand entrance to the city at Piazza del Popolo. From Viterbo they would follow the Via Cassia

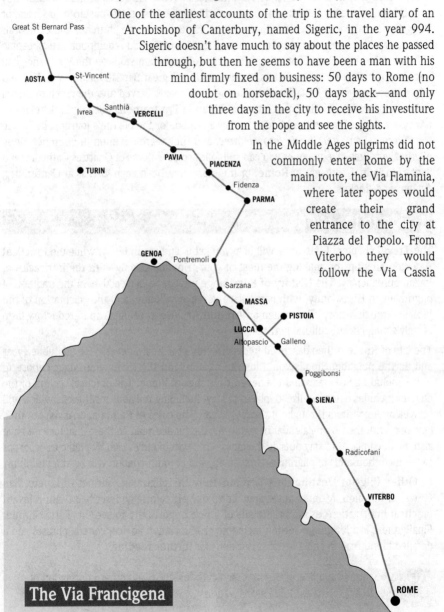

The Via Francigena

3

southwards and pass into Rome on what is now **Via Trionfale**, around the back side of Monte Mario, north of the Vatican. Here they would enjoy their first glimpse of the city—and a splendid panoramic view it is, roughly where Parco Mellina is today.

Pilgrims following the old routes to Rome will not find much to remind them of the journeys of their medieval forebears. The old hospices have mostly disappeared, or exist only as half-forgotten ruins. Remains of a few can still be seen, as at **Altopascio** near Lucca, or **Poggibonsi**, between Lucca and Siena. Of course the art of the churches and cathedrals remains, and we can reflect on their sculpted themes of sin and redemption just as people did when they were new. Sometimes, churches at important stops on the Via Francigena were decorated partly with pilgrims in mind, as in the great Baptistry at **Parma**. And you might keep an eye out for labyrinths, like the small mazes carved into the porch of **Lucca** Cathedral, San Michele in **Pavia**, and San Pietro in **Pontremoli**. The labyrinth seems to have been understood in the Middle Ages as a symbol for the pilgrim's journey. In France they were called *chemins de Jerusalemme*, and they were common in churches along pilgrimage routes, like the ones you can still follow on the floors of Chartres Cathedral and Santa Maria in Trastevere in **Rome**, or the many that have been lost, as at Canterbury, Amiens and Rheims.

Guide to the Guide

The **Travel** chapter of this guide will help you get to and around Italy, while the **Practical A–Z** contains tips on making the most of your trip, and coping with the intricacies of Italian bureaucracy. The **History of Pilgrimage** provides a perspective on the tradition of pilgrimage in Christianity, with particular reference to Rome, and the celebration of the Jubilee through history. The section on **Art and Architecture** offers an introductory taste of Italy's magnificent cultural heritage.

The city of **Rome** is then described in detail, with a calendar of events for the Jubilee year and all the neighbourhoods you'll love to explore and the sights you might choose to visit—including St Peter's and the Seven Churches of Rome. The practical section of the chapter includes extensive lists of places to stay, including religious institutions which will be welcoming visitors throughout the Holy Year. The cities of **Padua** and **Assisi** are then covered, with their own calendar of events for the Jubilee year. In these chapters we have also included places to stay outside the cities—but within easy reach by public transport or car—since thousands of pilgrims are expected, and accommodation will be at a premium.

In **Other Pilgrim Destinations Around Italy** the pilgrimage shrines of Loreto, San Giovanni Rotondo, Monte Sant'Angelo and Pompei are briefly described (with relevant practical information) as well as details of a rare opportunity to see the Turin Shroud. Finally there is a **language** section including pronunciation advice, general phrases and a detailed menu reader; and a list of suggestions for **further reading**.

⊕ Throughout the guide, this symbol indicates practical and other information of particular relevance to the Jubilee celebrations.

Travel

By Air

From the UK and Ireland

Flying is obviously the quickest and most painless way of getting to Italy from the UK. There are direct flights from over half a dozen British airports; Rome and Venice have the greatest choice of year-round services, though there are also flights to Perugia, Verona and Bologna. Scheduled services are, in the main, more expensive than charters although there are a couple of low-cost airlines whose scheduled flight prices can compete with the very lowest charter fares (*see* below).

major carriers

> **Alitalia**: London, ✆ (020) 7602 7111; Dublin, ✆ (01) 844 6035.
> **British Airways**: ✆ (0345) 222 111.
> **KLM UK**: ✆ (0870) 507 4074.
> **Meridiana**: ✆ (020) 7839 2222.
> **Sabena**: ✆ (020) 8780 1444.
> **Lufthansa**: ✆ (0345) 737 747.
> **Aer Lingus**: Dublin, ✆ (01) 705 3333; Belfast, ✆ (0645) 737 747.

Return fares vary greatly, depending on the season. The best-value deals are usually **Apex** or **SuperApex** fares, for which you must book seven days ahead, and stay a Saturday night in Italy—no alterations or refunds are possible without high penalties. Return scheduled fares range typically from around £200 off-season; midsummer fares will probably be well over £250. Full fares on the major carriers can be as high as £500. There are cheaper fares on offer (around £140), but these often have restrictions and involve flying via another European destination.

low-cost carriers

Go: ✆ (0845) 605 4321, a branch of British Airways, operates flights between London Stansted and Bologna, Venice and Rome.

Ryanair: ✆ (0541) 569 569, offer flights from Stansted to Treviso.

charter flights

Many inexpensive charter flights are available to popular Italian destinations in summer, though you are unlikely to find the sort of rock-bottom bargains as, say, to Spain. You may find cheaper fares by combing the small ads in the travel pages, or from a specialist agent (use a reputable ABTA-registered one), which offer good student and youth rates too. The main problems with cheaper flights tend to be inconvenient or unreliable flight schedules, and booking restrictions. Take good travel insurance, however cheap your ticket is.

discount agencies and youth fares

Italy Sky Shuttle, 227 Shepherd's Bush Rd, London W6 7AS, ✆ (020) 8748 1333.
Italflights, 125 High Holborn, London WC1V 6QA, ✆ (020) 7405 6771.
Italy Sky Bus, 37 Harley Street, London W1N 1DB, ✆ (020) 7631 3444.

Trailfinders, 215 Kensington High Street, London W8, ℘ (020) 7937 5400.
Budget Travel, 134 Lower Baggot Street, Dublin 2, ℘ (01) 661 1866.
Untied Travel, Stillorgan Bowl, Stillorgan, Dublin, ℘ (01) 288 4346/7.

Besides saving 25 per cent on regular flights, young people under 26 have the choice of flying on special discount charters.

Campus Travel, 52 Grosvenor Gardens, SW1, ℘ (020) 7730 3402, with branches at most UK universities; *www.campustravel.co.uk*
STA, 74 and 86 Old Brompton Rd, London SW7, ℘ (020) 7361 6161, and other branches.
USIT, Aston Quay, Dublin 2, ℘ (01) 679 8833, and other branches in Ireland.

From Mainland Europe

Air travel between Italy and other parts of Europe can be expensive, especially for short hops. Some airlines (**Alitalia, Qantas, Air France**, etc.) offer excellent rates on the European stages of intercontinental flights, and Italy is an important touchdown for many long-haul services to the Middle or Far East. Amsterdam, Paris and Athens are good centres to find cheap flights.

From the USA and Canada

The main Italian air gateways for direct flights from North America are Rome and Milan, though, if you're doing a grand tour, check fares to other European destinations (Paris or Amsterdam, for example) which may well be cheaper.

Alitalia: (USA) ℘ (800) 223 5730; (Canada) ℘ (800) 563 5954.
British Airways: ℘ (800) 247 9297.
Delta: ℘ (800) 241 414.
Air Canada: ℘ (800) 555 1212.
KLM: ℘ (800) 361 5330, operates from Toronto and Montreal.

It may be worth catching a cheap flight to London (New York–London fares are always very competitive) and then flying on from there. Prices are rather more from Canada, so you may prefer to fly from the States.

charters, discounts and special deals

For discounted flights, try the small ads in newspaper travel pages (e.g. *New York Times, Chicago Tribune, Toronto Globe & Mail*). Numerous travel clubs and agencies also specialize in discount fares, but may require an annual membership fee.

discount agencies and youth fares

Airhitch, 2472 Broadway, Suite 200, New York, NY 10025, ℘ (212) 864 2000.
Council Travel, 205 E 42nd Street, New York, NY 10017, ℘ (800) 743 1823. Major specialists in student and charter flights; branches all over the USA.
Last Minute Travel Club, 132 Brookline Avenue, Boston, MA 02215, ℘ (800) 527 8646.
Now Voyager, 74 Varick St, Suite 307, New York, NY 10013, ℘ (212) 431 1616, for courier flights.

Board Courier Services, ✆ (514) 633 0740, for courier flights from Canada.

STA, 48 East 11th Street, New York, NY 10003, ✆ (212) 627 3111, or freephone ✆ (800) 777 0112.

Travel Cuts 187 College Street, Toronto, Ontario M5T 1P7, ✆ (416) 979 2406. Canada's largest student travel specialists; branches in most provinces.

By Rail

From the UK and Europe

A train journey from London to Rome used to be something of a nightmare involving ferries and station changes and taking the best part of 24 hours. This experience can still be repeated, should you so desire it, and will cost you around £160 second-class return plus an extra £14 for a couchette. There is, however, following the opening of the Channel Tunnel and the construction of new fast rail networks throughout Europe, an alternative. Take a Eurostar to Paris and a high-speed Eurocity train to Italy and your journey could be reduced by as much as 12 hours. Unfortunately the price will increase to around £500. Train travel, at whatever speed, has its benefits—the opportunity it gives travellers to watch the changing scenery, to acclimatize themselves to new surroundings and take time to prepare for their arrival in a new country—but in an age of low-cost airlines, it is not much of an economy.

Rail Europe Travel Centre, (UK) 179 Piccadilly, London W1, ✆ (08705) 848 848; (USA) 226–230 Westchester Ave, White Plains, NY 10604, ✆ (914) 682 2999, or ✆ (800) 438 7245.

Eurostar, EPS House, Waterloo Station, London SE1, ✆ (0990) 186 186.

International Rail Centre, London Victoria Station, adjacent to Platform 2.

Eurotrain, 52 Grosvenor Gardens, London SW1, ✆ (020) 7730 3402.

Wasteels Travel, (UK) adjacent Platform 2, London Victoria Station, ✆ (020) 7834 7066; (USA) 5728 Major Boulevard, Suite 308, Orlando, FL 32819.

CIT, (UK) Marco Polo House, 3–5 Lansdowne Rd, Croydon, Surrey, ✆ (020) 8686 5533 (60p a minute), 🖷 (020) 8681 1712; (USA) 15 West 44th Street, 10th Floor, New York, NY 10036, ✆ (800) 248 7245, 🖷 (888) FAX CIT; (Canada) 1450 City Councillors St, Suite 750, Montreal H3A 2E6, ✆ (514) 845 4310.

The **Orient Express** deserves a special mention: it whirls you from London through Paris, Zurich, Innsbruck and Verona to Venice in a cocoon of traditional twenties and thirties glamour, with beautifully restored Pullman/wagon-lits. It's fiendishly expensive—and quite unforgettable for a once-in-a-lifetime treat. Current prices (including meals) are about £1095 per person (London–Venice one-way). Several operators offer packages including smart Venice hotels and return flights home. Contact **Venice-Simplon Orient Express,** Sea Container House, 20 Upper Ground, London SE1, ✆ (020) 7805 5100.

Interail (UK) or **Eurail** passes (USA/Canada) give unlimited travel for under-26s throughout Europe for one or two months. Various other cheap youth fares (BIJ tickets etc.) are also available; organize these through Rail Europe before you leave home.

If you are just planning to see Italy, inclusive rail passes may not be worthwhile. Fares on FS (*Ferrovie dello Stato*), the Italian State Railway, are among the lowest (km for km) in Europe. A month's full Interail pass costs £259 (£349 for those over 26), though you can now buy cheaper zonal passes covering three or four countries only. If you intend travelling extensively by train, one of the special Italian tourist passes may be a better bet (*see* 'Getting Around').

A convenient pocket-sized **timetable** detailing all the main and secondary Italian railway lines is now available in the UK, costing £6 (plus 50p postage). Contact **Accommodation Line Ltd**, 46 Maddox St, London W1; **Y Knot Travel**, Morley House, 1st Floor, 314–320 Regent Street, London W1; or **Italwings**, Travel & Accommodation, Linen Hall, Suite 217, 162–68 Regent Street, London W1R 5TB. If you wait until you arrive in Italy, however, you can pick up the Italian timetable (in two volumes) at any station for about L4,500 each.

By Road

by bus and coach

Eurolines, London Victoria Coach Station, ✆ (0990) 808 080, are booked in the UK through National Express (return ticket London–Rome £135; single £95; taking a good 34 hours). Within Italy you can obtain more information on long-distance bus services from any CIT office (*see* above).

by car

Italy is the best part of 24 hours' driving time from the UK, even if you stick to fast toll roads. Calais–Florence via Nancy, Lucerne and Lugano is about 1042km. The most scenic and hassle-free route is via the Alps but, if you take a route through Switzerland, expect to pay for the privilege (around £14 or SFr30 for motorway use). In winter the passes may be closed and you will have to stick to those expensive tunnels (one-way tolls range from about L37,000 for a small car). You can avoid some of the driving by putting your car on the train. **Express Sleeper Cars** run to Milan from Paris or Boulogne (infrequently in winter). The **Italian Auto Club** (ACI), ✆ 06 44 77, offers breakdown assistance.

To bring a GB-registered car into Italy, you need a **vehicle registration document**, **full driving licence** and **insurance papers** (these must be carried at all times when driving). Non-EU citizens should preferably have an **international driving licence** which has an Italian translation incorporated. Your vehicle should display a nationality plate indicating its country of registration. Before travelling, check everything is in perfect order. Minor infringements like worn tyres or burnt-out sidelights can cost you dear in any country. A **red triangular hazard sign** is obligatory; also recommended are a spare set of bulbs, a first-aid kit and a fire extinguisher. Spare parts for non-Italian cars can be difficult to find, especially Japanese models. Before crossing the border, fill her up; *benzina* is very expensive in Italy.

For more information on driving in Italy, contact the **AA**, ✆ (0990) 500 600, or **RAC**, ✆ (0800) 550 550 in the UK, and **AAA**, ✆ (407) 444 4000 in the USA.

Passports and Visas

EU nationals with a valid passport can enter and stay in Italy as long as they like. Citizens of the USA, Canada, Australia and New Zealand need only a valid passport to stay up to three months in Italy, unless they get a visa in advance from the Italian embassy or consulate in order to stay longer.

UK, 38 Eaton Place, London SW1X, ✆ (020) 7235 9371; 32 Melville Street, Edinburgh EH3 7HA, ✆ (0131) 226 3631; 2111 Piccadilly, Manchester, ✆ (0161) 236 3024.

Ireland, 63–65 Northumberland Road, Dublin, ✆ (01) 660 1744; 7 Richmond Park, Stranmillis, Belfast BT9 5EF, ✆ (01232) 668 854.

USA, 690 Park Avenue, New York, NY, ✆ (212) 737 9100; 12400 Wilshire Blvd, Suite 300, Los Angeles, CA, ✆ (213) 820 0622.

Canada, 136 Beverley Street, Toronto, ✆ (416) 977 1566.

Australia, Level 45, The Gateway Building, Macquarie Place, Circular Quay, Sydney 2000, NSW, ✆ (02) 2478 442.

New Zealand, 34 Grant Rd, Thorndon, Wellington, ✆ (04) 7473 5339.

France, 47 rue de Varennes, 73343 Paris, ✆ 01 45 44 38 90.

Germany, Karl Finkelnburgstrasse 49–51, 5300 Bonn 2, ✆ (0228) 82 00 60.

Netherlands, Herengracht 609, 1017 CE Amsterdam, ✆ (3120) 624 0043.

By law you should register with the police within eight days of your arrival in Italy. In practice this is done automatically for most visitors when they check in at their first hotel.

Customs

EU nationals over the age of 17 can now import a limitless amount of goods for personal use. Non-EU nationals have to pass through the Italian Customs which are usually benign. How the frontier police manage to recruit such ugly, mean-looking characters to hold the sub-machine guns and dogs from such a good-looking population is a mystery, but they'll let you be if you don't look suspicious and haven't brought along more than 200 cigarettes or 100 cigars, or not more than a litre of hard drink or three bottles of wine, a couple of cameras, a movie camera, 10 rolls of film for each, a tape-recorder, radio, record-player, one canoe less than 18ft, sports equipment for personal use, and one TV (though you'll have to pay for a licence for it at Customs). You can take the same items listed above home with you without hassle—but not of course your British pet. USA citizens may return with $400 worth of merchandise—keep your receipts. Pets must always be accompanied by a bilingual Certificate of Health from your local Veterinary Inspector.

Currency

There are no limits to how much money you bring into Italy: legally you may not export more than L20,000,000 in Italian banknotes, a sum unlikely to trouble many of us, though officials rarely check.

A selection of companies is listed below. They specialize in tours to popular pilgrimage sites, and some have planned tours to coincide with the celebration of the Jubilee and Holy Year in 2000. Not all of them are necessarily ABTA-bonded; we recommend you check before booking. It's also worth checking the travel sections of the Sunday papers, or contacting your local diocesan office for details of pilgrimage tours organized in your area.

in the UK

Alternative Travel Group, 69–71 Banbury Road, Oxford OX2 6PE, ✆ (01865) 315 678; beautifully organized walking tours, including two special walks for the Millennium: the Via Francigena, a 23-day trip, following the ancient route from Canterbury to Rome; and Paths to Rome, an 18-day trip following pilgrim paths from Siena to Rome.

St Peter's Pilgrims, 87a Rushey Green, London SE6 4AF, ✆ (020) 8244 8844, ✆ (020) 8697 2466, *www.stpeter.co.uk*; tours to Rome and Assisi.

Tangney Tours, Pilgrim House, Station Court, Borough Green, Kent TN15 8AF, ✆ (0800) 783 1178; tours to Rome and Turin.

Kensington Travel, 26 Thackeray Street, London W8 5ET, ✆ (020) 7937 9861; Catholic pilgrimages to Italy and elsewhere.

Pilgrimage Options, ✆ (01706) 713 966

Rosary Pilgrimage Apostolate, 12 Farleigh Cres, Lawns, Swindon SN3 1JY, ✆ (01793) 422 714; tours to Rome, Padua, Assisi, San Giovanni Rotondo, Turin.

Pax Travel, 152–156 Kentish Town Road, London NW1 9QB, ✆ (020) 7485 3003, ✆ (020) 7485 3006; tailor-made pilgrimages to Rome and Assisi.

McCabe Pilgrimages, 53–55 Balham Hill, London SW12 9DR, ✆ (0800) 980 8188; pilgrimages to Italy.

in the USA/Canada

Unitours, 411 West Putnam Avenue, Greenwich, CT ✉ 06830, ✆ (203) 629 3900, ✆ (800) 777 7432, or ✆ (203) 629 1905; special Jubilee pilgrimages concentrating heavily on Rome, with trips to Assisi and Florence.

Catholic Pilgrimage Tours, 35 South 13th Street, Allentown, PA ✉ 18102, ✆ (800) 455 5514, or ✆ (610) 434 3201, ✆ (610) 435 3874; thirty special tours already set including: Holyweek in Rome and the Holy Land; Shrines of Italy.

Jubilee Promotions Itc., 7231 Eastern Ave, Suite B177, Las Vegas, NV ✉ 89119, ✆ (702) 263 9540, ✆ (702) 263 9530; touring Italy for many important dates on the Holy Year Calendar including: World Youth Day and Opening of the Holy Door.

ITS International Tours, 3013 20th Street Suite B, Metairie, LA ✉ 70002, ✆ (800) 892 7729, or ✆ (504) 831 0843, ✆ (504) 837 2920; customized tours all over Italy.

Best Catholic Pilgrimages, 1 East Superior Street, Suite 510, Chicago IL ✉ 60611, ✆ (312) 944 3958, 🖷 (312) 944 3352; tailor-made pilgrimages and set itineraries e.g. Rome for the Millennium; the Holy Lands for the Pope's Jubilee visit in March.

Inspirational Tours, Inc., 5433 Westheimer, Suite 600, Houston, TX ✉ 77056, ✆ (800) 231 6287, or ✆ (713) 961 2785, 🖷 (713) 961 7496; especially Assisi.

Franciscan Pilgrimage Programs, 1648 S. 37th Street, Milwaukee, WI ✉ 53215-1724, ✆ (414) 383 9870, 🖷 (414) 383 0335; emphasis on Franciscan spirituality—short and 28-day pilgrimages. Especially Assisi and Rome.

206 Tours, 325 Middle Country Road, Smithtown, NY ✉ 11787, ✆ (800) 206 8687, 🖷 (516) 361 3682; set programmes: great Jubilee trip to Rome with excursions to Florence and Assisi; custom-made tours for groups of 20 plus.

Family Travel, 424 Bridge Street, Ashland OR ✉ 97520, ✆ (800) 826 7165, or ✆ (541) 488 3074, 🖷 (541) 488 3067; total package tours for any sized family or group.

Little Flower Tours and Travel, 145 Fieldstone Road, Staten Island, New York 10314, *www.littleflowertours.com*

Getting Around

Italy has an excellent network of airports, railways, highways and byways and you'll find getting around fairly easy—until one union or another takes it into its head to go on strike (to be fair they rarely do it during the high holiday season). There's plenty of talk about passing a law to regulate strikes, but it won't happen soon if ever. Instead, learn to recognize the word in Italian: *sciopero* (SHO-per-o), and do as the Romans do—quiver with resignation. There's always a day or two's notice, and strikes usually last only a day, just long enough to throw a spanner in the works if you have to catch a plane. Keep your ears open and watch for notices posted in the stations.

By Air

Air traffic within Italy is intense, with up to ten flights a day on popular routes. Domestic flights are handled by Alitalia, ATI (its internal arm) or Avianova. Air travel makes most sense when hopping between north and south. Shorter journeys are often just as quick (and usually much less expensive) by train or even bus, if you take travelling to the airport and check-in times into account.

Mainland cities with airports include Ancona, Bari, Bergamo, Bologna, Brindisi, Florence, Genoa, Lamezia Terme (near Catanzaro), Milan, Naples, Parma, Pisa, Reggio Calabria, Turin, Trieste, Venice and Verona, all of which have direct flights to and from Rome.

Domestic flight costs are comparable to those in other European countries, and a complex system of discounts is available. Each airport has a bus terminal in the city; ask about schedules as you purchase your ticket to avoid hefty taxi fares. Baggage allowances vary between airlines. Tickets can be bought at CIT offices and other large travel agencies.

FS national train information: © 1478 888 088 (*open 7am–9pm*);
www.fs-on-line.com

Italy's national railway, the **FS** (*Ferrovie dello Stato*) is well run, inexpensive and often a pleasure to ride; some of the trains are sleek and high-tech, but much of the rolling stock hasn't been changed for fifty years. Possible FS unpleasantnesses you may encounter, besides a strike (and there is supposed to be a moratorium on strikes during 2000), are delays, crowding (especially at weekends and in the summer), and crime on overnight trains, where someone rifles your bags while you sleep. Reserve a seat in advance (*fare una prenotazione*): the fee is small and can save you hours standing in some train corridor. On the more expensive trains, and for sleepers and couchettes on overnight trains, **reservations** are mandatory. Check when you purchase your ticket that the date is correct; tickets are only valid the day they're purchased unless you specify otherwise.

It is easier to buy **tickets** at a travel agent in one of the city centres. Fares are strictly determined by the kilometres travelled. The system is computerized and runs smoothly, at least until you try to get a reimbursement for an unused ticket (usually not worth the trouble). Be sure you ask which platform (*binario*) your train arrives at; the big permanent boards in the stations are not always correct. Always remember to stamp your ticket (*convalidare*) in the not-very-obvious yellow machines at the head of the platform before boarding the train. Failure to do so could result in a fine. If you get on a train without a ticket you can buy one from the conductor, with an added 20 per cent penalty. You can also pay a conductor to move up to first class or get a couchette, if there are places available.

There is a fairly straightforward **hierarchy of trains**. At the bottom of the pyramid is the humble, sometimes excruciatingly slow, *Locale* (euphemistically known sometimes as an *Accelerato*) which often stops even where there's no station in sight. When you're checking the schedules, beware of what may look like the first train to your destination—if it's a *Locale*, it will be the last to arrive. A *Diretto* stops far less, an *Expresso* just at the main towns. *Intercity* trains whoosh between the big cities and rarely deign to stop. *Eurocity* trains link Italian cities with major European centres. Both of these services require a supplement—some 30% more than a regular fare.

Above these are the *ETR 500 pendolino* trains, similar to the French TGV, which can travel at up to 186mph. Reservations are free, but must be made at least five hours before the trip, and on some trains there are only first-class coaches. The super-swish, super-fast (Florence–Rome in 1½ hours) *Eurostars* make very few stops, have both first and second class carriages, and carry a supplement which includes an obligatory seat reservation.

The FS offers several **passes**. The 'Flexi Card' (marketed as a 'Freedom Pass' in the UK) allows unlimited travel for either four days within a month (L206,000), 8 days within a month (L287,000), or 12 days within a month (L368,000)—plus seat reservations and supplements on Eurostars. The *Kilometrico* allows 3000kms of travel, made on a maximum of 20 journeys, and is valid for two months (2nd Class L206,000, 1st Class 338,000); one advantage is that it can be used by up to five people at the same time—however, supplements are payable on *Intercity* trains. Other discounts are available for day returns, families, senior citizens and the under-26s.

Refreshments on routes of any great distance are provided by bar cars or trolleys; you can usually get sandwiches and coffee from vendors along the tracks at intermediary stops. Station bars often have a good variety of take-away travellers' fare; consider at least investing in a plastic bottle of mineral water, since there's no drinking water on the trains.

Besides trains and bars, Italy's stations offer other **facilities**. Most have a *deposito*, where you can leave your bags for hours or days for a small fee. The larger ones have porters (who charge L1500–2000 per piece) and some even have luggage trolleys; major stations have an *albergo diurno* ('day hotel', where you can take a shower, get a shave and have a haircut, etc.), information offices, currency exchanges open at weekends (not at the most advantageous rates, however), hotel-finding and reservation services, kiosks with foreign papers, restaurants, etc. You can also arrange to have a rental car awaiting you at your destination—Avis, Hertz and Maggiore are the firms most widespread in Italy.

Beyond that, some words need to be said about riding the rails on the most serendipitous national line in Europe. The FS may have its strikes and delays, its petty crime and bureaucratic inconveniences, but when you catch it on its better side it will treat you to a dose of the real Italy before you even reach your destination. If there's a choice, try for one of the older cars, depressingly grey outside but fitted with comfortably upholstered seats, Art Deco lamps and old pictures of the towns and villages of the country. The washrooms are invariably clean and pleasant. Best of all, the FS is relatively reliable, and even if there has been some delay you'll have an amenable station full of clocks to wait in; some of the station bars have astonishingly good food (some do not), but at any of them you may accept a well-brewed cappuccino and look blasé until the train comes in. Try to avoid travel on Friday evenings, when the major lines out of the big cities are packed.

By Coach and Bus

Inter-city coach travel is sometimes quicker than train travel, but also a bit more expensive. The Italians aren't dumb; you will find regular coach connections only where there is no train to offer competition. Coaches almost always depart from the vicinity of the train station, and tickets usually need to be purchased before you get on. In many regions they are the only means of public transport and well used, with frequent schedules. If you can't get a ticket before the coach leaves, get on anyway and pretend you can't speak a word of Italian; the worst that can happen is that someone will make you pay for a ticket.

City buses are the traveller's friend. Most cities (at least in the north) label routes well; all charge flat fees for rides within the city limits and immediate suburbs (*c.* L1500). Bus tickets must always be purchased before you get on, either at a tobacconist's, a newspaper kiosk, in bars, or from ticket machines near the main stops. Once you get on, you must 'obliterate' your ticket in the machines in the front or back of the bus; controllers stage random checks to make sure you've punched your ticket. Fines for cheats are about

L50,000, and the odds are about 12 to 1 against a check, so many passengers take a chance. If you're good-hearted, you'll buy a ticket and help some overburdened municipal transit line meet its annual deficit.

By Car

The advantages of driving in Italy generally outweigh the disadvantages, but before you bring your own car or hire one, consider the kind of holiday you're planning. If you're only planning on visiting the cities, you'd be better off not driving at all: parking is impossible, traffic impossible, deciphering one-way streets, signals and signs impossible. But for touring the countryside a car gives immeasurable freedom. Third-party **insurance** is a minimum requirement in Italy (and you should be a lot more than minimally insured, as many of the locals have none whatever!). Obtain a Green Card from your insurer, which gives proof that you are fully covered. Also get hold of a **European Accident Statement** form, which may simplify things if you are unlucky enough to have an accident. Always insist on a full translation of any statement you are asked to sign. Breakdown assistance insurance is obviously a sensible investment.

Petrol (*benzina*, unleaded is *benzina senza piombo*, and diesel *gasolio*) is still very expensive in Italy (around L1800 per litre). Many petrol stations close for lunch in the afternoon, and few stay open late at night, though you may find a 'self-service' where you feed a machine nice smooth L10,000 notes. Motorway (*autostrada*) tolls are quite high (the journey from Milan to Rome on the A1 will cost you around L60,000). Rest stops and petrol stations along the motorways stay open 24 hours.

Italians are famously anarchic behind a wheel. The only way to beat the locals is to join them by adopting an assertive and constantly alert driving style. Bear in mind the maxim that he/she who hesitates is lost (especially at traffic lights, where the danger is less great of crashing into someone at the front than being rammed from behind). All drivers from boy racers to elderly nuns seem to tempt providence by overtaking at the most dangerous bends, and no matter how fast you are hammering along the *autostrada*, plenty will whizz past at apparently supersonic rates. North Americans used to leisurely speeds and gentler road manners may find the Italian interpretation of the highway code especially stressful. Speed limits (generally ignored) are officially 130kph on motorways, 110kph on main highways, 90kph on secondary roads, and 50kph in built-up areas. Speeding fines may be as much as L500,000, or L100,000 for jumping a red light (a popular Italian sport). If you are undeterred, you may actually enjoy driving in Italy, at least away from the congested tourist centres. Signposting is generally good, and roads are well maintained. Some are feats of engineering that the Romans themselves would have admired—bravura projects suspended on cliffs, crossing valleys on vast stilts and winding up hairpins.

Buy a good road map (the Italian Touring Club series is excellent). The **Automobile Club of Italy** (ACI), Viale C. Colombo 261, Rome, ✆ 06 514 971 or Vai Marsala 8, Rome, ✆ 06 495 9352, is a good friend to the foreign motorist. Besides having bushels of useful information and tips, they can be reached from anywhere by dialling ✆ 116—also use this number to find the nearest service station. If you need major repairs, the ACI can make sure the prices charged are according to their guidelines.

Hiring a car (*autonoleggio*) is simple but not particularly cheap. Remember to take into account that some hire companies require a deposit amounting to the estimated cost of the hire. The minimum age limit is usually 25 (sometimes 23) and the driver must have held their licence for over a year. Most major rental companies have offices in airports or main stations, though it may be worthwhile checking prices of local firms. If you need a car for longer than three weeks, leasing may be a more economic alternative. The National Tourist Office has a list of firms in Italy that hire caravans (trailers) or camper vans. Non-residents are not allowed to buy cars in Italy.

It is probably easiest to arrange your car hire with a domestic firm before you depart and, in particular, to check out fly-drive discounts.

Avis, (UK) ✆ (0990) 900 500; (USA) ✆ (800) 331 1084.

Hertz, (UK) ✆ (0990) 996 699; (Ireland), ✆ (01) 660 2255; (USA), ✆ (800) 654 3001; (Canada) ✆ (800) 263 0600.

National Car Rental, ✆ (0870) 600 0044.

Car Rental Direct, (UK) ✆ (020) 7625 7166.

hitch-hiking

It is illegal to hitch on the *autostrade*, though you may pick up a lift near one of the toll booths. Don't hitch from the city centres, head for suburban exit routes. For the best chances of getting a lift, travel light, look respectable and take your shades off. Hold a sign indicating your destination if you can. Risks for women are lower in northern Italy than in the more macho south, but it is not advisable to hitch alone. Two or more men may encounter some reluctance.

By Motorcycle or Bicycle

Mopeds, vespas and scooters are the vehicles of choice for a great many Italians. You will see them everywhere. In the traffic-congested towns this is a ubiquity born of necessity; when driving space is limited, two wheels are always better than one. Despite the obvious dangers, there are clear benefits to moped-riding in Italy. For one thing it is cheaper than car hire and can prove an excellent way of covering a town's sites in a limited space of time. Furthermore, because Italy is such a scooter-friendly place, car drivers are more conditioned to their presence and so are less likely to hurtle in to them when taking corners. Nonetheless, you should only consider hiring a moped if you have ridden one before (Italy's hills and alarming traffic are no place to learn) and, despite local examples, you should always wear a helmet. Also, be warned that some travel insurance policies exclude claims resulting from scooter or motorbike accidents.

You can hire a bicycle in most Italian towns. Alternatively, if you bring your own bike, check the airlines' policy on transporting them. Bikes can be transported by train in Italy, either with you or within a couple of days—apply at the baggage office (*ufficio bagagli*).

Practical A–Z

Children

Children are the royalty of Italy, pampered, often obscenely spoiled, probably more fashionably dressed than you are, and never allowed to get dirty. Surprisingly, most of them somehow manage to be well-mannered little charmers. If you're bringing your own *bambini* to Italy, they'll receive a warm welcome everywhere.

Many hotels offer advantageous rates for children and most of the larger cities have permanent **Luna Parks**, or funfairs. Rome's version in its EUR suburb is huge and charmingly old-fashioned (a great trade-off for a day in the Vatican Museums). Apart from endless quantities of pizza, spaghetti and ice cream, children love the **Bomarzo Monster Park** in northern Lazio (a collection of huge, weird 16th-century follies); the fairy-tale playground of **Città della Domenica** in Perugia; and the whole city of **Venice**.

If a **circus** visits town, you're in for a treat: it will either be a sparkling showcase of daredevil skill or a poignant, family-run version of Fellini's *La Strada*.

Climate and When to Go

'*O Sole Mio*' notwithstanding, all of Italy isn't always sunny; it rains just as much in Rome every year as in London, and Turin's climate in the winter is said to be about the same as that of Copenhagen.

Summer comes on dry and hot in the south and humid and hot in much of the northern lowlands and inland hills; Venice tends to swelter. You can probably get by without an umbrella, but take a light jacket for cool evenings. For average touring, August is probably the worst month to stump through Italy. Transport facilities are jammed to capacity, prices are at their highest, and the large cities are abandoned to hordes of tourists while the locals take to the beach.

Spring and **autumn** are perhaps the loveliest times to go; the weather is mild, places aren't crowded, and you won't need your umbrella too much, at least until November. **Winter** is the best time to go if you want the art and museums to yourself. Beware though, it can rain and rain.

Crime

There is a fair amount of petty crime in Italy—purse-snatchings, pickpocketing, minor thievery of the white collar kind (always check your change) and car break-ins and theft—but violent crime is rare. Nearly all mishaps can be avoided with adequate precautions. Scooter-borne purse-snatchers can be foiled if you stay on the inside of the pavement and keep a firm hold on your property (sling your bag-strap across your body, not dangling from one shoulder); pickpockets strike in crowded buses or trams and gatherings; don't carry too much cash, and split it so you won't lose the lot at once. In cities and popular tourist sites, beware groups of scruffy-looking women or children with placards, apparently begging for money. They use distraction techniques to perfection. The smallest and most innocent-looking child is generally the most skilful pickpocket.

If you are targeted, the best technique is to grab hold sharply of any vulnerable possessions or pockets and shout furiously. (Italian passers-by or plain-clothes police will often come to your assistance if they realize what is happening.) Be extra careful in train stations, don't leave valuables in hotel rooms, and always park your car in garages, guarded lots or on well-lit streets, with portable temptations well out of sight.

Purchasing small quantities of soft drugs for personal consumption is technically legal in Italy, though what constitutes a small quantity is unspecified, and if the police don't like you to begin with, it will probably be enough to get you into big trouble.

Political terrorism, once the scourge of Italy, has declined greatly in recent years, mainly thanks to special quasi-military squads of black-uniformed national police, the *Carabinieri.* Local matters are usually in the hands of the *Polizia Urbana*; the nattily dressed *Vigili Urbani* concern themselves with directing traffic, and handing out parking fines. If you need to summon any of them, dial ✆ **113**.

Disabled Travellers

Italy has been relatively slow off the mark in its provision for disabled visitors. Cobblestones, uneven or non-existent pavements, the appalling traffic conditions, crowded public transport and endless flights of steps in many public places are all disincentives. Progress is gradually being made, however. A national support organization in your own country may well have specific information on facilities in Italy, or will at least be able to provide general advice.

The Italian tourist office, or CIT (travel agency) can also advise on hotels, museums with ramps and so on. If you book rail travel through CIT, you can request assistance. Once in Italy, you can ring the disabled cooperative, ✆ 167 179 179, for advice on accommodation and travel.

Royal Association for Disability & Rehabilitation (RADAR), 12 City Forum, 250 City Road, London EC1V 8AF, ✆ (020) 7250 3222, sells a guide, *Holidays & Travel Abroad: A Guide for Disabled People* (£5).

Mobility International, 228 Borough High Street, London SE1, ✆ (020) 7403 5688; or West Broadway, Eugene OR, USA, ✆ (541) 343 1284.

Society for the Advancement of Travel for the Handicapped (SATH), 347 Fifth Avenue, Suite 610, New York, NY 10016, ✆ (212) 447 7284.

Australian Council for the Rehabilitation of the Disabled (ACROD), 55 Charles Street, Ryde, New South Wales, ✆ (02) 9809 4488.

Florence, (UK) Lungarno Corsini 2, © 055 284 133; (USA) Lungarno Vespucci 38, © 055 239 8276.

Milan, (Australia) Via Borgagna 2, © 02 7601 1330; (Canada) Via Vittorio Pisani 19, © 02 669 7451; (UK) Via San Paulo 7, © 02 723 001; (USA) Largo Donegani 1, © 02 2900 1841.

Naples, (UK) Via Crispi 122, © 081 663 511; (USA) Piazza Repubblica 2, © 081 583 8111.

Rome, (Australia) Via Alessandria 215, © 06 852 721; (Canada) Via Zara 30, © 06 440 3028; (Ireland) Largo Nazareno 3, © 06 678 2541; (New Zealand) Via Zara 28, © 06 440 2928; (UK) Via XX Settembre 80/a, © 06 482 5441; (USA) Via V. Veneto 119/a, © 06 46741.

Turin, (UK) Via Saluzzo, 60, © 011 650 9202, ✉ 011 657 157.

Festivals

There are literally thousands of festivals answering to every description in Italy. Every *comune* has at least one or two honouring patron saints, at which the presiding Madonna is paraded through the streets decked in fairy lights and gaudy flowers. Shrovetide and Holy Week are great focuses of activity. *Carnival,* after being suppressed and ignored for decades, has been revived in many places, displaying the gorgeous music and pageantry of the *Commedia dell'Arte* with Harlequin and his motley crew. In Venice, the handmade carnival masks now constitute a new art form and make popular souvenirs.

In Rome the Pope himself officiates at the Easter ceremonies. Other festivals are more earthily pagan, celebrating the land and the harvest in giant phallic towers. Some are purely secular affairs sponsored by political parties (especially the Communists and Social-ists), where everyone goes to meet friends. There are great costume pageants dating back to the Middle Ages or Renaissance like the Sienese *Palio* (a bareback horserace), an endless round of carnivals, music festivals, opera seasons and antique fairs. Relaxed village *festas* can be just as enjoyable as (or more so than) the big national crowd-pullers. Outsiders are nearly always welcome.

Whatever the occasion, eating is a primary pastime at all Italian jamborees, and all kinds of regional specialities are prepared. Check at the local tourist office for precise dates, which alter from year to year, and often slide into the nearest weekend.

Feb–March	Shrovetide Carnivals all over Italy, especially in **Venice** (boat procession).
March–April	Holy Week and Easter celebrations: processions **Bari**; Scoppio del Carro (Explosion of the Cart), **Florence**; Good Friday procession led by the Pope, **Rome**.

May	Feast of San Nicola, **Bari.**
	Feast of San Gennaro (first of three such occasions when the faithful assemble in **Naples** cathedral to await the miraculous liquefaction of a phial of the saint's blood).
	Vogolonga, **Venice** (the 'long row' from San Marco to Burano).
June 21	Infiorata, **Genzano** (Rome) and **Spello** (Umbria) (Corpus Domini celebrations with flower decorations).
	Feast of St Antonio, **Padua.**
	Festa dei Gigli, **Nola** (Naples) ('lily' procession—the lillies in this instance are large wooden towers).
July	Feast of the Redeemer, **Venice** (fireworks and gondola procession).
	Umbria Jazz Festival in **Perugia.**
July and August	Palio, **Siena**—bareback horserace (held twice).
	Verona Outdoor Opera Season.
September	Feast of San Gennaro, **Naples.**
	Luminaria di Santa Croce, **Lucca** (torchlit procession).
October	Feast of St Francis, **Assisi.**
November	Festa della Salute, **Venice.**
December	Advent and Christmas celebrations.
	Christmas Fair of the *presepi*, **Naples.**

Food and Drink

There are those who eat to live and those who live to eat, and then there are the Italians, for whom food has an almost religious significance, unfathomably linked with love, La Mamma and tradition. In this singular country, where millions of otherwise sane people spend much of their waking hours worrying about their digestion, standards both at home and in the restaurants are understandably high. Few Italians are gluttons, but all are experts on what is what in the kitchen; to serve a meal that is not properly prepared and more than a little complex is tantamount to an insult.

For the visitor this national culinary obsession comes as an extra bonus to the senses— along with Italy's remarkable sights, music, and the warm sun on your back, you can enjoy some of the best tastes and smells the world can offer, prepared daily in Italy's kitchens and fermented in its countless wine cellars. Eating *all'Italiana* is not only delicious and wholesome, but now undeniably trendy. Foreigners flock here to learn the secrets of Italian cuisine and the even more elusive secret of how the Italians can live surrounded by such delights and still fit into their sleek Armani trousers.

Breakfast (*colazione*) in Italy is no lingering affair, but an early morning wake-up shot to the brain: a *cappuccino* (espresso with hot foamy milk, often sprinkled with chocolate—

incidentally first thing in the morning is the only time of day at which any self-respecting Italian will touch the stuff), a *caffè latte* (white coffee) or a *caffè lungo* (a generous portion of espresso), accompanied by a croissant-type roll, called a *cornetto* or *briosce*, or a fancy pastry. This repast can be consumed in any bar and repeated during the morning as often as necessary. Breakfast in most Italian hotels seldom represents great value.

Lunch (*pranzo*), generally served around 1pm, is the most important meal of the day for the Italians, with a minimum of a first course (*primo piatto*—any kind of pasta dish, broth or soup, or rice dish or pizza), a second course (*secondo piatto*—a meat dish, accompanied by a *contorno* or side dish—a vegetable, salad, or potatoes usually), followed by fruit or dessert and coffee. You can, however, begin with a platter of *antipasti*—the appetizers Italians do so brilliantly, ranging from warm seafood delicacies, to raw ham (*prosciutto crudo*), salami in a hundred varieties, lovely vegetables, savoury toasts, olives, pâté and many many more. There are restaurants that specialize in *antipasti*, and they usually don't take it amiss if you decide to forget the pasta and meat and just nibble on these scrumptious hors-d'œuvres (though in the end it will probably cost more than a full meal). Most Italians accompany their meal with wine and mineral water—*acqua minerale*, with or without bubbles (*con* or *senza gas*), which supposedly aids digestion—concluding their meals with a *digestivo* liqueur. *Cena*, the **evening meal**, is usually eaten around 8pm. This is much the same as *pranzo* although lighter, without the pasta; a pizza and beer, eggs or a fish dish. In restaurants, however, they offer all the courses, so if you have only a sandwich for lunch you can have a full meal in the evening.

In Italy the various terms for types of **restaurants**—*ristorante*, *trattoria* or *osteria*—have been confused. A *trattoria* or *osteria* can be just as elaborate as a restaurant, though rarely is a *ristorante* as informal as a traditional *trattoria*. Unfortunately the old habit of posting menus and prices in the windows has fallen from fashion, so it's often difficult to judge variety or prices. Invariably the least expensive eating place is the *vino e cucina*, a simple establishment serving simple cuisine for simple everyday prices. It is essential to remember that the fancier the fittings, the fancier the **bill**, though neither of these points has anything at all to do with the quality of the food. If you're uncertain, do as you would at home—look for lots of locals. When you eat out, mentally add to the bill (*conto*) the bread and cover charge (*pane e coperto*, between L2000 and L4000), and a 15% service charge. This is often included in the bill (*servizio compreso*); if not, it will say *servizio non compreso*, and you'll have to do your own arithmetic. Additional tipping is at your own discretion, but never do it in family-owned and family-run places.

People who haven't visited Italy for years and have fond memories of eating full meals for under a pound will be amazed at how much **prices** have risen; though in some respects eating out in Italy is still a bargain, especially when you figure out how much all that wine would have cost you at home. In many places you'll often find restaurants offering a *menu turistico*—full, set meals of usually meagre inspiration for L20,000–30,000. More imaginative chefs often offer a *menu degustazione*—a set-price gourmet meal that allows you to taste their daily specialities and seasonal dishes. Both of these are cheaper than if you had ordered the same food *à la carte*.

Restaurant price categories

very expensive	over L80,000
expensive	L50,000–80,000
moderate	L30,000–50,000
cheap	below L30,000

When you leave a restaurant you will be given a receipt (*scontrino* or *ricevuto fiscale*) which according to Italian law you must take with you out of the door and carry for at least 60 metres. If you aren't given one, it means the restaurant is probably fudging on its taxes and thus offering you lower prices. There is a slim chance the tax police (*Guardia di Fianza*) may have their eye on you and the restaurant, and if you don't have a receipt they could slap you with a heavy fine.

As the pace of modern urban life militates against traditional lengthy homecooked repasts with the family, followed by a siesta, alternatives to sit-down meals have mushroomed. Many office workers now behave much as their counterparts elsewhere in Europe and consume a rapid snack at lunchtime, returning home after a busy day to throw together some pasta and salad in the evenings.

The original Italian fast food alternative, a buffet known as the 'hot table' (*tavola calda*) is becoming harder and harder to find among the international and made-in-Italy fast food franchises of various descriptions; bars often double as *panicotecas* (which make hot or cold sandwiches to order, or serve *tramezzini*, little sandwiches on plain, square white bread that are always much better than they look); outlets selling pizza by the slice (*al taglio*) are common in city centres. At any grocer's (*alimentari*) or market (*mercato*) you can buy the materials for countryside or hotel-room picnics; some will make the sandwiches for you.

What comes as a surprise to many visitors is the tremendous regional diversity at the table; often next to nothing on the menu looks familiar, disguised by a local or dialect name. Expect further mystification, as many Italian chefs have wholeheartedly embraced the concept of *nouvelle cuisine*, or rather *nuova cucina*, and are constantly inventing dishes with even more names. If your waiter fails to elucidate, the menu decoder at the back of this book may help.

In northern Italy, look for dishes prepared with butter and cream. Egg pasta and *risotto* are favourite first courses, while game dishes, liver, *bollito misto* (mixed boiled meats), *ossobuco* (veal shin cooked in tomato sauce), seafood and sausages appear as main courses. Towards the Trentino-Adige the cooking displays hearty Austrian influences, with goulash and smoked meats with rye bread. Sometimes you may find dishes served with *polenta* (a pudding or cake of yellow maize flour), a brick-heavy substance to be approached with caution.

Central Italy is the land of beans and chick peas, game, tripe, salt cod (*baccala*), *porchetta* (whole roast pork with rosemary), Florentine steaks, *saltimbocca alla romana* (veal scallops with ham and sage), and freshwater fish in interesting guises. Tuscan and Umbrian cooking uses fresh, simple, high-quality ingredients flavoured with herbs and olive oil, and the local *porcini* mushrooms or truffles.

The further south you go, the spicier and oilier things get, and the richer the puddings and cakes. Modern Romans are as adventurous at the table as their classical ancestors, and include some stomach-churning offal in their diets. But the capital is an excellent place to delve into any style of regional cooking, with dozens of restaurants from all over Italy. Southern Italy is the land of homemade pasta, wonderful vegetables and superb seafood, often fried or laced with olive oil. Naples, of course, is the birthplace of pizza, and home of rich tomato sauces. Regional specialities are often seasoned with condiments like capers, anchovies, lemon juice, oregano, olives and fennel.

Wine and Spirits

Italy is a country where everyday wine is cheaper than Coca-Cola or milk, and where nearly every family owns some vineyards or has some relatives who supply most of their daily needs—which are not great. Even though they live in one of the world's largest wine-growing countries, Italians imbibe relatively little, and usually only at meals.

If Italy has an infinite variety of regional dishes, there is an equally bewildering array of **regional wines**, many of which are rarely exported because they are best drunk young. Even wines that are well known and derided abroad, like Chianti or Lambrusco, can be wonderful new experiences when tasted on their home turf. Unless you're dining at a restaurant with an exceptional cellar, do as the Italians do and order a carafe of the local wine (*vino locale* or *vino della casa*). You won't often go wrong.

Most Italian wines are named after the grape and the district they come from. If the label says DOC (*Denominazione di Origine Controllata*) it means that the wine comes from a specially defined area and was produced according to a certain traditional method. DOCG (*Denominazione d'Origine Controllata e Garantia*) is allegedly a more rigorous classification, indicating that the wines not only conform to DOC standards, but are tested by government-appointed inspectors. *Classico* means that a wine comes from the oldest part of the zone of production, though is not necessarily better than a non-Classico. *Riserva*, *superiore* or *speciale* denotes a wine that has been aged longer and is more alcoholic; *recioto* is a wine made from the outer clusters of grapes, with a higher sugar and therefore alcohol content.

Other Italian wine words are *spumante* (sparkling), *frizzante* (pétillant), *amabile* (semi-sweet), *abbocato* (medium dry), *passito* (strong sweet wine made from raisins). *Rosso* is red, *bianco* white; between the two extremes lie *rubiato* (ruby), *rosato*, *chiaretto* or *cera-suolo* (rosé). *Secco* is dry, *dolce* sweet, *liquoroso* fortified and sweet. *Vendemmia* means vintage, a *cantina* is a cellar, and an *enoteca* is a wine-shop or museum where you can taste and buy wines.

The regions of Piedmont, Tuscany and Veneto produce Italy's most prestigious red wines, while Friuli-Venezia Giulia and Trentino-Alto Adige are the greatest regions for white wines. King of the Tuscans is the mighty Brunello di Montalcino (DOCG), an expensive blockbuster. Pinot Grigio and the unusual Tocai make some of the best whites. But almost every other corner of Italy has its vinous virtues, be it the Orvieto of Umbria or the Frascati of Lazio. The well-known Valpolicella, Bardolino and Soave are produced on the shores of Lake Garda.

Italy turns its grape harvest to other uses too, producing Sicilian **Marsala**, a famous fortified wine fermented in wooden casks, ranging from very dry to flavoured and sweet; and **vin santo**, a sweet Tuscan speciality often served with almond biscuits. **Vermouth** is an idea from Turin made of wine flavoured with Alpine herbs and spices. Italians are fond of post-prandial brandies (to aid digestion)—**Stock** or **Vecchia Romagna** appear on the best-known Italian brandy bottles. **Grappa** is a rough, Schnapps-like spirit drunk in black coffee after a meal (a *caffè corretto*). Other drinks you'll see in any Italian bar include **Campari**, a red bitter drunk on its own or in cocktails; **Fernet Branca**, **Cynar** and **Averno** (popular aperitif/digestifs); and a host of liqueurs like **Strega**, the witch potion from **Benevento**, apricot-flavoured **Amaretto**, cherry **Maraschino**, aniseed **Sambuca** or herby **Millefiori**.

Health and Emergencies

You can insure yourself for almost any possible mishap—cancelled flights, stolen or lost baggage and health. Check any current policies you hold to see if they cover you while abroad, and under what circumstances, and judge whether you need a **traveller's insurance** policy for the journey. Travel agencies sell them, as well as insurance companies.

Citizens of EU countries are entitled to **reciprocal health care** in Italy's National Health Service and a 90% discount on prescriptions (bring **Form E111** with you). The E111 does not cover all medical expenses (no repatriation costs, for example, and no private treatment), and it is advisable to take out separate travel insurance for full cover. Citizens of non-EU countries should check carefully that they have adequate insurance for any medical expenses, and the cost of returning home. Australia has a reciprocal health care scheme with Italy, but New Zealand, Canada and the USA do not. If you already have health insurance, a student card, or a credit card, you may be entitled to some medical cover abroad.

In an **emergency**, dial ℗ **115** for fire and ℗ **113** for an ambulance (*ambulanza*) or to find the nearest hospital (*ospedale*). Less serious problems can be treated at a *Pronto Soccorso* (casualty/first aid department) at any hospital clinic (*ambulatorio*), or at a local health unit (*Unita Sanitarial Locale*—USL). Airports and main railway stations also have **first-aid posts**. If you have to pay for any health treatment, make sure you get a receipt, so that you can make any claims for reimbursement later.

Dispensing **chemists** (*farmacia*) are generally open from 8.30am to 1pm and from 4 to 8pm. Pharmacists are trained to give advice for minor ills. Any large town will have a *farmacia* that stays open 24 hours; others take turns to stay open (the address rota is posted in the window).

No specific **vaccinations** are required or advised for citizens of most countries before visiting Italy; the main health risks are the usual travellers' woes of upset stomachs or the effects of too much sun. Take a supply of **medicaments** with you (insect repellent, anti-diarrhœal medicine, sun lotion and antiseptic cream), and any drugs you need regularly.

Most Italian doctors speak at least rudimentary English, but if you can't find one, contact your embassy or consulate for a list of English-speaking doctors.

Jubilee (*Giubileo*) 2000

✠ The Great Jubilee of the year 2000 will be celebrated by Catholics worldwide. Italy is expecting between 20 and 30 million visitors, who will travel to the principal pilgrimage destinations to receive indulgences—remissions of temporal punishment—through the act of pilgrimage and through performing specific actions at their destination: passing through the Holy Door of one of the Patriarchal Basilicas, celebration of Mass, the stations of the cross or charitable works.

The following organizations have been set up to help visitors during the Jubilee:

Peregrinatio Ad Petri Sedem, Piazza Pio XII 4, ✆ 06 6988 4896, 🖷 06 6988 5617, in front of St Peter's, is the official Vatican office for the placement of pilgrims in Rome.

The Central Welcoming Committee for Jubilee 2000, Piazza San Marcello 4, Rome ✉ 00187, ✆ 06 696 221, 🖷 06 699 24853, sells the **Pilgrims' Electronic Card** (*L65.000*), whose benefits include the use of public transport in Rome and admission to some or all of the big Jubilee events. To obtain it before you travel, call ✆ 06 7298 3331 (English language line).

Maps

The maps in this guide are for orientation only and to explore in any detail it is worth investing in a good, up-to-date regional map before you arrive from any of the following bookshops:

Stanford's, 12–14 Long Acre, London WC2 9LP, ✆ (020) 7836 1321.

The Travel Bookshop, 13 Blenheim Crescent, London W11 2EE, ✆ (020) 7229 5260.

The Complete Traveller, 199 Madison Ave, New York, NY 10016, ✆ (212) 685 9007.

Excellent maps are produced by **Touring Club Italiano**, **Michelin** and **Istituto Geografico de Agostini**. They are available at all major bookshops in Italy and sometimes at news stands. Italian tourist offices are helpful and can often supply good area maps and town plans.

Money

It's a good idea to order a wad of lire from your home bank to have on hand when you arrive in Italy, the land of strikes, unforeseen delays and quirky banking hours (*see* below). Take great care how you carry it, however (don't keep it all in one place). The easiest and best way to change money is by using your ATM card. The machines, usually in city centres, take cards from all English-speaking countries, are open 24 hours a day, the rate is the bank wholesale exchange rate (the best you can get), and there is no fee other than the service charge of a couple dollars. Otherwise you can change money at your hotel, or in private exchange offices in airports of city centres. Remember that Italians indicate decimals with commas and thousands with full points.

On 1 January 1999 Italy joined the first wave of European Monetary Union, thus making the **euro** its official new currency (and the lira a denomination thereof). In the short term this is unlikely to make much of a difference to the lives of either Italians or tourists—euro notes and coins are not due to be introduced until the launch of the second stage of monetary union on 1 January 2002, and the lira will continue to be used during the three year transitional period. The only visible difference that you will notice is that prices are now usually displayed in both lire and euros.

National Holidays

Most museums, as well as banks and shops, are closed on the following national holidays.

1 January (New Year's Day)

6 January (Epiphany)

Easter Monday

25 April (Liberation Day)

1 May (Labour Day)

15 August (Assumption, also known as *Ferragosto*, the official start of the Italian holiday season)

1 November (All Saints' Day)

8 December (Immaculate Conception)

25 December (Christmas Day)

26 December (*Santo Stefano*, St Stephen's Day)

In addition to these general holidays, many towns also take off their patron saint's day.

Opening Hours and Museums

Although it varies from region to region, most of Italy closes down at 1pm until 3 or 4pm to eat and properly digest the main meal of the day. Afternoon hours are from 4 to 7, often from 5 to 8 in the hot summer months. Bars are often the only places open during the early afternoon. In any case, don't be surprised if you find anywhere in Italy unexpectedly closed (or open for that matter), whatever its official stated hours.

banks:	*open Mon–Fri 8.30–1 and 3–4, closed weekends and on local and national holidays (see above).*
shops:	*open Mon–Sat 8–1 and 3.30–7.30.* Some supermarkets and department stores stay open throughout the day; hours vary according to season and are shorter in smaller centres.

Government-run dispensers of red tape (e.g. visa departments) often stay open for quite limited periods, usually during the mornings (*Mon–Fri*). It pays to get there as soon as they open (or before) to spare your nerves in an interminable queue. Anyway, take something to read, or write your memoirs.

museums and galleries

Many of Italy's museums are magnificent, many are run with shameful neglect, and many have been closed for years for 'restoration' with slim prospects of reopening in the foreseeable future. With at least one work of art per inhabitant, Italy has a hard time financing the preservation of its national heritage; enquire at the tourist office to find out exactly what is open and what is 'temporarily' closed before setting off on a wild-goose chase.

churches

Italy's churches have always been a prime target for art thieves and as a consequence are usually locked when there isn't a sacristan or caretaker to keep an eye on things. All churches, except for the really important cathedrals and basilicas, close in the afternoon at the same hours as the shops, and the little ones tend to stay closed. Always have a pocketful of coins for the light machines in churches, or whatever work of art you came to inspect will remain clouded in ecclesiastical gloom. Don't do your visiting during services, and don't come to see paintings and statues in churches the week preceding Easter—you will probably find them covered with mourning shrouds.

In general, Sunday afternoons and Mondays are dead periods for the sightseer—you may want to make them your travelling days. Places without specified opening hours can usually be visited on request—but it is best to go before 1pm. We have listed the hours of important sights and museums, and specified which ones charge admission. Entrance charges vary widely; major sights are fairly steep (L10,000 plus), but others may be completely free. EU citizens under 18 and over 65 get free admission to state museums, at least in theory.

Packing

You simply cannot overdress in Italy; whatever grand strides Italian designers have made on the international fashion merry-go-round, most of their clothes are purchased domestically, prices be damned. Whether or not you want to try to keep up with the natives is your own affair. It's not that the Italians are very formal; they simply like to dress up with a gorgeousness that adorns their cities just as much as those old Renaissance churches and palaces. The few places with dress codes are the major churches and basilicas (no shorts, sleeveless shirts or strappy sundresses—women should tuck a light silk scarf in a bag to throw over their shoulders), casinos, and a few posh restaurants.

Your electric appliances will work in Italy if you adapt and convert them to run on 220 AC with two round prongs on the plug.

Post Offices

post offices: *usually open Mon–Sat 8–1; in large cities 8–6 or 7.*

Dealing with *la posta italiana* has always been a risky, frustrating, time-consuming affair. It is one of the most expensive and slowest postal services in Europe. Even buying the right stamps requires dedicated research and saintly patience. One of the scandals that mesmerized Italy in recent years involved the minister of the post office, who disposed of literally tons of backlog mail by tossing it in the Tiber. When the news broke, he was replaced—the new minister, having learned his lesson, burned all the mail the post office was incapable of delivering.

Not surprisingly, fed-up Italians view the invention of the fax machine as a gift from the Madonna. From these harsh judgements, however, we must exempt the Vatican City, whose special postal service (on angelic wings?) knocks spots off the rest of the country for speed and efficiency. If you're anywhere in Rome, be sure to post your mail in the Holy See. You need to buy the special Vatican stamps, which provide a tidy profit for the papal coffers.

To have your mail sent *poste restante* (general delivery), have it addressed to the central post office (*Fermo Posta*) and expect three to four weeks for it to arrive. Make sure your surname is clearly written in block capitals. To pick up your mail you must present your passport and pay a nominal charge. Stamps (*francoboli*) are available in post offices or at tobacconists (*tabacchi*, identified by their blue signs with a white T). Prices fluctuate.

You can also have money telegraphed to you through the post office; if all goes well, this can happen in a mere three days, but expect a fair proportion of it to go into commission.

Shopping

'Made in Italy' has become a byword for style and quality, especially in fashion and leather, but also in home design, ceramics, kitchenware, jewellery, lace and linens, glassware and crystal, chocolates, bells, Christmas decorations, hats, straw work, art books, engravings, handmade stationery, gold and silverware, bicycles, sports cars, woodworking, a hundred kinds of liqueurs, aperitifs, coffee machines, gastronomic specialities, and antiques (both reproductions, and the real thing).

If you are looking for antiques, be sure to demand a certificate of authenticity—reproductions can be very good. To get your antique or modern art purchases home, you will have to apply to the Export Department of the Italian Ministry of Education and pay an export tax as well; your seller should know the details. Non-EU citizens should save all receipts for Customs.

Italians don't much like department stores, but there are a few chains—the classiest is the oldest, Rinascente, while COIN stores often have good buys in almost the latest fashions. Standa and UPIM are more like Woolworths; they have good clothes selections, housewares, etc., and often contain basement supermarkets. The main attraction of Italian shopping, however, is to buy classy luxury items; for less expensive clothes and household items you can nearly always do better at home. Prices for clothes are generally very high.

Telephones

Public telephones for international calls may be found in the offices of **Telecom Italia**, Italy's telephone company. They are the only places where you can make reverse-charge calls (*a erre*, collect calls) but be prepared for a wait, as all these calls go through the operator in Rome. Rates for long-distance calls are among the highest in Europe. Calls within Italy are cheapest after 10pm; international calls after 11pm.

Most phone booths now take either coins (L100, 200, 500 or 1000) or phone cards (*schede telefoniche*), available in L5000, L10,000 and sometimes 15,000 amounts at tobacconists and news-stands—you have to snap off the small perforated corner in order to use them. In smaller villages you can usually find *telefoni a scatti*, with a meter on it, in at least one bar (a small commission is generally charged). Try to avoid telephoning from hotels, which often add 25% to the bill.

Direct calls may be made by dialling the international prefix (for the UK 0044, Ireland 00353, USA and Canada 001, Australia 0061, New Zealand 0064). If you're calling Italy from abroad, dial 39 first. Many places have public fax machines, but the speed of transmission may make costs very high.

Time

Italy is on Central European Time, one hour ahead of Greenwich Mean Time and six hours ahead of Eastern Standard Time. From the last weekend of March to the end of September, Italian Summer Time (daylight saving time) is in effect.

Toilets

Frequent travellers have noted a steady improvement over the years in the cleanliness of Italy's public conveniences, although as ever you will only find them in places like train and bus stations and bars. Ask for the *bagno*, *toilette* or *gabinetto*; in stations and the smarter bars and cafes there are washroom attendants who expect a few hundred lire for keeping the place decent. You'll probably have to ask them for paper (*carta*). Don't confuse the Italian plurals; s*ignori* (gents), *signore* (ladies).

Tourist Offices

> **tourist information offices:** *open 8–12.30 or 1 and 3–7, possibly longer in summer. Few open on Saturday afternoons or Sundays.*

Known as EPT, APT or AAST, information booths provide hotel lists, town plans and terse information on local sights and transport. Queues can be maddeningly long. If you're stuck, you may get more sense out of a friendly travel agency than an official tourist office. Nearly every city and province now has a web page, and you can often book your hotel direct through the Internet.

UK, 1 Princes Street, London W1R 8AY, ✆ (020) 7408 1254; **Italian Travel Centre**, Thomas Cook, 30 St James's Street, London SW1A 1HB, ✆ (020) 7853 6464.

USA, 630 Fifth Ave, Suite 1565, New York, NY 10111, ✆ (212) 245 4822; 12400 Wilshire Blvd, Suite 550, Los Angeles, CA 90025, ✆ (310) 820 0098; 500 N. Michigan Ave, Suite 1046, Chicago, IL 60611, ✆ (312) 644 0990.

Australia, c/o Italian Embassy, 61–69 Macquarie St, Sydney 2000, NSW, ✆ (02) 9247 8442.

Canada, 1 Place Ville Marie, Suite 1914, Montréal, Quebec H3B 3M9, ✆ (514) 866 7667.

N. Zealand, c/o Italian Embassy, 36 Grant Road, Thomdon, Wellington, ✆ (04) 736 065.

Tourist and travel information may also be available from **Alitalia** (Italy's national airline) or **CIT** (Italy's state-run travel agency) offices in some countries.

Websites

The following websites should be updated regularly and are a good source of the latest information on Jubilee arrangements and events.

www.vatican.va	official Vatican Jubilee 2000 website; information, Papal documents and letters, etc.
www.catholic.net	Jubilee Resources: links, information and a countdown to the Jubilee Year 2000
www.nccbuscc.org	Jubilee Year 2000—Third Millennium Page; comprehensive site from the US National Conference of Catholic Bishops
www.cin.org	Catholic Information Network—Jubilee 2000; documents, resources and info about the Jubilee year and beyond
www.AmericanCatholic.org	American Catholic Online—Millennium Monthly newsletter
www.jubil2000.org	official site of Central Committee of the Great Jubilee of the Year 2000; masses of practical information, history etc.
www.roma2000.it	practical info for visitors: hotels, restaurants, museums, etc.
www.assisionline.com	practical info for visitors: hotels, restaurants, museums, etc.

All accommodation in Italy is classified by the Provincial Tourist Boards. Price control, however, has been deregulated since 1992. Hotels now set their own tariffs, which means that in some places prices have rocketed. After a period of rapid and erratic price fluctuation, tariffs are at last settling down again to more predictable levels under the influence of market forces.

The quality of furnishings and facilities has generally improved in all categories in recent years. Many hotels have installed smart bathrooms and electronic gadgetry. At the top end of the market, Italy has a number of exceptionally sybaritic hotels, furnished and decorated with real panache. But you can still find plenty of older-style hotels and *pensioni*, whose eccentricities of character and architecture (in some cases undeniably charming) may frequently be at odds with modern standards of comfort or even safety.

The following phrases will come in useful when you are looking for somewhere to stay: *pernottamento e prima colazione* (bed and breakfast), *mezza pensione* (half board) and *pensione completa* (full board).

Hotel price categories

Category	Double with bath
luxury (*****)	L450–800,000
very expensive (****)	L300–450,000
expensive (***)	L200–300,000
moderate (**)	L120–200,000
cheap (*)	up to L120,000

If all the predictions for visitor numbers to Italy for the Jubilee come true, accommodation in Italy, especially in and around all the major pilgrimage sites, will be chock-a-block throughout the year. Try to book before you arrive in Italy, and be prepared to stay a little way out of town (we have provided extra listings for hotels in the regions around Padua and Assisi in the relevant chapter, which are easily reached by public transport).

Religious Houses

⊕ Many convents and other religious institutions will provide inexpensive accommodation to all-comers during the Jubilee year. For a complete listing write to: Vicariato di Roma, Piazza S. Giovanni 6, ✉ 00184 Rome; or to the Rome Tourist Board, Via Parigi 11, ✉ 00185 Rome. For Parish group bookings, contact Peregrinatio Ad Petri Sedem, Piazza Pio XII 4, ✉ 00120 Vatican City State, ✆ 06 6988 4896, ✉ 06 6988 5617, just off St Peter's Square. But don't forget that in Rome information is passed by word of mouth. If none of the convents listed on pp.134–35 has space for you, they'll certainly know of others that might.

The Paulist Fathers at Santa Susanna (the American Church in Rome) have set up a cheerful website offering tips on accommodation and other practical information for Rome: *www.santasusanna.org/html*

Italia Sixtina has an excellent website: *www.sixtina.com*

Giubileum Rents, ℗ 06 4425 2224, www.giubileumrents.com organizes short-term lets of apartments in Rome

Hotels and Guesthouses

Italian *alberghi* come in all shapes and sizes. They are rated from one to five stars, depending what facilities they offer (not their character, style or charm). The star ratings are some indication of price levels, but for tax reasons not all hotels choose to advertise themselves at the rating to which they are entitled, so you may find a modestly rated hotel just as comfortable (or more so) than a higher rated one. Conversely, you may find a hotel offers few stars in hopes of attracting budget-conscious travellers, but charges just as much as a higher-rated neighbour. *Pensioni* are generally more modest establishments, though the distinction between these and ordinary hotels is becoming rather blurred. *Locande* are traditionally an even more basic form of hostelry, but these days the term may denote somewhere fairly chic. Other inexpensive accommodation is sometimes known as *alloggi* or *affittacamere*. There are usually plenty of cheap dives around railway stations; for somewhere more salubrious, head for the historic quarters. Whatever the shortcomings of the décor, furnishings and fittings, you can usually rely at least on having clean sheets.

Price lists, by law, must be posted on the back of the door of every room, along with meal prices and any extra charges (such as air-conditioning, or even a shower in cheap places). Many hotels display two or three different rates, depending on the season. Low-season rates may be about a third lower than peak-season tariffs. During high season you should always book ahead to be sure of a room (a fax reservation may be less frustrating to organize than one by post, and certainly more likely to reach its destination).

If you have paid a deposit, your booking is valid under Italian law, but don't expect it to be refunded if you have to cancel. Tourist offices publish annual regional lists of hotels and pensions with current rates, but do not generally make reservations for visitors. Major city business hotels may offer significant discounts at weekends.

Main railway stations generally have accommodation booking desks; inevitably, a fee is charged. Chain hotels or motels are generally the easiest hotels to book, though not always the most interesting to stay in. Top of the list is CIGA (*Compagnia Grandi Alberghi*) with some of the most luxurious establishments in Italy, many of them grand, turn-of-the-century places that have been exquisitely restored. Venice's legendary Cipriani is one of its flagships. The French consortium *Relais et Châteaux* specializes in tastefully indulgent accommodation, often in historic buildings. At a more affordable level, one of the biggest chains in Italy is *Jolly Hotels*, always reliable if not all up to the same standard; these can generally be found near the centres of larger towns. Many motels are operated by the ACI (Italian Automobile Club) or by AGIP (the oil company) and usually located along major exit routes.

If you arrive without a reservation, begin looking or phoning round for accommodation early in the day. If possible, inspect the room (and bathroom facilities) before you book, and check the tariff carefully. Italian hoteliers may legally alter their rates twice during the year, so printed tariffs or tourist board lists (and prices quoted in this book!) may be out of date. Hoteliers who wilfully overcharge should be reported to the local tourist office. You will be asked for your passport for registration purposes.

Prices listed in this guide are for double rooms, and you can expect to pay about two-thirds the rate for single occupancy. Extra beds are usually charged at about a third more of the room rate. Rooms without private bathrooms generally charge 20–30% less, and most offer discounts for children sharing parent's rooms, or children's meals. A *camera singola* (single room) may cost anything from about L25,000 upwards. Double rooms (*camera doppia*) go from about L60,000 to L250,000 or more. If you want a double bed make sure you specify a *camera matrimoniale*. Breakfast is usually optional in hotels, though obligatory in *pensioni*. You can usually get better value by eating breakfast in a bar or café.

Hostels and Budget Accommodation

There aren't many youth hostels (*alberghi* or *ostelli per la gioventù*) in Italy, but they are generally pleasant and sometimes located in historic buildings. The **Associazione Italiana Alberghi per la Gioventù** (Italian Youth Hostel Association, or AIG) is affiliated to the International Youth Hostel Federation. For a full list of hostels, contact AIG at Via Cavour 44, 00184 Roma (✆ 06 487 1152, ✉ 06 488 0492). An international membership card will enable you to stay in any of them. Cards can usually be purchased on the spot, or you can obtain one in advance from:

UK, Youth Hostels Association of England and Wales, 8 St Stephens Hill, St Albans, ✆ (01727) 855 215.

USA, American Youth Hostels Inc., Box 37613, Washington DC 20013-7613, ✆ (202) 783 6161.

Australia, Australian Youth Hostel Association, 60 Mary Street, Surry Hills, Sydney, NSW 2010, ✆ (02) 9621 1111.

Canada, Canadian Hostelling Association, 1600 James Naismith Drive, Suite 608, Gloucester, Ontario K1B 5N4, ✆ (613) 237 7884.

Religious institutions also run hostels; some are single sex, others accept Catholics only. Rates are usually somewhere between L15,000 and L20,000, including breakfast. Discounts are available for senior citizens, and some family rooms are available. You generally have to check in after 5pm, and pay for your room before 9am. Hostels usually close for most of the daytime, and many operate a curfew. During the spring, noisy school parties cram hostels for field trips. In the summer, it's advisable to book ahead. Contact the hostels directly.

If you're travelling in a group or with a family, self-catering can be the ideal way to experience Italy. The National Tourist Office has lists of agencies in the UK and USA which rent places on a weekly or fortnightly basis. The small ads in the weekend papers are crammed with suggestions, especially for Tuscany. If you have set your heart on a particular region, write to its tourist office and ask for a list of agencies and owners, who will send brochures or particulars of their accommodation. Maid service is included in the more glamorous villas; ask whether bed linen and towels are provided. A few of the larger operators are listed below.

in the UK and Ireland

Citalia, Marco Polo House, 3–5 Lansdowne Road, Croydon CR9 1LL, ✆ (020) 8686 5533.

Eurovillas, 36 East Street, Coggeshall, Essex CO6 1SH, ✆ (01376) 561156.

Inghams, 10–18 Putney Hill, London SW15 6AX, ✆ (020) 8780 4450.

Interhome, 383 Richmond Road, Twickenham, Middx TW1 2EF, ✆ (020) 8891 1294.

International Chapters, 47–51 St John's Wood High Street, London NW8 7NJ, ✆ (020) 7722 9560.

Magic of Italy, 227 Shepherds Bush Road, London W6 7AS, ✆ (020) 8748 7575.

Topflight, D'Olier Chambers, D'Olier Street, Dublin 2, ✆ (01) 679 9177.

Vacanze in Italia, Manor Courtyard, Bignor, Pulborough, West Sussex RH20 1QD, ✆ (01798) 7426.

in the USA

CIT, ✆ (800) 248 8687; in New York, ✆ (212) 730 2121, who can also arrange fly-drive rental car packages.

At Home Abroad, 405 East 56th Street 6-H, New York, NY 10022-2466, ✆ (212) 421 9165, ✆ 752 1591, *athomabrod@aol.com*

CUENDET: Rentals for Italy (and Elsewhere!), ✆ (800) 726 7602 *www.rentvillas.com*

Hideaways International, 767 Islington Street, Portsmouth, NH 03801, ✆ (617) 486 8955.

Homeowners International, 1133 Broadway, New York, NY 10010, ✆ (212) 691 2361.

RAVE (Rent-a-Vacation Everywhere), 135 Meigs Street, Rochester, New York, NY 14607, ✆ (716) 246 0760.

Life under canvas is not the fanatical craze it is in France, nor necessarily any great bargain, but there are over 2000 sites in Italy, particularly popular with holidaymaking families in August, when you can expect to find many sites at bursting point. Unofficial camping is generally frowned on and may attract a stern rebuke from the local police. Camper vans (and facilities for them) are increasingly popular. You can obtain a list of local sites from any regional tourist office. Campsite charges generally range from about L6–8000 per adult; tents and vehicles additionally cost about L7000 each. Small extra charges may also be levied for hot showers and electricity. A car-borne couple could therefore spend practically as much for a night at a well-equipped campsite as in a cheap hotel. To obtain a camping carnet and to book ahead, write to the **Centro Internazionale Prenotazioni Campeggio**, Casella Postale 23, 50041 Calenzano, Firenze, ✆ 055 882 381, ✆ 055 882 3918 (ask for their list of campsites with the booking form). The **Touring Club Italiano** (TCI) publishes a comprehensive annual guide to campsites throughout Italy which is available in bookshops for L29,500. Write to: TCI, Corso Italia 10, Milan, ✆ 02 85261/✆ 02 852 6245.

Women Travellers

Italian men, with the heritage of Casanova, Don Giovanni and Rudolph Valentino as their birthright, are very confident in their role as Great Latin Lovers, but the old horror stories of gangs following the innocent tourist maiden and pinching her bottom are way behind the times. Italian men these days are often exquisitely polite and flirt on a much more sophisticated level, especially in the more 'Europeanized' north.

Still, women travelling alone may frequently receive hisses, wolf-whistles and unsolicited comments (complimentary or lewd, depending on your attitude) or 'assistance' from local swains—usually of the balding, middle-age-crisis variety. A confident, indifferent poise is usually the best policy. Failing that, a polite 'I am waiting for my *marito*' (avoiding damaged male egos which can turn nasty), followed by a firm '*no!*' or '*Vai via!*' (Scram!) will generally solve the problem. Flashers and wandering hands on crowded buses may be an unpleasant surprise, but rarely present a serious threat (unless they're after your purse).

Risks can be greatly reduced if you use common sense and avoid lonely streets or parks and train stations after dark. Choose hotels and restaurants within easy and safe walking distance of public transport. Travelling with a companion of either sex will buffer you considerably from such nuisances (a guardian male, of course, instantly converts you into an inviolable chattel in Italian eyes). Two women travelling together may still find they attract unwanted advances, particularly in the south. Avoid hitch-hiking alone in Italy.

A History of Pilgrimage

Staff, Scrip and Tunic: Two Millennia of Christian Pilgrimage

Pilgrimage is common to all the great religions, and to all times. The annual festivals where the nomadic tribes of ancient Israel would meet and dance around their sanctuary were called *hag*, a word that comes from the same Semitic root as the Arabic *haj*, meaning the all-important Muslim pilgrimage to Mecca. Jesus himself, in the trips to Jerusalem mentioned in the gospels, was following the custom of **festival pilgrimages**. Israel knew three of these each year, and in them the population of Jerusalem increased as much as fivefold. The main festival occurred at the time of the modern Passover, or Easter, so that a considerable proportion of the people of Israel would in fact have been present when Jesus was crucified.

In **Christianity**, the idea of pilgrimage developed slowly and naturally. Not much is heard of it until the 3rd century, when the earliest graffiti on the walls of the Roman catacombs attests to the visits of the faithful at the tombs of the martyrs. In the 4th century, after the conversion of Constantine and the establishment of the Church under Theodosius, their numbers greatly increased, both in Rome and in the Holy Land. One of the early visitors to Jerusalem was Helen, the pious mother of Constantine; she came as a pilgrim, but also to oversee the construction of the church complex her son was building at the Holy Sepulchre, and it was there that according to legend she discovered the True Cross.

In the early days, the **rituals** of the pilgrimage were still, like so many other features of Christian practice, strongly influenced by the pagan past. Many of the first pilgrims came to be cured of diseases, and would spend the nights sleeping in the basilicas hoping for a cure, as their ancestors had done in the sanctuaries of Aesclepius, the god of healing. All pilgrims would commonly practise the *refrigeratum*, or ritual banquet around the tombs of the saints, a pagan legacy which was expressly forbidden by Pope Damasus in the 4th century.

The end of the Roman Empire, and the growing insecurity around the Western world, did not stop Christians from seeking out the sources of their faith. Nor was pilgrimage confined to **Rome** and **Jerusalem**. Other popular sites included places mentioned in the Bible, especially **Nazareth** and **Jericho**, as well as the once-great city of **Antioch** not far to the north, which had an important collection of Christian martyrs of its own. **Egypt**, where the fathers of the desert had initiated Christian monasticism, became a popular destination among monks looking for inspiration and guidance for their communities back home. Even in the west of Europe, graves of early bishops or martyrs from the imperial persecutions attracted pilgrims, notably St Martin at **Tours**, and St Vincent in **Saragossa**, which became the national pilgrimages of the Franks in Gaul and the Visigoths in Spain.

The City to Where All Roads Lead

But from the beginning, the eyes of most wayfaring Christians were turned towards **Rome**. After 476 no longer a capital of empire, the Rome of the popes was now a spiritual capital, a holy city. As Leo I put it, in a document from the 5th century: 'Rome, stained in its first founding by the blood of Remus, slain by his brother Romulus, is made new in the blood of martyrs, shed by the new founders, brothers in sanctity, Peter and Paul.'

In one sense, pilgrimage came naturally to a world that had for so long looked to Rome as its political and spiritual centre. After the fall of the Empire, **popes** assumed the old role of the emperors as dispensers of justice. Under the Empire, any condemned prisoner who was a Roman citizen could 'appeal unto Caesar', as had St Paul, who came to Rome in the year 62. Now, Church tribunals would often send felons to Rome for **penance**, or to get the pope's advice in difficult cases. One such case is that of an Anglo-Saxon named Wulfin, who murdered six priests; they sent him to Rome and he was there told to endow a church and six monks to pray for his soul in perpetuity. By the 9th century, as a contemporary writer expressed it, 'penance was synonymous with going to Rome'.

For all that, it was not the presence of the Pope, but the **tombs of the martyrs** that brought so many people to Rome. Reverence for the first saints, the men and women who had died for their faith, had been the strength, the essence of Christianity in the difficult early centuries. By the 300s this reverence had transformed itself into a **cult of relics**, in which the remains of Peter and the rest were attributed magical virtues, and even occasioned miracles. Relics Rome had in plenty, and they would be the main attraction for centuries to come. In the troubles of the dark ages, so many raids and sieges disturbed the rest of the martyrs in the catacombs that the Church gradually moved their bones into new churches dedicated to them. The process began as early as the 5th century, and was first carried out on a large scale by Pope Paul I beginning in 757.

Not content with the relics of the holy martyrs, the Romans over the centuries had accumulated a historic treasure trove of dubious items, including an urn full of manna, the genuine Ark of the Covenant, the tablets of Moses and even the loaves and fishes that Jesus had used to feed the multitude. It was a credulous age, but sincere pilgrims might smile at these as they came to pray at the tomb of St Peter. Another attraction, and the one that always drew the largest crowds when it was exhibited, was the *Sudarium*, supposedly the cloth with which Veronica had wiped Jesus' brow while he was carrying the cross, and which bore the image of his face.

It may come as a surprise to hear of so many people traveling so far in what we have learned to call the 'Dark Ages'. But people do have a way of getting around, even in the most uncertain of times, and the rulers of the day, both princes and bishops, did what they could to make the trip safer and easier for the growing waves of pilgrims. The first **hostels**, or *xenodochie*, began to appear in the 6th century, usually attached to monasteries; many included hospitals, for pilgrims often suffered from diseases, and were travelling to Rome in the hope of a cure. Some rulers were particularly solicitous of pilgrims' welfare. Charlemagne often welcomed them into his own court, and the Lombard kings of Italy built well-equipped **hospices** on the roads to Rome and Monte Sant'Angelo

Nor were accommodations lacking in Rome. One feature of this age was the national hostels, or *scholae*, that grew up to serve the needs of pilgrims. Again, it is surprising to learn that the first and largest of these was created by a small nation very far from Rome—the English. King Ina of Wessex founded their *Schola Saxonum* in 717; part of this much-rebuilt complex survives as the **Hospital of Santo Spirito in Sassia**, on Borgo

Santo Spirito. A *schola Francorum* came next, endowed by Charlemagne himself (who also financed an elaborate centre for the reception of pilgrims in Jerusalem, courtesy of his good relations with Caliph Haroun al-Rashid). Both of these *scholae* were near St Peter's, though the Lombards, the Frisians and others built theirs in other parts of the city.

As pilgrimage became an established part of Christianity, other destinations began to draw the attention of the faithful. In this period, devotion to St Michael was increasingly important throughout Europe, especially among soldiers and knights. **Monte Sant'Angelo**, high on a mountain in the Gargano Peninsula of Puglia, became the national shrine of the Lombards after their fleet won a great victory over the Arabs in 663 nearby on St Michael's Day. Lombard kings endowed the site with churches and hospices, but men of other nations came too—among them the Normans, whose visits as pilgrims perhaps convinced them to come down and conquer southern Italy. Monte Sant'Angelo remained one of the leading pilgrimage sites in Europe until about the 9th century, when its temporary control by the Orthodox Byzantines decreased its attraction for Westerners. Pilgrims who once travelled all the way to the Gargano now began to visit a more convenient centre: **Mont-St-Michel** in Normandy. Most important of all the new pilgrimages was **Compostela**, out at the end of the world in the far northwestern corner of Spain, where the remains of the apostle, St James the Greater, were discovered in the 9th century. Compostela gradually replaced **Saragossa** as the national shrine of Christian Spain, though it was nearly as popular among the French.

The coming of a millennium focuses minds on spiritual things, and there seems to have been a great increase in pilgrimages around 980, especially to Palestine. Many Christians dreamed of being in Jerusalem for the thousandth anniversary of Jesus' crucifixion in 1033, but politics got in the way. The fanatical **Caliph Al-Hakim** began persecuting pilgrims around 1010; he also destroyed the Church of the Holy Sepulchre in Jerusalem. Worse yet, after the Battle of Manzikert in 1071 the Seljuk Turks occupied almost all of what is now Turkey. A stroll through the medieval Balkans and Anatolia had never been easy, and now it became almost impossible. The closing of the Holy Land, of course, was a direct motivation for the **First Crusade**, proclaimed by Pope Urban II in 1095. Urban also granted a 'plenary' indulgence for anyone going on the Crusade—equal to penance for a whole life's worth of sins.

This idea of **indulgences** seems to have been invented in the Frankish Church in the 10th century, where it took the form of a simple cash payment for sins. Alms-giving was a common sort of penance, it was rationalized, so why should a contribution to the servants of God, with their many charitable enterprises, not be a fitting recompense for sins? After the Crusades, papal indulgences were gradually introduced as a reward for pilgrimages. The great increase came during the papacies of Alexander III (d.1181), who extended it to Compostela, Nicholas IV (d. 1292) and Celestine V, a simple hermit from Abruzzo who became a surprise compromise choice for pope in 1294. Celestine had founded a church back home in the city of L'Aquila, called Santa Maria di Collemaggio; as pope, he granted an indulgence for visiting it (the custom is maintained to this day; to receive it pilgrims pass through the Holy Door, which is opened once a year on August 28). For Rome itself, a program of visits was gradually developed to obtain the indulgence, taking in the '**Seven Churches**': San Pietro and San Paolo Fuori le Mure, the most important, but also Santa Maria Maggiore, San Giovanni in Laterano, Santa Croce in Gerusalemme, with its relic of the true cross, San Lorenzo and San Sebastiano on the Appian Way.

Pilgrim Practicalities

Why walk halfway across Europe? In the Middle Ages, the question would not even need to be asked. Spiritual journeys were an accepted part of life, and their motivations varied as much as the length of the trip, from the heights of inspired devotion to the most candid pious innocence. One writer in the 1300s noted French peasants typically vowing to walk to St-Martial in Limoges if God would protect their cows from the horrible English, or help them find some lost pennies.

Wherever they were going, or why, there were **established procedures** for all pilgrims to follow. Before they set on their way, they were expected to clear their debts and make a will—that is, if they were fortunate enough to own any property. The wealthy often got in the mood by making large charitable gifts. Particularly devout ones might hand over everything to the Church, with the proviso that, if they returned safely, they would have the use of their property for the rest of their lives.

That, at times, could be problematical. One historian has estimated that over half the pilgrims setting out for Rome for the 1350 Jubilee never made it back home. In normal years, though, pilgrims could travel in relative security. There was always plenty of company on the roads to Rome, and pilgrims commonly joined up in **convoys**, like the merry company in Chaucer's *Canterbury Tales*, as much for companionship as for safety. Throughout the Middle Ages both secular and clerical authorities did the best they could to look after pilgrims, who enjoyed a special legal status. A substantial body of international law, the *lex peregrinorum*, developed, protecting pilgrims from arbitrary detention or seizure of goods; local barons or princes who transgressed it might be excommunicated.

Certain things every pilgrim had to have. First of all a **staff**—practical for long walks through Europe, but also a well-understood sign of spiritual intent. Sometimes priests would bestow the staff on a departing pilgrim in a ceremony similar to the dubbing of a knight; in French the staff was called a *bourdon*: a lance, symbolic of the fight against the Devil. The other indispensibles were a **scrip** (leather pouch) and a distinctive sort of **tunic** (called in medieval England a *sclaevin*, though fashions for pilgrims changed over the centuries like everything else). These were practical too, but medieval writers, living in their animated cosmos where every simple thing carried deeper levels of meaning, found ingenious ways of allegorizing them; one clerical scribe explained that staff, bag and tunic, duly blessed by the local priest before the pilgrim's departure, should remind him of the elemental virtues: faith, hope and charity.

Even royalty made a show of following the custom. **King Canute** came down in 1027, with his scrip, cloak and staff like everyone else. Another visitor from up north was a Scottish king named **Macbeth**, who made it to Rome in 1050 with perhaps quite a few sins to atone for; it isn't recorded what he was wearing. These two would no doubt have come on horseback, and they might have managed 30 miles in a day—or as little as five, over roads that had not been improved since the fall of the Roman Empire. Less opulent burghers and clerics might make the trip on a mule or donkey. A pilgrim on foot—the vast majority of them— would be lucky to cover ten miles a day in the best of circumstances.

One thing remained constant: whatever class you were travelling, a pilgrimage was an **expensive** proposition. Especially in Jubilee years, the traffic was terrific and innkeepers along the way could charge accordingly. In Rome itself, the crush of people made it even worse. For the Jubilee of 1350, you paid 13 pennies a night for the privilege of sleeping in the same bed with three other people. However spiritually edified by the experience, few pilgrims seem to have come home with a good opinion of Rome. English writer Walter Map, in the 12th century, reckoned that ROMA stood for *Radix Omnium Malarum Avaritia*: 'avarice, the root of all evil'. Pilgrim Desiderius Erasmus, some 400 years later, dryly noted that he considered the Roman innkeepers' chances of salvation 'limited'.

Pilgrims came home from the holy city confirmed in their faith, perhaps, but travel 'broadened the man' in more secular ways. Pilgrims saw the marvels of ancient Rome, and acquired a greater respect for the past. The artists and scholars among them learned new ideas and techniques from the Italians. Most importantly, meeting Christians from all over Europe and sometimes beyond helped to confirm **the community of the faith**.

They brought home other things too. Rome was a great market for **antiquities**, and occasionally even bulk loads of marble, pillaged from the ancient ruins. Many pilgrims, both clerical and secular, however, were after something much more portable and valuable— **holy relics**. By fair means or foul, they got hold of tiny bits of bone or even entire bodies, shipping them home to endow the countless new churches of booming medieval Europe. The Germans had a particular reputation for it. On more than one occasion, when word got out that a particularly important relic was going north, the Romans started a riot.

More commonly, each pilgrim would bring back some sort of **souvenir** to prove he had made the trip. In Jerusalem, they were given **palm leaves** from the 'Grove of Abraham': hence the English word and common surname *Palmer* (people of Spanish descent can trace a pilgrim to Rome in their ancestry from the equally common surname *Romero*). At Compostella, the common insignia of a pilgrim to St James was a **cockle-shell**, fixed to the cap or tunic. The Spaniards, in the 12th century, were the first to think of making leaden badges with pins, in the shape of a cockle shell. The idea spread to other centres, in Italy and elsewhere, and by the late Middle Ages some determined travellers could be seen with many badges adorning their hats—just as some do today.

By the 13th century, even papal indulgences weren't enough to keep the faithful coming to Rome. Competition from other centres was putting Peter's See in the shadows: first **Assisi**, where the impetus to popular religion given by St Francis and the Franciscans naturally found an expression in pilgrimage after Francis' canonization in 1228. Already, Franciscans were claiming that the saint had received a special plenary indulgence from Pope Honorius III for pilgrims visiting the Porziuncola. It was controversial, but it paid; Assisi was the most important pilgrimage site in Italy in the 1300s.

Other major centres were **Santiago de Compostela** and **Mont-St-Michel**, along with the new pilgrimage at **Canterbury**, which grew up after the murder of Thomas Becket in 1170. Becket came to be considered by many as a holy martyr, and reports of miracles multiplied; after his canonization in 1173, Canterbury attracted pilgrims from across Europe, especially France. Also, in this great age of devotion to the Virgin Mary, numerous new pilgrimages sprang from apparitions or miraculous images of the Virgin, as at **Chartres** and **Rocamadour** in France, **Mariazell** in Austria, and **Montserrat** in Catalunya.

Rome itself was full of troubles, from the sack by the Norman Robert Guiscard in 1084 to the short-lived revolution of Arnold of Brescia in in 1145, and the continuous gang warfare between noble Roman houses like the Colonna and Orsini. By the 1200s most of the *scholae* were closing down, and Rome was becoming a very quiet place. At the end of the century, however, a surprise event would bring the Roman pilgrimage back to life.

The Roman Jubilee

'Jubilee' is a Hebrew word, meaning a ram's horn. In ancient times this instrument proclaimed the beginning of the great celebrations held every fifty years in Israel, a **holy year** when slaves were freed, debts forgiven, and seized property was restored; in these years the land remained uncultivated, according to the Bible, and the people had to live on what they had stored from the years previous. For Christians, the idea of 'jubilee' started with the **Crusades**; in a metaphorical sense the liberation of the Holy Land was to be a great celebration, greater than ever the Hebrews knew. Even for a fighting Crusader, of course, the trip to the Holy Land was also a kind of **pilgrimage**, and it was only natural that all these ideas became intertwined in the Christian mind. There were other influences at work too: perhaps a faint memory of the hundred-year festivals of ancient Rome called the *ludi saeculares*.

Whatever the source, these ideas all came together at the first, utterly spontaneous **1300 Jubilee**. Around New Years' Day, huge crowds of pilgrims, from Italy and beyond, began marching into Rome, claiming that this year had been declared a special one, with a plenary indulgence decreed by a pope a hundred years before. This was news to Boniface VIII. No one knows how the rumour started, or where, but with all the people flooding into the city, full of expectations, Boniface allowed himself to be convinced. He had a bull (written mandate) proclaiming the Jubilee, *Antiquarium Relatio*, out by 22 February.

Among the pilgrims present was Dante Alighieri, and it seems to have made a considerable impression on him. His *Commedia* begins on Good Friday of 1300, and there are several references in it to his experience in Rome; a bridge in the *Inferno* is even designed after the Ponte Mollo, which carried the pilgrims over the Tiber to St Peter's, an early landmark in the art of traffic control:

Come i Roman per l'essercito molto,
L'anno del giubileo, su per lo ponte
Hanno a passar la gente molto colto;

Che dall'un lato tutti hanno la fronte
Verso l' castello, e vanno a San Pietro;
Dall'altra sponda vanno verso il monte.

Inferno, XVIII, 28–32

(As the Romans, in the year of the Jubilee, had to arrange it to pass the polite crowds over the bridge/That on one side everyone faced the castle [Castel Sant'Angelo], and proceeded to St Peter's, while on the other side they passed towards the mountain.)

Pope Boniface's surprise turned out to be by no means an unpleasant one. The Jubilee of 1300 was a tremendous success, and quite profitable for both the Pope and the Romans; one account records the priests literally raking in the money—with rakes—cast by pilgrims in front of the high altar of St Peter's. The gossips claimed they were pulling in 1000 livres a day. People would gossip about such things, even in a Jubilee year.

In fact, the numerous enemies of the much-despised Boniface turned the Jubilee into an argument against him, with cries of **commercialism** that were probably not at all deserved. For Boniface, disgrace and death were only a few years away, and for Rome, the Jubilee was to be only a kind of farewell party before one of the most dismal centuries in the city's long history. In 1305, with the election of the French Pope **Clement V**, the papacy prepared to move to Avignon; preparations were hastened along when the popes' abode, the Lateran Palace, burned to the ground in 1308.

Rome was destitute, and the Romans were doing the best they could to gain back their lost trade; some of them were busy forging papal bulls, declaring new indulgences for pilgrimages to the city. In 1342 they got up a delegation of nobles, commons and clerics to send to Avignon, asking the pope to grant another Jubilee for the year 1350. **Clement VI** was amenable, and preparations were made for what was to prove the absolute worst Christian journey since the ragtag Crusade of Peter the Hermit.

Fate welcomed in the **1350 Jubilee** with an earthquake, which knocked the top off the campanile of St Peter's and damaged many other of the city's churches. News travelled slowly back then, and perhaps a million pilgrims were already on their way. As we have seen, only half of them managed to make the round trip in safety.

Conditions were unsettled throughout Europe, to say the least; England and France were in the middle of the **Hundred Years' War**, and the **Black Death** had roared through Europe only two years previously. Northern Italy was especially thick with bands of robbers in 1350, most of them German, but plenty of them Italian as well. Even Roman hoodlums were getting in on the act. Worrying that all the choice marks would be taken before they even reached the city, they are recorded as organizing expeditions to Tuscany, hoping to bag a few wealthy pilgrims while there were still some left.

Of the crowned heads of the day, only King Louis of Hungary managed to come. Edward III of England, too busy wrecking France to have time for penance, sent a clever archbishop to Avignon to get the indulgence for him, arguing with cunning sophistries that princes were too wound up with the cares of state, and deserved special treatment. Pope Clement said nothing doing; if you wanted the indulgence you had to come to Rome. Both Edward and the King of France actually forbade their subjects to make the trip, worrying about the loss of men and money from their war efforts. Fortunately for the Romans it was still the Middle Ages and few people paid their rulers any mind—though quite a few Englishmen returned home to find that the King had sequestered their property.

Rome actually did well by this Jubilee, but it wasn't enough to repair the fortunes of a city the papacy had abandoned. After 1354 the Church had split into political schism, and back in Avignon the popes reigning there were doing anything they could to raise money. In 1382 they tried to move the indulgences granted for visiting the churches of Rome to those of Marseilles; few Christians were convinced. Pope **Boniface IX**, reigning in Rome, declared a Jubilee in 1390, which was formally condemned from Avignon.

In **1400**, Rome saw another spontaneous Jubilee like the one in 1300; no pope declared it, but everybody came, drawn by the magic of the turn of a century. On the other hand, an official Jubilee in 1423 was a failure. The Church had been reunited, and **Martin IV** reigned back in Rome, but the city was at its lowest ebb; visitors reported that St Peter's often looked abandoned in daytime, while wolves sniffed around it at night. For those who did come, visiting the **catacombs**, nearly forgotten for centuries, once again became popular. The biggest shows were still the public displays of the Sudarium; some fortunate foreign pilgrims got 14,000 years off purgatory just for seeing it. Rome was in a bad way.

Slowly but surely, however, the city and the papacy were recovering from the long abandonment and the schism. A regular **Jubilee** was proclaimed for 1450, and extensive preparations were made, but this one proved to be as full of trouble as the one a century before. A summer epidemic chased most of the pilgrims out into the countryside; when they returned in the autumn, so did the disease. On December 19th, a day when the Sudarium was to be displayed, panic broke out on the Ponte Mollo, the bridge Dante described in the *Inferno*, and the only one near the Vatican. A Roman nobleman tried to drive his carriage over against the traffic and 200 pilgrims tumbled into the Tiber; some of their bodies were found as far downsteam as Ostia.

For all that, the Jubilee was considered a success. Both the Church and the Romans had learned a bit about accommodating the crowds, and things were considerably more organized than in previous Holy Years. 1,022 *alberghi* were ready to receive pilgrims, and these were joined by the national hostels, refounded after their decline in the 13th century. The English hostel had been the first to be rebuilt, in 1362, thanks to a rosary-maker named John Shepard and his wife Alice, and now a score of others followed, serving nations as diverse as the Hungarians and the Catalans. Most importantly, the Church had the foresight to buy up stores of grain and wine, so no one went hungry and pilgrims were able to enjoy a slight respite from the usual Roman price-gouging; still, food was dear enough and thousands of pilgrims slept rough in the porticos of the great basilicas.

Sojourners in a World of Sceptics

Through the 15th and 16th centuries pilgrims still came to Rome, and Jubilees passed in majestic succession; Rome enjoyed a rebirth at the height of the Renaissance, but in this new age the Church would face the most serious **crisis** in its history. And in the troubles of the **Reformation** and the grey age that followed, even the idea of pilgrimage would be called into question.

Along with the Middle Ages, a lot of the old communal sense of life and spirituality was passing too. Reformers denied the efficacy of holy relics, and condemned the idea of indulgences; many of them were willing to throw the idea of pilgrimage out with all the other things they saw as mere medieval superstitions. As the religious impulse turned inwards, men who would become **Protestants** and even many of those who remained with the Church began to see **faith** and **prayer** as the only things that mattered; journeys and ceremonies were a pointless distraction. Instead of a pilgrimage, a doctor of theology at Paris in 1423 recommended saying ten Paternosters a day, as a real pilgrim would walk ten miles. In Italy an unusual fashion took hold, a sort of virtual pilgrimage whereby the benefits of the real thing could be gained without leaving home. To that end, artists created the first versions of the *Monte Sacro*, a kind of pilgrimage in miniature, with a series of chapels on a hill, each representing a stage of the Passion; one of the first was built at **Varallo** in Piedmont in 1520, where it can still be seen.

Martin Luther had been a pilgrim in Rome, and he was not impressed. In those days, part of the pilgrimage ritual was to climb on one's knees the **Scala Santa** at St John Lateran, the staircase brought from Jerusalem where Jesus had departed Pilate's palace on the way to the crucifixion. Luther had got halfway up when he heard a voice saying 'The just shall live by faith alone, not by penance'; whereupon he stood up, walked back down and went home to Germany to start the Reformation. Luther and **Calvin** both believed that all pilgrimages should be abolished, and in lands that went over to Protestantism, most of them were. As the religious struggle became increasingly fanatical, important pilgrimage sites under Protestant control were sacked or destroyed, as at Tours, where the body of St Martin was publicly burned by the Huguenots in 1562.

On the Catholic side, the **Council of Trent** in 1563 confirmed the veneration of saints and the usefulness of pilgrimages, as well as the efficacy of indulgences. The great Renaissance and Baroque rebuilding of Rome, well under way at this time, was largely undertaken with pilgrims in mind. **Piazza del Popolo**, just inside the Porta Flaminia, was redeveloped under Sixtus V, with its obelisk and twin churches—probably the most spectacular front door of any city in the world. New streets were laid out from there, to facilitate the movement of people around the city and connect the great basilicas, from Via del Babuino, under Sixtus, to Via Merulana between S. Maria Maggiore and the Lateran, under Gregory XVIII. **St Peter's** itself, the showpiece of the renewed Church, was not completed until 1626, with Bernini's colonnades in front to embrace the vast crowds

The **1550 Jubilee**, held at the height of the religious wars, did not attract large numbers of pilgrims, but with the recovery of the **Counter-reformation** Church things slowly got back to normal, and bigger crowds than ever came for the Holy Years of 1575 and 1600. In the Baroque era, Rome was sharing the devotion of pilgrims with a relatively new destination: **Loreto**, near Ancona in the Marches, where the home of Mary was said to have miraculously transported itself from Nazareth. Like Assisi, Loreto proved a refreshing contrast to the worldliness of Rome. In the 16th century it had come under the influence of the **Jesuits**, the new order that, among its many other activities, was attempting to develop a new spiritual basis for pilgrimage in response to the times. The French philosopher **Montaigne**, who visited in 1581, claimed that there was more sincere religiosity there than in any place he had ever seen. Ironically Jean **Descartes**, whose metaphysics and mathematics did more than anything to undermine the spiritual conception of life, was a fervent Catholic who made a pilgrimage to Loreto in 1623. So, at about the same time, did **Galileo**.

Led by the Jesuits, the Church throughout the 1600s exerted itself to put an end to abuses and practices considered superstitious, and many of the features of pilgrimage came under attack. In the eyes of these **modernizers**, many of Europe's local pilgrimages had turned into simple popular festivals. These they tried to reform, and in many cases they put an end to the veneration of relics considered doubtful. One thing Protestants and Catholics shared in this hard-boiled century was a conspicuous loss of any feeling for the poor as fellow Christians. Many came to look on pilgrimage as a lazy man's way of avoiding work. Even in Catholic countries touched by the modern spirit, pilgrims were often regarded as little more than tramps. This sentiment perhaps reached its height under that Most Catholic Monarch **Louis XIV**. During his reign many of France's hospices were closed by royal decree, and pilgrims without expensive permits from the authorities were rounded up and pressed into the navy.

Hard times only got worse in the 'Age of Enlightenment', and not only for Rome. With a hostile Ottoman Empire in control of Palestine, voyages there slowed to a trickle. Besides Loreto, the only really thriving pilgrimages were in places like Czestochowa in **Poland**, or St Patrick's Purgatory at Lough Derg in **Ireland**. Under the French revolutionary governments, pilgrimage was considered a 'counter-revolutionary activity', and Napoleon expanded the ban on it to all the lands under French control. After the old order was restored, the Church celebrated with a joyous and thoroughly successful Jubilee in 1825. Some 400,000 attended, mostly Italians, since the faithful in many other countries, even Catholic France and Austria, were in one way or another discouraged from the trip by their governments. Many of those who attended came in the traditional pilgrim costume of the old days.

It was to be the only Jubilee of the century. In 1850, Rome was under occupation by French troops, and still recovering from Mazzini and Garibaldi's unsuccessful revolt. 1875 found the city the new capital of a united Italy, with the Pope in self-imposed seclusion in the Vatican. Pope **Leo XIII** finally opened the Holy Doors again in 1900, in a Jubilee marked by the canonization of **St Rita of Cascia**, whose tomb in Umbria has since become a pilgrimage destination in its own right.

One of many. The most remarkable and unexpected turn to pilgrimage in our time has been the spontaneous gatherings of people around **apparitions of the Virgin Mary**: at Lourdes in 1858, at Fatima in 1917, and at a score of other places around the world. After decades in which the pilgrimage of Santiago seemed a doomed medieval relic, now every year more and more pilgrims walk the long road across northern Spain to Compostela. **Assisi** too has found new life, with a modern generation for whom the teachings of St Francis seem to have a special resonance. And in the Gargano, not far from the ancient shrine at Monte Sant'Angelo, tens of thousands each year come to **San Giovanni Rotondo**, the home of Padre Pio, a simple priest who received the stigmata like St Francis, was beatified in 1999, and is expected soon to become a saint.

On **Christmas Eve 1999**, the Holy Doors of the Roman basilicas once more will swing open for a Jubilee year, one in which some 20 million Catholics are expected to visit Italy. Not many of them will be walking, or even riding mules. But they need only take a brief look at the history to see how they are part of a profound and venerable tradition, one that has its source in the people, and that has found the inspiration to adapt to changing times and tides for, at the time of writing, precisely two thousand years.

Art and Architecture

You'd have to spend your holiday in a baggage compartment to miss Italy's vast piles of architecture and art. The Italians estimate there is at least one work of art per capita in their country, which is more than anyone could see in a lifetime—especially since so much of it is locked away in museums that are in semi-permanent 'restoration'. Although you may occasionally chafe at not being able to see certain frescoes, or at finding a famous palace completely wrapped up in the ubiquitous green netting of the restorers, the Italians on the whole bear very well the burden of keeping their awesome patrimony dusted off and open for visitors. Some Italians find it insupportable living with the stuff all around them; the futurists, for instance, were worried that St Mark's in Venice might be blown up by foreign enemies in the First World War—but only because they wanted to do it themselves, as was their right as Italian citizens.

To give a chronological account of the first Italian artists is an uncomfortable task. The peninsula's mountainous terrain saw many isolated developments, and many survivals of ancient cultures even during the days of the sophisticated Etruscans and Romans. Most ancient of all, however, is the palaeolithic troglodyte culture on the Riviera, credited with creating some of the first artworks in Europe—chubby images of fertility goddesses. The most remarkable works from the Neolithic period up until the Iron Age are the thousands of graffiti rock incisions in several isolated Alpine valleys north of Lake Iseo, especially the Val Camonica, where these ancient outdoor masterpieces are protected in a national park. After 1000 BC Italic peoples all over the peninsula were making geometrically painted pots, weapons, tools and bronze statuettes. The most impressive culture, however, was the tower-building, bronze-working Nuraghe civilization on Sardinia, of which echoes are seen in many cultures on the mainland.

Etruscan and Greek (8th–2nd centuries BC)

With the refined, art-loving Etruscans we begin to have architecture as well as art. Not much has survived, thanks to the Etruscans' habit of building in wood and decorating with terracotta, but we do have plenty of distinctive rock-cut tombs, the best of which are at Cerveteri and Tarquinia; many of them contain exceptional frescoes that reflect Aegean Greek styles. The best of their lovely sculptures, jewellery, vases, and much more, are in the museums in **Rome** (Villa Giulia—where you can also see a reconstructed temple façade), Chiusi, Volterra and Tarquinia. There are also fine Etruscan holdings in Perugia, and in the archaeology museums in Florence and Bologna.

The Etruscans imported and copied many of their vases from their ancient Greek contemporaries, from Greece proper and the colonies of Magna Graecia in southern Italy. The

Doric temple at Paestum is the best-surviving Greek structure on the peninsula (there are many others in Sicily); of the many other excavated Greek cities, usually only foundations remain. The archaeological museums in Naples, Bari and the **Vatican** contain some of the most impressive collections of ancient Greek vases, statues, and other types of art.

Roman (3rd century BC–5th century AD)

Italian art during the Roman hegemony is mostly derivative of the Etruscan and Greek, with a special talent for mosaics, wall paintings, glasswork and portraiture; architecturally, the Romans were brilliant engineers, the inventors of concrete and grand exponents of the arch. Even today their constructions such as aqueducts, amphitheatres, bridges, baths, and the Pantheon are most impressive. Of course, **Rome** itself has no end of ancient monuments; also in the vicinity there is Ostia Antica, Rome's ancient port, and Tivoli, site of Hadrian's great villa. Rome also has a stellar set of museums filled with Roman antiquities—the National Museum (now split in two), the Vatican Museum, the Capitoline Museums and the Museum of Roman Civilization at EUR. Naples is the other outstanding destination for Roman art, with the ruins of ancient Pompeii and Herculaneum on its outskirts, and a spectacular museum, not only of artefacts found in the Pompeii excavations, but also of statues from Rome dug up by Renaissance collectors like the Farnese. Other impressive Roman monuments may be seen in Verona (the arena, gates and theatre complex); the museum and excavations of Aquileia; the temples in Brescia and **Assisi**; and odds and ends in Fiesole, Bologna, Perugia, Cori (in Lazio) and Spoleto.

Early Middle Ages (5th–10th centuries)

After the fall of the Roman Empire, civilization's lamp flickered most brightly in Ravenna, where Byzantine mosaicists adorned the glittering churches of the Eastern Exarchate. Theirs was to be the prominent style in pictorial art and architecture until the 13th century. Apart from Ravenna, there are fine mosaics and paintings in **Rome**, in churches such as Sant'Agnese, San Clemente and Santa Prassede. In Rome the Italian preference for basilican churches and octagonal baptistries began in Constantine's day, and the development of Christian art and architecture through the Dark Ages can be traced there better than anywhere else. There are also many paintings in the catacombs of Rome and Naples. Other good Ravenna-style mosaics may be seen in the cathedrals of Aquileia and Torcello in Venice, where the fashion lingered long enough to create St Mark's.

'Lombard' art, really the work of the native population under Lombard rule, revealed an original talent in the 7th–9th centuries, especially evident in the churches of Cividale del Friuli, in the works in the cathedral of Monza, in and around Spoleto, and in the Abbey of San Salvatore in Brescia. A new style, presaging the Romanesque, may be seen in Sant'Ambrogio in Milan.

Romanesque (11th–12th centuries)

At this point, when an expansive society made new advances in art possible, north and south Italy went their separate ways, each contributing distinctive styles in sculpture and architecture. We also begin to learn the identities of some of their makers. The great Lombard cathedrals, masterworks of brick art and adorned with blind arcading, bas-reliefs and lofty campaniles, are best exemplified at Modena (by the master builder-sculptor Wiligelmo), San Michele in Pavia, Cremona Cathedral, and the Santo Stefano complex in Bologna. In Verona the cathedral and San Zeno were embellished by Guglielmo's talented student Nicolò; in Parma the great baptistry by Benedetto Antelami is a milestone in the synthesis of sculpture and architecture.

The rapidly accumulating wealth of Pisa permitted the undertaking of the cathedral—the largest building programme in Italy in a thousand years; its exotic style owed something to contacts with the Muslim world, but the inspiration for the design was completely original—in part a very conscious attempt to recapture the grandeur of the ancient world. Florence developed its own black and white style, exemplified in amazing buildings like the baptistry and San Miniato. Interesting variations appeared in the other Tuscan cities, each showing some Pisan stripes or Florentine rectangles.

In the south, Byzantine and Muslim influences helped create a very different tendency. Amalfi and Caserta built a Saracenic cathedral and cloister dating from this period; Amalfi's was adorned with incised bronze doors from Constantinople in a style that was copied all over the south, notably at Trani and **Monte Sant'Angelo** in Puglia. The tradition of Byzantine painting and mosaics continued, mostly in Sicily. From Muslim geometrical patterns, southern artists acquired a taste for intricate designs using enamel or marble chips in church furnishings and architectural trim—as seen in pulpits and candlesticks in the churches of Salerno, Ravello, and many others. The outstanding architectural advance of this period is the Pugliese Romanesque, as shown in cathedrals in almost every Puglian city (including **Monte Sant'Angelo**, Trani and Bari), a style closely related to contemporary Norman and Pisan work.

This period also saw the erection of urban skyscrapers by the nobility, family fortress-towers built when the *comuni* forced local barons to move into the towns. Larger cities once had literally hundreds of them, before the townspeople succeeded in getting them demolished. San Gimignano and Ascoli Piceno have the most surviving examples. In many cases extremely tall towers were built simply for decoration and prestige. Bologna's Garisendi and Asinelli Towers, along with Pisa's Campanile, are the best examples of medieval Italy's occasional disdain for the horizontal.

Late-Medieval–Early-Renaissance (13th–14th centuries)

In many ways this was the most exciting and vigorous phase in Italian art history, an age of discovery when the power of the artist was almost like that of a magician. Great imaginative leaps occurred in architecture, painting and sculpture, especially in Tuscany. From Milan to Assisi a group of masons and sculptors known as the Campionese Masters built magnificent brick cathedrals and basilicas. Some of their buildings reflect the Gothic style of the north (most spectacularly Milan), while in Como Cathedral you can see the transition from that same Gothic to Renaissance. In **Venice** an ornate, half-oriental style called Venetian-Gothic still sets the city's palaces and public buildings apart, and influenced the exotic Basilica di Sant'Antonio in **Padua**. This was also an era of transition in sculpture, from stiff Romanesque stylization to the more realistic, classically inspired works of the great Nicola Pisano and his son Giovanni (in the churches of Pisa, Pistoia and Siena) and his pupil Arnolfo di Cambio (Florence). Other outstanding works of the 14th century are Lorenzo Maitani's cathedral in Orvieto and the Scaliger tombs of **Verona** by the Campionese Masters.

Painters, especially in Rome and Siena, learned from the new spatial and expressive sculpture. Most celebrated of the masters in the dawn of the Italian Renaissance is, of course, the solemn Giotto, whose greatest works are the fresco cycles in **Padua** and **Assisi**. In the town of St Francis you can also see some excellent works by Giotto's merrier contemporaries from Siena. That city's artists, Duccio di Buoninsegna, Simone Martini and Pietro and Ambrogio Lorenzetti, gave Italy its most brilliant exponents of the International Gothic style—though they were also important precursors of the Renaissance. Northern European Gothic never made much headway in Italy, though French Cistercians did build fine abbey churches like those at San Galgano in Tuscany and Fossanova in Lazio, and the English-financed Sant'Andrea in Vercelli. The south had relatively little to contribute during this period, but Naples developed its own neo-Gothic architecture, and unique geometrically patterned church façades appear at L'Aquila and Brindisi.

Rome, for one of the few times in its history, achieved artistic prominence with home-grown talent. The city's architecture from this period (as seen in the campaniles of Santa Maria in Cosmedin and Santa Maria Maggiore) has largely been lost under Baroque remodellings, but the paintings and mosaics of Pietro Cavallini and his school, and the intricate, inlaid stone pavements and architectural trim of the Cosmati family and their followers, derived from the Amalfi Coast style, can be seen all over the city; both had an influence that extended far beyond Rome itself.

The Renaissance (15th–16th centuries)

The origins of this high-noon of art are very much the accomplishment of quattrocento Florence, where sculpture and painting embarked on a totally new way of educating the eye. The idea of a supposed 'rediscovery of antiquity' has confused the understanding of the time. In general, artists broke new ground when they expanded from the traditions of medieval art; when they sought merely to copy the forms of ancient Greece and Rome, the imagination often faltered. Florentine art soon became recognized as the standard of the age, and examples can be seen everywhere in Tuscany. By 1450 Florentine artists were spreading the new style to the north, especially Milan, where Leonardo da Vinci and Bramante spent several years; the collections in the Brera and other galleries, the *Last Supper*, and the nearby Certosa di Pavia are essential works of the Renaissance. Other good museum collections are in **Rome**, Parma, **Turin** and Bergamo. Michelangelo and Bramante, among others, carried the Renaissance to **Rome**, where it thrived under the patronage of enlightened popes.

The most significant art in the north came out of Venice, which had its own distinct school led by Mantegna and Giovanni Bellini; one of the best painters of the school, the fastidious Carlo Crivelli, did much of his work in the Marche. In Perugia Perugino was laying the foundations of the Umbrian school, in which Raphael and Pinturicchio earned their stripes. In Orvieto Cathedral, the Tuscan painter Signorelli left a *Last Judgement* that inspired Michelangelo. Piero della Francesca was the most important non-Florentine painter before Raphael; his revolutionary works are at Urbino, Sansepolcro and Arezzo. Southern Italy, trapped in a decline that was even more artistic than economic, hardly participated at all, though examples of the northerners' art can be seen in Naples (the Triumphal Arch in the Castel Nuovo).

Despite the brilliant triumphs in painting and sculpture, the story of Renaissance architecture is partially one of confusion and retreat. Florence, with Brunelleschi, Alberti and Michelozzo, achieved its own special mode of expression, a dignified austerity that proved difficult to transplant elsewhere. In most of Italy the rediscovery of the works of Vitruvius, representing the authority of antiquity, killed off Italians' appreciation of their own architectural heritage; with surprising speed the dazzling imaginative freedom of medieval architecture was lost forever. Some fine work still appeared, however, notably Codussi's palaces and churches in Venice.

High Renaissance and Mannerism (16th century)

At the beginning of the cinquecento Michelangelo, Raphael and Leonardo held court at the summit of European art. But as Italy was losing her self-confidence, and was soon to lose her liberty, artistic currents tended toward the dark and subversive. More than anyone it was Michelangelo who tipped the balance from the cool, classical Renaissance into the turgid, stormy, emotionally fraught movement labelled Mannerism. Among the few painters left in exhausted Florence, he had the brilliant Jacopo Pontormo and Rosso Fiorentino to help. Other painters lumped in with the Mannerists, such as Giulio Romano in Mantua and Il Sodoma around Siena, broke new ground while maintaining the discipline and intellectual rigour of the early Renaissance. Elsewhere, and especially among the fashionable Florentine painters and sculptors, art was decaying into mere interior decoration.

For **Venice** it was a golden age, with Titian, Veronese, Tintoretto, Sansovino and Palladio, whose works may be seen throughout Venetia. In Cremona, Milan, and other lucky galleries, you can see works by Arcimboldo, the cinquecento surrealist.

In architecture, attempts to recreate ancient styles and the classical orders won the day. In Milan, and later in **Rome**, Bramante was one of the few architects able to do anything interesting with it, while Michelangelo's great dome of St Peter's put a cap on the accomplishments of the Renaissance. Other talented architects found most of their patronage in **Rome** which after the 1520s became Italy's centre of artistic activity: Ligorio, Peruzzi, Vignola and the Sangallo family among them.

Baroque (17th–18th centuries)

Rome continued its artistic dominance to become the Baroque capital, where the socially irresponsible genius of artists like Bernini and Borromini was approved by the Jesuits and indulged by the tainted ducats of the popes. As an art designed to induce temporal obedience and psychical oblivion, its effects are difficult to describe, but the three great churches along Corso Vittorio Emanuele, Bernini's Piazza Navona fountains and St Peter's colonnades, are fine examples. More honest cities such as Florence and Venice chose to sit out the Baroque, though Florence at first approved the works of 16th-century proto-Baroque sculptors like Ammannati, Giambologna and Cellini. Not all artists fit the Baroque mould; genius could survive even in a dangerous, picaresque age, most notably in the person of Michelangelo (works in Milan and **Rome**).

The south of Italy, with its long tradition of religious emotionalism, found the Baroque entirely to its tastes, though few towns could afford to build much. Naples could, and the Monastery of San Martino by Cosimo Fanzago marks the apotheosis of Neapolitan Baroque. Painting and sculpture even flourished while they were dying in northern Renaissance towns; southern art's eccentricity climaxed in the Sansevero Chapel. A very different sort of Baroque appeared in the deep south, where the studied excess seemed to strike a deep chord in the popular psyche. Much of it is in Sicily, though the Spanish-looking city of Lecce developed a Baroque style that lasted from the 16th to the late 18th century, consistent and beautiful enough to make as impressive an architectural ensemble as any medieval or Renaissance city in the north.

Turin's town plan, churches, palaces and royal hunting lodges, designed by the priest Guarini and the early 18th-century Sicilian Juvarra, are the most elegant representations of the Baroque spirit in northern Italy. This was a great age of palaces and ornate Italian gardens, most famously in Tivoli, Isola Bella in Lake Maggiore, Villa Borghese and innumerable other locations in and around **Rome**, as well as around **Padua** and Vicenza.

Neoclassicism and Romanticism (late 18th–19th centuries)

Baroque was a hard act to follow, and at this time Italian art and architecture almost cease to exist. Two centuries of stifling oppression had taken their toll on the national imagination, and for the first time Italy not only ceased to be a leader in art, but failed even to make significant contributions. The one bright spot was Venice, where Giambattista Tiepolo and son adorned the churches and palaces of the last days of the Serenissima. Other Venetians, such as Canaletto and Guardi, painted their famous canal scenes for Grand Tourists. In the 19th century the *Macchiaioli*, the Italian Impressionist movement led by Giovanni Fattori, was centred in Florence. In sculpture the neoclassical master Canova stands almost alone, a favourite in the days of Napoleon. His best works may be seen in the Villa Carlotta, on Lake Como, in **Rome**'s Villa Borghese and at Possagno. In architecture it was the age of grand opera houses, many designed by the Bibiena family of Bologna. The Gallerias in Milan and Naples (late 19th century) and the extravagances of the Piedmontese Alessandro Antonelli (**Turin** and Novara) are among the most impressive public buildings, and the neoclassical royal palaces at Caserta and Stra near Venice the grandest private addresses.

20th Century

The turn-of-the-century Italian Art Nouveau—known as Liberty Style—failed to spread as widely as its counterparts in France and central Europe. There are a few good examples in Milan, but the best are linked with the burgeoning tourist industry: the construction of Grand Hotels, casinos and villas, especially in Venice, the Lakes, the Riviera, Pésaro, Viareggio and the great spas at Merano, Montecatini and San Pellegrino. Two art movements attracted international attention: futurism, a response to Cubism, concerned with the relevancy to the present, a movement led by Boccioni, Severini and Balla (best seen in the National Gallery of Modern Art, **Rome**, and in Milan); and the mysterious, metaphysical world of De Chirico; while Modigliani, Morandi and Carrà were masters of silences. Their works, among others, are displayed in the museums of **Rome**, Venice and Milan. Architecture in this century reached its (admittedly low) summit in the Fascist period (the EUR suburb in Rome, and public buildings everywhere in the south). Mussolinian architecture often makes us smile, but, as the only Italian school in the last 200 years to have achieved a consistent sense of design, it presents a challenge to all modern Italian architects—one they have so far been unable to meet.

In **Turin** and Milan you can see the works of the most acclaimed Italian architect of this century, Pier Luigi Nervi; good post-War buildings are very difficult to find, and the other arts have never yet risen above the level of dreary, saleable postmodernism. Much of the Italians' artistic urge has been sublimated into the shibboleth of Italian design—clothes, sports cars, suitcases, kitchen utensils, etc. At present, though business is good, Italy is generating little excitement in these fields. Europe expects more from its most artistically talented nation; after the bad centuries of shame and slumber, a free and prosperous Italy may well find its own voice and its own style to help interpret the events of the day. If Italy ever does begin to speak with a single voice, whatever it has to say will be worth hearing.

Rome

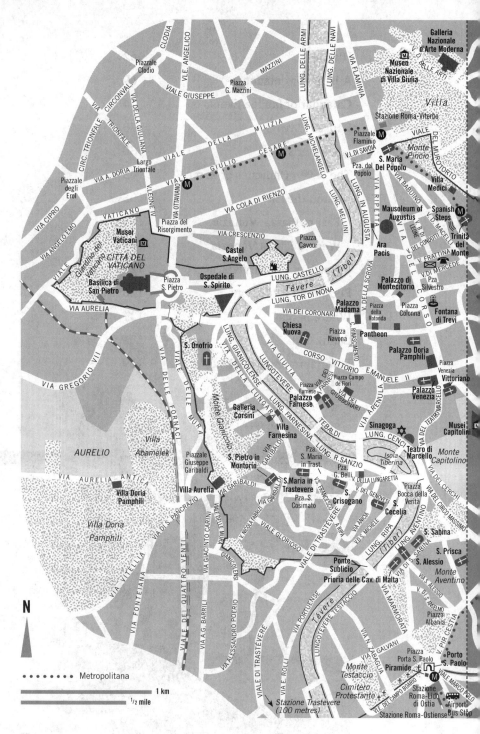

Galleria
Nazionale
d'Arte Moderna

Museo
Nazionale
di Villa Giulia

Villa

Stazione Roma-Viterbo

Piazzale
Clodio

VLE. ANGELICO

CLODIA

Piazza
G. Mazzini

MAZZINI

LUNG. DELLE ARMI

LUNG. DELLE NAVI

VIA FLAMINIA

BELLE ARTI

VIALE GIUSEPPE

VIALE DELLA GIULIANA

VIA DELLA GIULIANA

VIA DELLA

MILIZIA

LUNG. MICHELANGELO

Piazzale
Flaminio

M

VIALE

DEL MURO TORTO

Monte
Pincio

S. Maria
Del Popolo

Villa
Medici

CIRC. TRIONFALE

VIA A. DORIA

Largo
Trionfale

VIALE

GIULIO

CESARE

M

V.LD DI SAVOIA

Pza. del
Popolo

VIA FLAMINIA

LUNG. IN RIPETTA

VIA BABUINO

Piazzale
degli
Eroi

VIA CIPRO

VIA LEONE IV

VIA OTTAVIANO

VIA COLA DI RIENZO

LUNG. MELLINI

LUNG. IN AUGUSTA

Mausoleum of
Augustus

Ara
Pacis

Spanish
Steps

M

Trinità
del Monte

V. DEL CONDOTTI

V. FRATTINA

V.D.I MERCEDE

VATICANO

VIA ANGELO EMO

VIALE

Musei
Vaticani

M

Piazza del
Risorgimento

VIA CRESCENZIO

Piazza
Cavour

LUNG. CASTELLO

VIA DELLA SCROFA

Palazzo di
Montecitorio

Piazza
Colonna

V.D. DI MERCEDE

Pza
Silvestro

CITTÀ DEL
VATICANO

Giardino del
Vaticano

Castel
S.Angelo

Ospedale di
S. Spirito

Tévere

(Tiber)

Fontana
di Trevi

Basílica di
San Pietro

Piazza
S. Pietro

LUNG. TOR DI NONA

VIA DEI CORONARI

Palazzo
Madama

Piazza
della
Rotonda

Piazza
Colonna

CORSO

VIA AURELIA

S. Onofrio

Chiesa
Nuova

Piazza
Navona

Pantheon

Palazzo Doria
Pamphili

VIA GREGORIO VII

VIALE DELLE MURA

VIA DELLE FORNACI

VIA GIANICOLENSE

VIA GIULIA

CORSO VITTORIO EMANUELE II

Piazza
Venezia

VIA DEL TEATRO MARCELLO

Vittoriano

Galleria
Corsini

LUNGOTEVERE

Monte Gianicolo

LUNG. FARNESINA

LUNG. LUNGARA

Piazza
Farnese

Piazza Campo
de' Fiori

Palazzo
Farnese

VIA DEI
GIUBBONARI

VIA ARENULA

Palazzo
Venezia

Musei
Capitolini

AURELIO

Villa
Abamelek

Villa
Farnesina

VIA GARIBALDI

Piazzale
Giuseppe
Garibaldi

S. Pietro in
Montorio

Pza.
S. Maria
in Trast.

Sinagoga

LUNG. CENCI

LUNG. R. SANZIO

Isola
Tiberina

Teatro di
Marcello

Monte
Capitolino

*Villa Doria
Pamphili*

Villa Doria
Pamphili

VIA AURELIA ANTICA

Villa Aurelia

VIA GARIBALDI

Pza
G. Belli

V. DELLA LUNGARETTA

S.Maria in
Trastevere

Pza. S.
Cosimato

S.
Crisogano

V. DEL GENOVESI

S.
Cecelia

Piazza
Bocca della
Verità

VIA DEL CIRCO MASSIMO

VIA DI S. SABINA

VIA DEL CERCHI

VIALE GLORIOSO

VIA NICOLA FABRIZI

VIALE DI TRASTEVERE

VIA S. FRANCESCO A RIPA

V. ANICA

V.D. S. MICHELE

LUNG. RIPA

VIA AVENTINO

S. Sabina

Monte
Aventino

VIA VITELLIA

VIA DI S. PANCRAZIO

VIA GIACINTO CARINI

VIALE DEI QUATTRO VENTI

VIA A.G. BARRILI

VIALE DI TRASTEVERE

Ponte
Sublicio

Prioria delle Cav. di Malta

S. Alessio

VIA DI S. SABINA

S. Prisca

VIA DI S. ALESSIO

VIA DI S. ANSELMO

Piazza
Albania

VIA PIR CESTIA

VIA FONTEIANA

VIA ALESSANDRO POERIO

VIALE GIACINTO CARINI

GIANICOLENSI

VIA E. ROLLI

VIA PORTUENSE

LUNGOTEVERE TESTACCIO

Tévere

(Tiber)

VIA MARMORATA

VIA N. ZABAGLIA

VIA GALVANI

Piazza
Porta S. Paolo

Piramide

Porto
S. Paolo

VIALE MARCO POLO

N

• • • • • • • • Metropolitana

1 km

½ mile

Monte
Testaccio

Cimitero
Protestante

VIA DEL CAMPO BOARIO

Stazione
Roma-Lido
di Ostia

Airport
Bus Stop

↓ Stazione Trastevere
(100 metres)

Stazione Roma-Ostiense

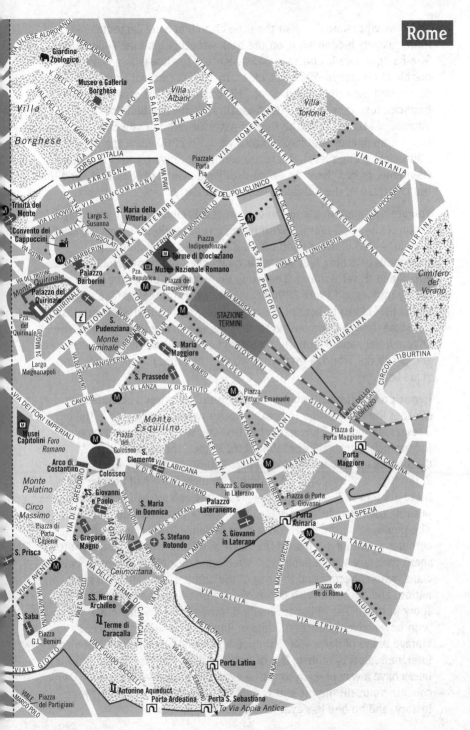

Rome

59

To know what Rome is, visit the little church of San Clemente, unobtrusively hidden away on the back streets behind the Colosseum. The Baroque façade conceals a 12th-century basilica with a beautiful marble choir screen 600 years older. In 1857 a cardinal from Boston discovered the original church of 313, one of the first great Christian basilicas, just underneath. And beneath *that* are two buildings and a Temple of Mithras from the time of Augustus; from it you can walk out into a Roman alley that looks exactly as it did 2000 years ago, now some 28ft below ground level. There are commemorative plaques in San Clemente, placed there by a Medici duke, a bishop of New York, and the last chairman of the Bulgarian Communist Party.

You are not going to get to the bottom of this city, whether your stay is for three days or a month. With its legions of headless statues, acres of paintings, 913 churches and megatons of artistic sediment, this metropolis of aching feet will wear down even the most resolute of travellers (and travel writers). The name Rome passed out of the plane of reality into legend some 2200 years ago, when princes as far away as China first began to hear of the faraway city and its invincible armies. At the same time the Romans were cooking up a personified goddess, the Divine Rome, and beginning the strange myth of their destiny to conquer and pacify the world, a myth that would still haunt Europe a thousand years later.

In our prosaic times, though, you may find it requires a considerable effort of the imagination to break through to the past Romes of the Caesars and popes. They exist, but first you will need to peel away the increasingly thick veneer of the 'Third Rome', the burgeoning, thoroughly up-to-date creation of post-Reunification Italy. Ancient Rome at the height of its glory had perhaps a million and a half people; today there are four million, and at any given time at least half of them will be pushing their way into the Metro train while you are trying to get off. The popes, for all their centuries of experience in spectacle and ceremony, cannot often steal the show in this new Rome, and have to share the stage with a deplorable overabundance of preposterous politicians, with *Cinecittà* and the rest of the cultural apparatus of a great nation, and of course with the tourists, who sometimes put on the best show in town. The old guard Romani, now a minority in a city swollen with new arrivals, bewail the loss of Rome's slow and easy pace, its vintage brand of *dolce vita* that once impressed other Italians, let alone foreigners. Lots of money, lots of traffic and an endless caravan of tour buses have a way of compromising even the most beautiful cities. Don't concern yourself; the present is only one snapshot from a 2600-year history, and no one has ever left Rome disappointed.

One thing is certain; Rome is going to be a very crowded place in the year 2000. Major Church events like World Youth Day already have all their places booked, and estimates of the total number of visitors expected over the course of the year range from 20 to 30 million. The *Agenzia Romana per la Preparazione del Giubileo*, which has done considerable research, comes up with a conservative prediction of 16 million Italians and 10 million foreigners. They say the busiest period will be between April and September, with a peak in May. The Vatican and national authorities, along with Rome and the Lazio regional government, are working like beavers to get all their ambitious plans finished by Christmas Eve, the Jubilee's official opening. With such a huge undertaking, you might expect some delays and confusion—and, this being Italy, you will not be disappointed.

Already the Jubilee preparations are giving Italians the chance to 'make polemics', as they say in the press. Big infrastructure projects, such as the extension of the Metropolitana and the new Tiburtina railway station, are way behind schedule. Rome figures it has only half the hotel rooms it needs; people blame the situation on the hotel owners' lobby, which wants to keep their establishments full. Traffic might prove an even worse nightmare. Even with a big new Papal parking lot on the Janiculum, no one has any idea where all the tour buses are going to fit. Chronic gridlock is a distinct possibility; it's already an everyday reality in many districts. Rome will be getting more than its share of Lazio's 980 new traffic wardens (who will probably make things even worse). Meanwhile, the government and the trade unions are discussing a strike moratorium for the year 2000. If that comes true, it will prove an unimaginable blessing for beleaguered pilgrims in the land of the surprise transport sciopero.

Rome has accomplished an impressive amount in order to lick its monuments into shape for the occasion. Many of the city's major museums are thoroughly restored and ready to show off their treasures to the world: the Palazzo Barberini, the Etruscan Museum at the Villa Giulia, the Calcografia Nazionale/Istituto per l'Arte Grafica, the Galleria Nazionale d'Arte Moderna e Contemporanea in the Villa Borghese, and the Palazzo Braschi on Piazza Navona, the last of the great Roman family palaces and now home to the wonderful collections of the Museo di Roma. The restoration of the Capitoline Museums has been finished, along with a new 'Roman Garden', and Rome's Eternal Project—the Museo Nazionale at the Baths of Diocletian—has moved a few more plodding steps closer to completion; already large parts of the complex are open that haven't been seen for decades. In addition, new museum spaces have been developed to house contemporary art and special exhibitions: the Galleria Comunale d'Arte Moderna e Contemporanea in the old Peroni Brewery, and the Centro per le Arti Contemporanee in the former Montello Barracks, and the Scuderie Papali (Papal stables), part of the Palazzo Quirinale that has long been neglected: an impressive space, that will now be filled with art.

Among the architectural treasures of the city, the Imperial Fora have just been refurbished and reopened after major new excavations; they've been at work on the Colosseum too, and for the Jubilee year there will be special tours of parts of the amphitheatre that have long been off-limits. Near Piazza Venezia on Via delle Botteghe Oscure, the Crypta Balbi, the cellars of the ancient Theatre of Balbus, are being restored to house a new museum of medieval Rome. And at the southern edge of the walls at Porta Latina, the Parco delle Tombe di Via Latina offers a look at some remarkable, newly restored ancient tombs.

Not a city noted for architecture—for the last two hundred years at least—Rome nevertheless has two important new buildings to greet the millennium: first, American Richard Meyer's *Chiesa del 2000* at Tor Tre Teste in suburban Centocelle, a striking, free-form structure that has been likened to a 'sail lightly filled with the breeze'. Meyer is also working on a new museum building for the Ara Pacis near the Tiber. The other major project is the Città della Musica, including Renzo Piano's long-delayed Auditorium di Roma; the works that began in 1995 were delayed from the start by the discovery of an important Republican-era archaeological site, which has been thoroughly excavated, and now integrated into the new complex.

History

The beginnings are obscure enough. Historians believe the settlement of the Tiber Valley began some time about 1000 BC, when an outbreak of volcanic eruptions in the Alban Hills to the south forced the Latin tribes down into the lowlands. Beyond that there are few clues for the archaeologists to follow. But remembering that every ancient legend conceals a kernel of truth— perhaps more poetic than scientific—it would be best to follow the accounts of Virgil, the poet of the empire, and Livy, the great 1st-century chronicler and mythographer. When Virgil wrote, in the reign of Augustus, Greek culture was an irresistible force in all the recently civilized lands of the Mediterranean. For Rome, Virgil concocted the story of Aeneas, fleeing from Troy after the Homeric sack and finding his way to Latium. Descent from the Trojans, however specious, connected Rome to the Greek world and made it seem less of an upstart. As Virgil tells it, Aeneas' son Ascanius founded Alba Longa, a city that by the 800s was leader of the Latin Confederation. Livy takes up the tale with Numitor, a descendant of Ascanius and rightful king of Alba Longa, tossed off the throne by his usurping brother Amulius. In order that Numitor should have no heirs, Amulius forced Numitor's daughter Rhea Silvia into service as a Vestal Virgin. Here Rome's destiny begins, with an appearance in the Vestals' chambers of the god Mars, staying just long enough to leave Rhea Silvia pregnant with the precocious twins Romulus and Remus.

When Amulius found out he of course packed them away in a little boat, which the gods directed up the Tiber to a spot near today's Piazza Bocca della Verità. The famous she-wolf looked after the babies, until they were found by a shepherd, who brought them up. When Mars revealed to the grown twins their origin, they returned to Alba Longa to sort out Amulius, and then returned (in 753 BC, traditionally) to found the city the gods had ordained. Romulus soon found himself constrained to kill Remus, who would not believe the auguries that declared his brother should be king, and thus set the pattern for the bloody millennium of Rome's history to come. The legends portray early Rome as a glorified pirates' camp, and the historians are only too glad to agree. Finding themselves short of women, the Romans stole some from the Sabines. Not especially interested in farming or learning a trade, they adopted the hobby of subjugating their neighbours and soon polished it to an art.

Seven Kings of Rome

Romulus was the first, followed by Numa Pompilius, who laid down the forms for Rome's cults and priesthoods, its auguries and College of Vestals. Tullius Hostilius, the next, made Rome ruler of all Latium, and Ancus Martius founded the port of Ostia. The next king, Tarquinius Priscus, was an Etruscan, and probably gained his throne thanks to a conquest by one of the Etruscan city-states. Tarquin made a city of Rome, building the first real temples, the Cloaca Maxima or Great Drain, and the first Circus Maximus. His successor, Servius Tullius, restored Latin rule, inaugurated the division between patricians (the senatorial class) and plebeians, and built a great wall to keep the Etruscans out. It apparently did not work, for as next king we find the Etruscan Tarquinius Superbus (about 534 BC), another great builder. His misfortune was to have a hot-headed son like Tarquinius Sextus, who imposed himself on a noble and virtuous Roman maiden named Lucretia (cf. Shakespeare's *Rape of Lucrece*). She committed public suicide; the enraged Roman patricians, under the leadership of Lucius Junius Brutus, chased out proud Tarquin and the Etruscan dynasty forever. The republic was established before the day was out, with Brutus as first consul, or chief magistrate.

The Invincible Republic

Taking an oath never to allow another king in Rome, the patricians designed a novel form of government, a republic (*res publica*—public thing) governed by the two consuls elected by the Senate, the assembly of the patricians themselves; later innovations in the Roman constitution would include a tribune, an official with inviolable powers elected by the Plebeians to protect their interests. The two classes fought like cats and dogs at home but combined with impressive resolve in their foreign wars. Etruscans, Aequi, Hernici, Volscii, Samnites and Sabines—all powerful nations—were defeated by Rome's citizen armies. Some of Livy's best stories come from this period, such as the taking of Rome by marauding Gauls in 390, when the cackling of geese awakened the Romans and saved the citadel on the Capitoline Hill.

By 270 BC Rome had eliminated all its rivals to become master of Italy. It had taken about 200 years, and in the next 200 Roman rule would be established from Spain to Egypt. The first stage had proved more difficult. In Rome's final victory over the other Italians, whole cities and tribes simply disappeared, their peoples joining the mushrooming population of Rome. After 270 it was much the same story, but on a wider scale. In the three Punic Wars against Carthage (264–146 BC) Rome gained almost the whole of the western Mediterranean; Greece, North Africa and Asia Minor were absorbed in small bites over the next 100 years. Rome's history was now the history of the western world.

Imperial Rome

The old pirates' nest had never really changed its ways. Rome, like old Assyria, makes a fine example of that species of carnivore that can only live by continuous conquest. When the Romans took Greece they first met Culture, and it had the effect on them that puberty has on little boys. After some bizarre behaviour, evidenced in the continuous civil wars (Sulla, Marius, Pompey, Julius Caesar), the Romans began tarting up their city in the worst way, vacuuming all the gold, paintings, statues, cooks, poets and architects out of the civilized East. Beginning perhaps with Pompey, every contender for control of the now constitutionally deranged republic added some great work to the city centre: Pompey's theatre, the Julian Basilica, and something from almost every emperor up to Constantine. Julius Caesar and Augustus were perhaps Rome's greatest benefactors, initiating every sort of progressive legislation, turning dirt lanes into paved streets and erecting new fora, temples and the vast network of aqueducts. In their time Rome's population probably reached the million mark, surpassing Antioch and Alexandria as the largest city in the western world.

It was Augustus who effectively ended the Republic in 27 BC, by establishing his personal rule and reducing the old constitution to formalities. During the imperial era that followed his reign, Rome's position as administrative and judicial centre of the empire kept it growing, drawing in a new cosmopolitan population of provincials from Britain to Mesopotamia. The city became the capital of banking and finance—and religion; Rome's policy was always to induct everyone's local god as an honorary Roman, and every important cult image and relic was abducted to the Capitoline Temple. The emperor himself was *Pontifex Maximus*, head priest of Rome, whose title derives from the early Roman veneration of bridges (*pontifex* means keeper of bridges). St Peter, of course, arrived, and was duly martyred in AD 67. His successor, Linus, became the first pope—or *pontiff*—first in the long line of hierophants who would inherit Rome's longstanding religious tradition.

For all its glitter, Rome was still the complete predator, producing nothing and consuming everything. No one with any spare *denarii* would be foolish enough to go into business with Romans, when the only real money was to be made from government, speculation or real estate. At times almost half the population of Roman citizens (as opposed to slaves) was on the public dole. Naturally, when things went sour they really went sour. Uncertain times made Aurelian give Rome a real defensive wall in 275. By 330 the necessity of staying near the armies at the front led the western emperors to spend most of their time at army headquarters in Milan. Rome became a bloated backwater, and after three sackings (Alaric the Goth in 410, Geiseric the Vandal in 455 and Odoacer the Goth in 476), there was no reason to stay. The sources disagree: perhaps 100,000 inhabitants were left by the year 500, perhaps as few as 10,000.

Rome in the Shadows

Contrary to what most people think, Rome did not ever quite go down the drain in the Dark Ages. Its lowest point in prestige undoubtedly came in the 14th century, when the popes were at Avignon. The number of important churches built in the Dark Ages (most, unfortunately, Baroqued later) and the mosaics that embellished them, equal in number if not in quality to those of Ravenna, testify to the city's importance. There was certainly enough to attract a few more sacks (Goths and Greeks in the 6th-century wars, Saracens from Africa in 746).

As in many other western cities, but on a larger scale, the bishops of Rome—the popes—picked up some of the pieces when civil administration disintegrated and extended their power to temporal offices. Chroniclers report fights between them and the local barons, self-proclaimed heirs of the Roman Senate, as early as 741. It must have been a fascinating place, much too big for its population though still, thanks to the popes, thinking of itself as the centre of the western world. The forum was abandoned, as were the gigantic baths, rendered useless as the aqueducts decayed. Almost all of the temples and basilicas survived, converted to Christian churches. Hadrian's massive tomb on the banks of the Tiber was converted into a fortress, the Castel Sant'Angelo, an impregnable haven for the popes in times of trouble.

The popes deserve credit for keeping Rome alive, but the tithe money trickling in from across Europe confirmed the city in its parasitical behaviour. With two outrageous forgeries, the 'Donation of Constantine' and the 'Donation of Pepin', the popes staked their claim to temporal power in Italy. Charlemagne visited the city after driving the Lombards out in 800; in St Peter's on Christmas Eve, Pope Leo III sneaked up behind the Frankish king and set an imperial crown on his head. The surprise coronation, which the outraged Charlemagne could or would not undo, established the precedent of Holy Roman Emperors having to cross over the Alps to receive their crown from the pope; for centuries to come Rome was able to keep its hand in the political struggles of all Europe.

Arnold of Brescia and Rienzo

Not that Rome ever spoke with one voice; over the next 500 years it was only the idea of Rome, as the spiritual centre of the universal Christian community, that kept the actual city of Rome from disappearing altogether. Down to some 20–30,000 people in this era, Rome evolved a sort of stable anarchy, in which the major contenders for power were the popes and noble families. First among the latter were the Orsini and the Colonna, racketeer clans who built fortresses for themselves among the ruins and fought like gangs in 1920s Chicago.

Very often outsiders would get into the game. A remarkable woman of obscure birth named Theodora took the Castel Sant'Angelo in the 880s; with the title of Senatrix she and her daughter Marozia ruled Rome for decades. Various German emperors seized the city, but were never able to hold it. In the 10th century, things got even more complicated as the Roman people began to assert themselves. Caught between the people and the barons, nine of the 24 popes in that century managed to get themselves murdered. The 1140s was a characteristic period of this convoluted history. A Jewish family, the Pierleoni, held power, and a Jewish antipope sat enthroned in St Peter's. Mighty Rome occupied itself with a series of wars against its neighbouring village of Tivoli, and usually lost. A sincere monkish reformer appeared, the Christian and democrat Arnold of Brescia; he recreated the Senate and almost succeeded in establishing Rome as a free *comune*, but in 1155 he fell into the hands of the German emperor Frederick Barbarossa, who sold him to the English pope (Adrian IV) for hanging.

Too many centuries of this made Rome uncomfortable for the popes, who frequently removed themselves to Viterbo. The final indignity came when, under French pressure, the papacy decamped entirely to Avignon in 1309. Pulling strings from a distance, the popes only made life more complicated. Into the vacuum they created stepped one of the noblest Romans of them all, later to be the subject of Wagner's first opera. Cola di Rienzo was the son of an innkeeper, but he had a good enough education to read the Latin inscriptions that lay on ruins all around him, and Livy, Cicero and Tacitus wherever he could find them. Obsessed by the idea of re-establishing Roman glory, he talked at the bewildered inhabitants until they caught the fever too. With Rienzo as Tribune of the People, the Roman Republic was reborn in 1347.

Power does corrupt, however, in Rome more than any spot on the globe, and an increasingly fat and ridiculous Rienzo was hustled out of Rome by the united nobles before the year was out. His return to power, in 1354, ended with his murder by a mob after only two months. Rome was now at its lowest ebb, with only some 15,000 people, and prosperity and influence were not to be restored until the reign of Pope Nicholas V after 1447.

The New Rome

The old papacy, before Avignon, had largely been a tool of the Roman nobles; periods when it was able to achieve real independence were the exception rather than the rule. In the more settled conditions of the 15th century, a new papacy emerged, richer and more sophisticated. Political power, as a guarantee of stability, was its goal, and a series of talented Renaissance popes saw their best hopes for achieving this by rebuilding Rome. By the 1500s this process was in full swing. Under Julius II (1503–13) the papal domains for the first time were run like a modern state; Julius also laid plans for the rebuilding of St Peter's, beginning the great building programme that transformed the city. New streets were laid out, especially Via Giulia and the grand avenues radiating from Piazza del Popolo; Julius' architect, Bramante, knocked down medieval Rome with such gay abandon that Raphael nicknamed him 'Ruinante'.

Over the next two centuries the work continued at a frenetic pace. Besides St Peter's, hundreds of churches were either built or rebuilt, and cardinals and noble families lined the streets with new palaces, imposing if not always beautiful. A new departure in urban design was developed in the 1580s, under Sixtus V, recreating some of the monumentality of ancient Rome. Piazzas linked by a network of straight boulevards were cleared in front of the major religious sites, each with an Egyptian obelisk. The New Rome, symbol of the Counter-Reformation and the majesty of the popes, was, however, bought at a terrible price. Besides the destruction of Bramante, buildings that had survived substantially intact for 1500 years were cannibalized for their marble; the popes wantonly destroyed more of ancient Rome than Goths or Saracens had ever managed. To pay for their programme, they taxed the economy of the Papal States out of existence. Areas of Lazio turned into wastelands as exasperated farmers simply abandoned them; the other cities of Lazio and Umbria were set back centuries in their development. The New Rome was proving as voracious a predator as the old.

Worst of all, the new papacy in the 16th century instituted terror as an instrument of public policy. In the course of the previous century the last vestiges of Roman liberty had been gradually extinguished. The popes tried to extend their power by playing a game of high-stakes diplomacy between Emperor Charles V of Spain and King Francis I of France, but reaped a bitter harvest in the 1527 sack of Rome. An out-of-control imperial army occupied the city for almost a year, causing tremendous destruction, while the disastrous Pope Clement VII looked on helplessly from the Castel Sant'Angelo. Afterwards the popes were happy to become part of the Imperial-Spanish system. Political repression was fiercer than anywhere else in Italy; the Inquisition was refounded in 1542 by Paul III, and book burnings, torture of freethinkers and executions became even more common than in Spain itself. .

The End of Papal Rule

By about 1610 there was no Roman foolish enough to get burned at the stake; at the same time workmen were adding the last stones to the cupola of St Peter's. It was the end of an era, but the building continued. A thick accretion of Baroque, like coral, collected over

Rome. Bernini did his Piazza Navona fountain in 1650, and the Colonnade for St Peter's 15 years later. The political importance of the popes, however, disappeared with surprising finality. As Joseph Stalin was later to note, the popes had plenty of Bulls, but few army divisions, and they drifted into irrelevance in the power politics of modern Europe during the Thirty Years War.

Rome was left to enjoy a decadent but pleasant twilight. A brief interruption came when revolutionaries in 1798 again proclaimed the Roman Republic, and a French army sent the pope packing. Rome later became part of Napoleon's empire, but papal rule was restored in 1815. Another republic appeared in 1848, on the crest of that romantic year's revolutionary wave, but this time a French army besieged the city and had the pope propped back on his throne by July 1849. Garibaldi, the republic's military commander, barely escaped with his life.

For twenty years Napoleon III maintained a garrison in Rome to look after the pope, and consequently Rome became the last part of Italy to join the new Italian kingdom. After the French defeat in the war of 1870, Italian troops blew a hole in the old Aurelian Wall near the Porta Pia and marched in. Pius IX, who ironically had decreed papal infallibility just the year before, locked himself in the Vatican and pouted; the popes were to be 'prisoners' until Mussolini's Concordat of 1929, by which they agreed to recognize the Italian state.

As capital of the new state, Rome underwent another building boom. New streets like Via Vittorio Veneto and Via Nazionale made circulation easier; villas and gardens disappeared under blocks of speculative building (everything around Stazione Termini, for example); long-needed projects like the Tiber embankments were built; and the new kingdom strove to impress the world with gigantic, absurd public buildings and monuments, such as the Altar of the Nation and the Finance Ministry on Via XX Settembre, as big as two Colosseums. Growth has been steady; from some 200,000 people in 1879, Rome has since increased twentyfold.

The Twentieth Century

In 1922 the city was the objective of Mussolini's 'March on Rome', when the Fascist leader used his blackshirt squads to demand, and win, complete power in the Italian government, though he himself famously made the journey into town by train, and in his best suit. Mussolini was one more figure who wanted to create a 'New Roman Empire' for Italy. For twenty years Piazza Venezia was the chosen theatre for his oratorical performances. He also had big ideas for the city itself: it was under Fascism that many of the relics of ancient Rome were first opened up as public monuments in order to remind Italians of their heritage, and Via dei Fori Imperiali was driven past the Forum, destroying some of the archaeological sites in the process. His greatest legacy was the EUR suburb, the projected site of a world exhibition for 1942, and a showcase of his preferred Fascist-classical architecture. At the end of the war it was only half-built, but the Italians, not wishing to waste anything, decided to finish the project, and it now houses a few of Rome's museums and sports venues.

Since the war Rome has continued to grow fat as the capital of the often ramshackle, notoriously corrupt political system thrown up by the Italian Republic, and the headquarters of the smug *classe politica* that ran it. Rome has been accused by Lombard regionalists of drawing off wealth from the productive areas of Italy in much the same way that it once demanded to be fed by the Empire; nevertheless, Romans have joined in Italy's 'Moral Revolution' of the last few years, abusing the old-style political bosses, despite the fact that a great many in this city of civil servants themselves benefited from the system.

The city has been led by a mayor from the Green Party since 1993. Preparations for the Holy Year 2000 have involved over 700 public works projects: façades are being restored, car parks added, museums refurbished and promises made for what will be one of the great tourist onslaughts of all time—officials are estimating as many as 30 million visitors over the year, most making the pilgrimage to the Vatican for the special blessing bestowed upon all who pass through the Holy Door at St Peter's, which will be opened on Christmas Day 1999 and resealed on 5 January 2001.

A Little Orientation

There's three things I want to see in Rome:
the Colosseum, St Peter's and the Acropolis.

a big-time tourist from Texas

Two Walls

Of Rome's earliest wall, built by King Servius Tullius before the republic, little remains; you can see one of the last surviving bits outside Stazione Termini. The second, built by Aurelian in 275 AD, is one of the wonders of Rome, though taken for granted. With its 19km length and 383 towers, it is one of the largest ever built in Europe—and certainly the best-preserved of antiquity. In places you can see almost perfectly preserved bastions and monumental gates.

Three Romes

Historians and Romans often think of the city in this way. Classical Rome began on the Palatine Hill, and its business and administrative centre stayed nearby, in the original Forum and the great Imperial Fora built around it. Many of the busiest parts lay to the south, where now you see only green on the tourist office's map. After Rome's fall these areas were never really rebuilt, and even substantial ruins like Trajan's Baths remain unexcavated. The Second Rome, that of the popes, had its centre in the Campus Martius, the plain west and north of the Capitoline Hill, later expanding to include the 'Leonine City' around St Peter's, and the new Baroque district around Piazza del Popolo and the Spanish Steps. The Third Rome, capital of United Italy, has expanded in all directions; the closest it has to a centre is Via del Corso.

Seven Hills

Originally they were much higher; centuries of building, rebuilding and river flooding have made the ground level in the valleys much higher, and emperors and popes shaved bits off their tops in building programmes. The **Monte Capitolino**, smallest but most important, now has Rome's City Hall, the Campidoglio, roughly on the site of ancient Rome's greatest temple, that of Jupiter Greatest and Best. The **Palatino**, adjacent to it, was originally the most fashionable district, and got entirely covered by the palaces of the emperors—the heart of the Roman Empire. The plebeian **Aventino** lies to the south of it, across the Circus Maximus. Between the Colosseum and the Stazione Termini, the **Esquilino**, the **Viminale** and the **Quirinale** stand in a row. The Quirinale was long the residence of the popes, and later of the Italian kings. Finally, there is the **Monte Celio** south of the Colosseum, now an oasis of parkland and ancient churches. Rome has other hills not included in the canonical seven: **Monte Vaticano**, from which the Vatican takes its name, **Monte Pincio**, including the Villa Borghese, and the **Gianicolo**, the long ridge above Trastevere the ancients called the Janiculum.

Fourteen Regions

Ancient Rome had neither street lights nor street signs; drunks trying to find their way home had a job on their hands. Modern Rome has plenty of both. Being Rome, of course the street signs are of marble. In the corner you will notice a small number in Roman numerals; this refers to the *rione*, or ward. In the Middle Ages, there were 14 of these, descendants of the 14 *regii* of the ancient city; even after the fall of Rome they maintained their organization and offered protection to their people in the worst of times. You can still see the heraldic symbols of several of the *rioni* on the sides of buildings which once marked their boundaries.

Getting There

by air

The main airport, **Leonardo da Vinci**, is usually referred to as **Fiumicino**, ✆ 06 65951. A taxi into Rome should cost about L70,000, including airport and luggage supplements. The next best way to get into town is by train. There are two rail links from the airport to the city: to Stazioni Trastevere, Ostiense, Tuscolana and Tiburtina (*every 20mins; L7000*), and a direct service to Stazione Termini, Rome's main rail station (*hourly; L15,000*). COTRAL buses run from outside the Arrivals hall to Stazione Ostiense, near Ⓜ Piramide (*hourly 10.20pm–7am; L6000*). The train takes about 30mins from Fiumicino to Tiburtina; the bus at least 50mins.

Rome's second airport, **Ciampino**, ✆ 06 794 941, is the base for a few passenger and charter flights. A COTRAL bus runs from here to the Anagnina stop at the southern end of the Metro A line, from where it's about 20mins to Stazione Termini (*daily 6.15am–10.20pm*).

Almost all long-distance trains arrive at and depart from the huge, chaotic but efficient **Stazione Termini**. The information and ticket windows are often terribly crowded, so allow plenty of time. There is a taxi stand in front, along with city buses to most points in Rome, and the main Metro Station is in the basement.

There are plenty of other stations: **Tiburtina** (Ⓜ Tiburtina), on the eastern edge of town, and **Ostiense** (Ⓜ Piramide), south of the Monte Aventino, serve some long distance north–south lines. During the night (*12 midnight–5am*), Stazione Termini is shut and trains stop at the other stations. A few trains to Tuscany and Umbria start from **Ostiense** and stop at **Trastevere**, on Viale Trastevere.

The Lazio transport authority, COTRAL, also operates its own little rail network: the **Roma-Nord** line to Viterbo, from their own station on Piazzale Flaminio, north of Piazza del Popolo, and a line to **Ostia** and the Lido, from Porta San Paolo (next to the main Stazione Ostiense FS) and the Ⓜ Magliana (Line B).

by bus

COTRAL buses serve almost every town in Lazio. They leave from different locations around the edge of Rome, depending on the destination: buses heading north northwest leave from Saxa Rubra (on the Roma-Nord rail line) and Lepanto (Ⓜ Lepanto); for the south, southwest and east, buses leave from Ⓜ Anagnina, Ⓜ EUR Fermi and Ⓜ Tiburtina. For details (in Italian) about schedules and fares, call freephone, ☏ 167 431 784 (*Mon–Fri 9–1 and 2–5*). Many companies offer long-distance bus services to and from Rome; check with the tourist office.

by road

All the *autostrade* converging on Rome run into the giant ring road, the *Grande Raccordo Anulare* or *GRA*. From there, good routes into the city are the Via Aurelia (SS1) from the west, the local SS201 *autostrada* from the airport in the southwest, and the A24 from the east. Rome is, as it has been for 2000 years, the hub of a network of ancient routes serving every direction, now transmogrified into state roads (SS) but retaining their old names, and they still provide the most direct means of escaping.

Getting Around

Looking at the map, Rome seems to be made for getting around on foot. This may be so in the *centro storico* around Piazza Navona, but elsewhere it's deceptive—blocks in the newer areas are huge and it will always take longer than you think to walk anywhere. The hills, the outsize scale and the traffic also make Rome a tiring place, but there is some pleasant strolling to be had in the old districts west of the Corso, around the Isola Tiberina, in old Trastevere and around the Monte Celio.

Special arrangements are being made to cope with the extraordinary influx of people and vehicles during the Jubilee year: there will be additional buses and trains laid on, as well as designated parking areas with extra spaces (indicated on the roads into the city centre). In typical Italian fashion, finalized details will not be available until the last minute, so make sure you check with tourist offices for the most up to date information before you set out.

by Metro

Rome's underground system is not particularly convenient as it seems to avoid the historic parts of the city; imagine trying to dig any sort of hole in Rome, with legions of archaeologists ready to pounce. The two lines, A and B, cross at Stazione Termini and will take you to the Colosseum, around the Monte Aventino, to Piazza di Spagna, San Giovanni in Laterano, San Paolo Fuori le Mura (Outside the Walls), Piazza del Popolo, or within eight blocks of St Peter's. Single tickets (*L1500*), also good for city buses—valid for 75mins from obliteration in the turnstile—are available from machines in Metro Stations and tobacconists, bars and kiosks.

by bus and tram

Buses are by far the best way to get around. Pick up a map of the bus routes from the **ATAC** (city bus company) booth outside Stazione Termini. For details (in Italian) about schedules and fares, call freephone, ✆ 167 431 784 (*Mon–Fri 9–1 and 2–5*). Bus tickets cost L1500, and are good for travel on any ATAC city bus or tram and one metro ride—within 75mins of the first use of the ticket—which must be stamped in the machines in the back entrance of buses or trams. There are also special-price full-day tickets (which also include the Metro), as well as weekly and monthly passes available from tobacconists. Most routes run frequently, and are often crowded.

by taxi

Official taxis (painted yellow or white) are in plentiful supply, and easier to get at a rank in one of the main piazzas than to flag down. They are quite expensive, with surcharges for luggage, on Sundays and after 10.30 at night (all explained in English on a laminated card in the taxi). Don't expect to find one when it's raining. To phone for a taxi, call ✆ 06 3570, or ✆ 06 4994; you don't pay extra for calling a cab, but expect to pay for the time it takes for it to reach you.

by car

Absolutely not recommended! Rome isn't as chaotic as Naples, but nearly so. Parking is expensive and difficult to find; many areas in the centre are closed to traffic (and the signs for them are hard to spot) and riddled with narrow, one-way streets. Rome and its cars are mortal enemies.

With all the special arrangements connected with the new millennium, the tourist information offices will be a particularly handy resource for visitors, and the city has added kiosks all over town with English-speaking staff. The main office is at **Via Parigi 5**, ✆ 06 4889 9253/✆ 06 4889 2255, three blocks north of Stazione Termini, just behind the Terme di Diocleziano (*open Mon–Fri 8.15–7.15, Sat 8.15–1.15*).

There are also offices inside **Stazione Termini** and at **Fiumicino Airport** (*open daily 8.15–7.15*), as well as the following kiosks (*open daily 9–6*): **Largo Goldoni**, ✆ 06 6813 6061; **Castel Sant'Angelo**, ✆ 06 6880 9707; **Fori Imperiali**, ✆ 06 6992 4307; **San Giovanni**, ✆ 06 7720 3535; **Stazione Termini**, ✆ 06 4890 6300; Piazza Sonnino (**Trastevere**), ✆ 06 5833 3457; **Via Nazionale** (next to Palazzo delle Esposizioni), ✆ 06 4782 4525; Piazza delle Cinque Lune (**Via del Corso**), ✆ 06 6880 9240; and **Santa Maria Maggiore**, ✆ 06 4788 0294. For the **Vatican City Information Office**, *see* p.77.

The **Hotel Reservation Service**, ✆ 06 699 1000 (*open daily 7am–10pm*) offers commission-free reservations at several hundred hotels in town. **Enjoy Rome**, Via Varese 39, ✆ 06 445 1843 (*open Mon–Fri 8.30–2 and 3.30–6.30, Sat 8.30–2*), also near Stazione Termini, is an efficient privately run English-speaking agency. Two agencies offer help in finding bed and breakfast accommodation: **Bed and Breakfast Italy**, ✆ 06 564 0716, and the **Bed and Breakfast Association of Rome**, ✆ 06 687 7348.

Two weeklies available from news-stands, *Romac'e'* (with a short English section at the back) and *Time Out* (in Italian), are the best sources of information on what's on in Rome in the arts, culture and entertainment.

24-hour pharmacies: Piram, Via Nazionale 228, ✆ 06 488 0754; **Arenula**, Via Arenula 73, ✆ 06 6880 3278, near Largo Argentina. Lists of duty pharmacists are also posted outside all other pharmacies.

By far the easiest and best way to change money is by using your ATM (cashpoint) card. The machines are just about everywhere in Rome, take cards from all English-speaking countries, are open 24 hours a day, the rate is the bank wholesale exchange rate (the best you can get), and there is no fee other than the service charge of a couple of dollars.

The best alternative is to change money at **American Express**, Piazza di Spagna 38, ✆ 06 67641 (*open Mon–Fri 9–5.30, Sat 9–12.30*); **Thomas Cook**, Via della Conciliazione 23–25, ✆ 06 6830 0435 (*open Mon–Sat 8.30–6, Sun 9–1.30*); and numerous money changing shops in the centre.

Main post office: in Piazza San Silvestro, ✆ 06 6771.

⊕ Calendar of Jubilee Events in Rome

December 1999

Fri 24	Feast of the Birth of the Lord; **St Peter's**: Midnight Mass, opening of Holy Door
Sat 25	Beginning of the Jubilee in Rome and around the world; Feast of the Birth of the Lord; **S Giovanni in Laterano** and **S Maria Maggiore**: Opening of Holy Door
	St Peter's: Mass during the day, papal 'Urbi et Orbi' Blessing
Fri 31	**St Peter's**: New Year's Eve Prayer vigil for the millennium

January 2000

Sat 1	World Day of Peace; Feast of Mary, Mother of God
Sun 2	Second Sunday after Christmas; Day for Children
Thurs 6	Feast of the Epiphany of the Lord; **St Peter's**: Episcopal Ordinations
Sun 9	Feast of the Baptism of the Lord; celebration of the sacrament of Baptism for children
Tues 18	Beginning of the Week of Prayer for Christian Unity; **S Paolo fuori le Mura**: Opening of Holy Door; Ecumenical celebration
Tues 25	Feast of the Conversion of St Paul, **S Paolo fuori le Mura**; ecumenical celebration for the conclusion of the Week of Prayer for Christian Unity

February 2000

Wed 2	Feast of the Presentation of the Lord; **St Peter's**: Liturgy of light
Fri 11	Memorial of Our Lady of Lourdes; **St Peter's**: Celebration of the Sacrament of the Anointing of the Sick
Tues 22	Feast of the See of St Peter; **St Peter's**
Fri 25–Sun 27	Convention on the implementation of the Second Vatican Ecumenical Council

March 2000

Sun 5	**St Peter's**: Beatification/Canonization
Wed 8	Ash Wednesday: Penitential procession from S Sabina to the Circus Maximus; Holy Mass and imposition of ashes
Thurs 9	Eucharistic Adoration, **S Paolo fuori le Mura**
Fri 10	Way of the Cross and penitential celebration, **S Giovanni in Laterano**
Sat 11	Recitation of the Rosary, **S Maria Maggiore**
Sun 12	First Sunday of Lent; **S Giovanni in Laterano**: Rite of Election and the enrolment of the names of the catechumens
Thurs 16	Eucharistic Adoration, **S Paolo fuori le Mura**
Fri 17	Way of the Cross and penitential celebration, **S Giovanni in Laterano**
Sat 18	Recitation of the Rosary, **S Maria Maggiore**
Sun 19	Second Sunday of Lent; First scrutiny of catechumens, **S Giovanni in Laterano**
Mon 20	Feast of St Joseph, Husband of the Blessed Virgin Mary
Thurs 23	Eucharistic Adoration, **S Paolo fuori le Mura**
Fri 24	Way of the Cross and penitential celebration, **S Giovanni in Laterano**
Sat 25	Feast of the Annunciation of the Lord; simultaneous celebration at **S Maria Maggiore**, Nazareth Basilica of the Annunciation, and all major Marian shrines
Sun 26	Third Sunday of Lent; Second scrutiny of catechumens, **S Giovanni in Laterano**
Thurs 30	Eucharistic Adoration, **S Paolo fuori le Mura**
Fri 31	Way of the Cross and penitential celebration, **S Giovanni in Laterano**

April 2000

Sat 1	Recitation of the Rosary, **S Maria Maggiore**
Sun 2	Fourth Sunday of Lent; Third scrutiny of catechumens, **S Giovanni in Laterano**
Thurs 6	Eucharistic Adoration, **S Paolo fuori le Mura**
Fri 7	Way of the Cross and penitential celebration, **S Giovanni in Laterano**
Sat 8	Recitation of the Rosary, **S Maria Maggiore**
Sun 9	Fifth Sunday of Lent; Rite of giving the Creed and the Lord's Prayer to the catechumens, **S Giovanni in Laterano**
Thurs 13	Eucharistic Adoration, **S Paolo fuori le Mura**
Fri 14	Way of the Cross and penitential celebration, **S Giovanni in Laterano**
Sat 15	Recitation of the Rosary, **S Maria Maggiore**
Holy Week	
Sun 16	Palm Sunday: **St Peter's Square**; Commemoration of the Lord's entry into Jerusalem and Holy Mass
Tues 18	Communal celebration of the sacrament of Penance with individual absolution, the **Patriarchal Basilicas**
Thurs 20	Holy Thursday; **St Peter's**: Chrism Mass; **S Giovanni in Laterano**: Mass in memory of the Last Supper
Fri 21	Good Friday; **St Peter's**: Celebration of the Lord's Passion; the Colosseum: Solemn Way of the Cross
Sun 23	Easter Sunday—the Resurrection of the Lord; **St Peter's**: Easter Vigil: Service of Light, Liturgy of the Word, Baptismal Liturgy (Celebration of the Rite of Christian Initiation of Adults), Eucharistic Liturgy; Mass during the day, 'Urbi et Orbi' Blessing

May 2000

Sat 6	Recitation of the Rosary, **S Maria Maggiore**
Sun 7	Third Sunday of Easter; **Colosseum**: Ecumenical service for the 'new martyrs
Sat 13	Recitation of the Rosary, **S Maria Maggiore**
Sun 14	Fourth Sunday of Easter; **St Peter's**: Holy Mass, Priestly Ordinations
Thurs 18	80th Birthday of the Holy Father; **St Peter's Square**: Holy Mass
Sat 20	Recitation of the Rosary, **S Maria Maggiore**
Sat 27	Recitation of the Rosary, **S Maria Maggiore**
Sun 28	Sixth Sunday of Easter; Holy Mass,
Wed 31	Vigil of the Feast of the Ascension of the Lord, **St Peter's**

June 2000

Thurs 1	Feast of the Ascension of the Lord, Holy Mass, **St Peter's**
Sat 10	Vigil of the Feast of Pentecost, **St Peter's Square**; Solemn Vigil of Pentecost
Sun 11	Feast of Pentecost, **St Peter's**; Day of Prayer for collaboration among all religions
Sun 18 the	Feast of the Holy Trinity, **S Giovanni in Laterano**; Celebration of the opening of International Eucharistic Congress
Thurs 22	Feast of the Body and Blood of Christ, Eucharistic procession, **S Giovanni in Laterano**
Sun 25	Closing of the International Eucharistic Congress
Thurs 29	Feast of the Apostles Peter and Paul; **St Peter's**: Holy Mass

August 2000

Sat 5	Vigil of prayer for the Feast of the Transfiguration of the Lord; **S Maria Maggiore**
Sun 6	Feast of the Transfiguration; **S Paolo fuori le Mura**
Mon 14	Vigil of the Feast of the Assumption of the Blessed Virgin Mary; **S Maria Maggiore**: Incense Rite of the Coptic Liturgy
Tues 15	Feast of the Assumption of the Virgin Mary; Opening of 15th World Youth Day
Sat 19–Sun 20	Vigil of prayer and Holy Mass; Conclusion of the 15th World Youth Day

September 2000

3 Sun	**St Peter's**: Beatification/Canonization
Fri 8	Feast of the Birth of the Blessed Virgin Mary
Thurs 14	Feast of the Exaltation of the Holy Cross, from the Basilica of the Holy Cross in Jerusalem to S Giovanni in Laterano; **S Giovanni in Laterano**: Stational Procession
Fri 15	Opening of the International Marian-Mariological Congress
Sun 24	Holy Mass; Conclusion of the International Marian-Mariological Congress

October 2000

Sat 7	Memorial of Our Lady of the Rosary; Recitation of the Rosary and torchlight procession
Sun 8	Holy Mass, **St Peter's**; Act of dedicating the new millennium to the protection of Mary
Sat 14–Sun 15	Third Worldwide Meeting of the Holy Father with Families
Sun 15	Holy Mass, **St Peter's Square**; Celebration of the Sacrament of Matrimony
Sat 21	Celebration of the Rosary, **S Maria Maggiore**
Sun 22	Holy Mass, **St Peter's**; World Mission Day
Sat 28	Recitation of the Rosary, **S Maria Maggiore**
Sun 29	Holy Mass, **Olympic Stadium**
Tues 31	First Vespers and Vigil of the Feast of All Saints; **St Peter's**

November 2000

Wed 1	Feast of All Saints; **St Peter's**: Beatification/Canonization
Sun 26	Feast of Christ the King; Holy Mass, **St Peter's**; Conclusion of the World Congress for the Apostolate of the Laity

December 2000

Sat 2	Vigil of the First Sunday of Advent; **St Peter's**
Sun 3	First Sunday of Advent; **S Paolo fuori le Mura**: Holy Mass
Fri 8	Feast of the Immaculate Conception, **S Maria Maggiore**
Sun 10	Second Sunday of Advent; **S Giovanni in Laterano**: Holy Mass
Sun 24	Feast of the Birth of Our Lord; Midnight Mass, **St Peter's**
Mon 25	Feast of the Birth of Our Lord; **St Peter's**: daytime Mass; 'Urbi et Orbi' Blessing
Sun 31	Prayer Vigil for the passage to the new millennium, **St Peter's**

January 2001

Mon 1	Feast of Mary Mother of God; **St Peter's**: Holy Mass; World Day of Peace
Thurs 5	Vigil of the Feast of the Epiphany of the Lord; **S Giovanni in Laterano, S Maria Maggiore** and **S Paolo fuori le Mura**: Holy Mass and Closing of Holy Doors; End of the Jubilee year
Fri 6	Feast of the Epiphany of the Lord; **St Peter's**: Closing of Holy Door

Vatican Practicalities

The **Vatican Information Office**, Piazza San Pietro, © 06 6988 4466 (*open daily 8–7*) is very helpful, and there are Vatican post offices on the opposite side of the square and inside the Vatican Museums for distinctive postcards home.

The information office arranges 2hr-long morning tours of the **Vatican Gardens**, easily Rome's most beautiful park, with a remarkable Renaissance jewel of a villa inside: the **Casino of Pius IV** by Pietro Ligorio and Peruzzi (1558–62; *open May–Sept Mon–Sat; Oct–April once a week; L18,000 per person; reserve a few days in advance with the information office*).

The entrance to the **museums** is on Viale Vaticano, to the north of Piazza San Pietro (*museums open Nov–Feb Mon–Sat 8.45–1.45, last admission 12.45; the rest of the year Mon–Sat 8.45–4.45, last admission 3.45; adm; the last Sun of each month and religious holidays 8.45–1.45, last admission 12.45; free*).

St Peter's (*open daily 7–7; Oct–Mar 7–6*) is closed when there are official ceremonies in the piazza, although visitors are allowed during mass. The dress code—no shorts, short skirts or sleeveless dresses—is strictly controlled by the papal gendarmes.

Underneath the crypt of St Peter's, archaeologists in the 1940s discovered a **street of Roman tombs**, perfectly preserved with many beautiful paintings (*open Mon–Sat 9–5; adm; tours can be arranged through the Uffizio degli Scavi, just to the left of St Peter's; in the summer book early as fragile conditions permit only 15 people at a time*). The rest of the Vatican is strictly off limits, patrolled by Swiss Guards (still recruited from the Catholic Swiss Cantons).

Michelangelo also designed the **wall** that since 1929 has marked the Vatican boundaries. Behind it are things most of us will never see: several small old churches, a printing press, the headquarters of *L'Osservatore Romano* and Vatican Radio (run, of course, by the Jesuits), a motor garage, a 'Palazzo di Giustizia' and even a big shop—everything the world's smallest nation could ever need. Modern popes, in glaring contrast to their predecessors, do not take up much space. The current Papal Apartments are in a corner of the Vatican Palace overlooking Piazza San Pietro; John Paul II usually appears to say a few electrically amplified words from his window at noon on Sundays.

For tickets to the Wednesday morning **papal audience**, usually held at 11am in the piazza (*May–Sept*) or in the Nervi Auditorium (*Oct–April*), apply in advance at the Papal Prefecture—through the bronze door in the right-hand colonnade of Piazza San Pietro (*open Mon and Tues 9–1, © 06 6988 3217*).

The only public entrances to Vatican City are through St Peter's Square and the Vatican Museums. Swiss Guards, dressed in a scaled-down version of the striped suits designed by either Michelangelo or Raphael, stand ready to smite you with their halberds if you try to push your way in elsewhere. The Vatican has its own stamps and postal service, which make it a tidy profit; it is also, like every postal system in the galaxy, more efficient than the Posta Italiana. The official language in Vatican City is Latin, though its own semi-official daily newspaper, *L'Osservatore Romano,* is in Italian (with a weekly digest in English) and its Vatican Radio broadcasts in 26 languages.

The Borgo

Another set of walls, originally built by Leo IV after the Saracen raid in 846, surrounds the Borgo, the small neighbourhood in the shadow of St Peter's. The word comes from the Anglo-Saxon *burgh,* or town, founded in the early 8th century by Anglo-Saxon kings and pilgrims. They were soon followed by the Franks and Frisians, who each built their own schola as a school and a hostel to protect their pilgrims from the wiles of Roman innkeepers. Today the Borgo, numbed by the predominance of its self-contained institutions, retains few memories of its English origins beyond its street names and the mediocrity of its restaurants. But it, too, has a mastodonic landmark of its own—the Castel Sant'Angelo (*see* p.94).

Piazza San Pietro

Not even all the photographs you've seen can quite prepare you for **Piazza San Pietro**. The gigantic proportions force you to suspend your normal visual belief; all is so superscale that only by constant reference to the measurements of man, a mere tiddlywink next to St Peter's 350ft-long façade, can you begin to digest its outrageous size.

Someone has calculated that there is room for about 300,000 people in the piazza, with no crowding. Few have ever noticed Bernini's little joke on antiquity; the open space almost exactly matches the size and dimensions of the Colosseum. Bernini would prefer us to see his **colonnade**, with its 284 massive columns and statues of 140 saints, as 'the arms of the Church embracing the world'—an ancient cliché, though perhaps exactly what patron and architect intended. Stand on either of the two dark stones at the foci of the elliptical piazza, and you will see the forest of columns resolve into neat rows, a subtly impressive optical effect. Bernini designed the colonnade so that the nobility could drive their carriages underneath to St Peter's, sheltered from sun or rain.

Flanked by two lovely fountains, luxuriantly spraying water all over the pavement—the one on the right by Carlo Maderno (1614), and the other, copied from it in 1667—the Vatican **obelisk**, though only average-size for an obelisk, is one of the most fantastical relics in all Rome. It comes from Heliopolis, the Egyptian city founded as a capital and cult centre by Ikhnaton, the half-legendary Pharaoh and religious reformer who, according to Sigmund

Freud and others, founded the first monotheistic religion, influencing Moses and all who came after. It arrived here apparently by divine coincidence; originally in the *spina* of Nero's Circus Vaticanus, it overlooked the martyrdom of St Peter. For a millennium and a half it remained in place, just to the left of the present basilica, until Sixtus V had it moved, accompanied by one of the city's favourite anecdotes.

Moving the Obelisk

 Sixtus V was no stuck-in-the-*sedia-gestatoria* pope, but a man of action, the only one, Queen Elizabeth I claimed, half-jokingly, who was worthy of her hand. One of his pet projects was to humble the ancient pagans of Rome, whose monuments, even in ruins, still threatened to overshadow the grandeur of the Church. In 1586 he ordered Domenico Fontana to move the obelisk to the piazza, to show how puny this heathen ornament was in comparison to the Biggest Church in the World.

The problem was, no one could remember how to move an obelisk. Fontana made careful, elaborate plans (Sixtus hinted that failure would mean the chopping block), and on 18 September 900 men, 150 horses and 47 cranes creaked into action. A vast crowd had gathered to watch, but the Pope insisted on perfect silence (underlined by the presence of a gallows) so the workmen could hear Fontana's orders. Slowly the obelisk was hauled upright by the ropes, then hesitated, the ropes too taut with the strain to finish the task. Suddenly the silence was broken by a Ligurian sailor's cry, 'Water on the ropes!' saving the obelisk and Fontana's neck. Sixtus showed his gratitude by giving the sailor's hometown of Bordighera the monopoly of supplying palm fronds to the Vatican on Palm Sunday. Originally the obelisk was topped by a golden ball, long believed to contain the ashes of Julius Caesar (though it proved empty when cracked open); now it has an iron cross, containing a sliver of the True Cross.

Off to the right of the square is a confusing cluster of buildings, the Vatican palaces. Since 1903, when the newly elected Pius X refused to move from the servants' quarters of the **Apostolic Palace** (the tallest building), where he stayed during the conclave, the popes have chosen to live there, behind the last two windows on the right, on the top floor.

On Sunday at noon John Paul II appears at the window and blesses the crowd in the piazza. The gallery along the right, the **Corridore del Bernini**, leads to the great **Bronze Door**, the ceremonial entrance to the Vatican for visiting dignitaries; it leads to the Scala Regia. On the left side are the Vatican information office, the bus stop for the Vatican Museums, post office, lavatories and first aid station. At the end is the **Arco delle Campane**, under St Peter's bells, guarded by the Swiss; if you're booking to see the necropolis, just tell them 'Ufficio degli Scavi'.

Open April–Sept daily 7–7; Oct–Mar daily 7–6; treasury open daily 9–6.30; adm; sacred grottoes open Oct–April 7–5; May–Sept 7–6; dome open Oct–Mar 8–5; April–Sept 8–6; adm.

It may be irreverent to say so, but old St Peter's was much cosier. Begun by Constantine over the Apostle's tomb in 324, it was a richly decorated basilica, in form much like S Paolo fuori le Mura, full of gold and mosaics, with a vast porch of marble and bronze in front, and a lofty campanile topped by the famous golden cockerel that everyone believed would some day crow to announce the end of the world. This St Peter's, where Charlemagne and Frederick II received their imperial crowns, was falling to pieces by the 1400s, conveniently in time for the popes and artists of the Renaissance to plan a replacement. The first to do so was Nicholas V, who, in about 1450, conceived an almost Neronian building programme for the Vatican, ten times as large as anything his ancestors could have contemplated—a complex that would have stretched all the way to Castel Sant'Angelo. It was not until Julius II realized that there was not enough room in the basilica for his planned tomb that he commissioned Bramante to demolish the old church and begin the new. His original plan called for a great dome over a central Greek cross. Michelangelo, who took over the work in 1546, basically agreed, and if he had had his way St Peter's might indeed have become the crowning achievement of Renaissance art everyone hoped it would be.

Unfortunately, despite nearly 200 years of construction and an expenditure of £460,000,000, too many popes and too many architects created instead of a masterpiece a monster of compromise. Raphael, who took over as architect after Bramante's death (nicknaming his former mentor 'Ruinante' for his summary demolition of much that was sacred and preservable in the old basilica), opted for a Latin cross. A number of architects succeeded him: Peruzzi returning to the Greek cross of Bramante, followed by Antonio da Sangallo the Younger, another advocate of the Latin cross. Paul III then summoned Michelangelo, aged 72, who reluctantly took over the mess, on the condition that the pope gave him a free hand (in return, he worked for free, too), whereupon he demolished everything da Sangallo had built and started afresh on Bramante's lines, though changing his plans for a Pantheon-type dome to a higher cupola modelled on Brunelleschi's dome over Florence Cathedral. But even this was reshaped by one of his successors, Giacomo della Porta, who completed it in 1590.

The most substantial tinkering came in 1605, when Paul V and his committee of cardinals decided on a Latin cross after all. Carlo Maderno was given the task of demolishing the portico of the old basilica to extend the nave, which had the unforeseen effect of blocking out the view of the dome, and he designed the façade (1612) with Paul V's name blazoned on top. But Maderno shouldn't be blamed for its disproportionate width: Bernini, who was in charge of decorating the interior, had the bright idea of adding twin campaniles to the flanks which were such a dismal failure that they were levelled to the same height as Maderno's façade. In the centre is the balcony from which the pope gives his *Urbi et Orbi* blessing at Easter and Christmas. On 18 Nov 1626, the supposed 1300th anniversary of the original basilica, Urban VIII consecrated the new St Peter's.

Some of the best art in St Peter's is in the **portico**, beginning with the oldest and hardest to see, Giotto's 1298 mosaic of Christ walking on water, called the *Navicella*, located in the tympanum over the central door; this has been so often moved and restored almost nothing remains of the original. At the extreme right end of the portico is Bernini's equestrian statue of *Constantine*, showing the emperor staring at the vision of the cross. There are five sets of bronze doors leading into the basilica, the work of some of Italy's leading modern sculptors.

St Peter's

50 m
50 yds

N

Portico

1 Statue of Constantine / Scala Regia	19 Altar of St Wenceslas	35 Leo the Great Tomb
2 Holy Door	20 Statue of St Peter	36 Alexander VII Monument
3 Crocetti's Door	21 High Altar / Bernini's	37 Cappella Clementina
4 Filarete's Door	Baldacchino	38 Pius VII Monument
5 Manzù Door	22 Confessio	39 Leo XI Monument
6 Minguzzi's Door	23 St Longinus / Entrance	40 Cappella del Coro
7 Giotto's Navicella	to Grottoes	41 Innocent VIII Monument
8 Statue of Charlemagne	24 St Helen	42 Pius X Monument
9 Michelangelo's Pietà	25 St Veronica	43 Cappella della Presentazione
10 Queen Christina Monument	26 St Andrew	44 John XXIII Monument
11 Cappella di S. Sebastiano	27 Tribune / Cathedra of St Peter	45 Clementina Sobieska Monument / stairs
12 Countess Matilda Monument	28 Urban VIII Monument	and down lift from dome
13 Innocent XII Monument	29 Paul III Monument	46 Monument to the Last Stuarts
14 Cappella del Smo. Sacramento	30 Guercino's St Petronilla	47 Baptistry
15 Gregory XIII Monument	31 Altar of the Navicella	48 Pius VIII Monument / entrance to
16 Cappella Gregoriana	32 Clement XIII Monument	St Peter's Treasury
17 Madonna del Soccorso	33 St Bruno	49 Sacristy
18 Lift up to Dome	34 Cappella della Colonna	

From right to left they are: the **Holy Door** (1950, by Vico Consorti), opened only in Holy Years; the next, by Venanzio Crocetti (1968); the famous central doors, from Old St Peter's, made by Antonio Filarete (1439–45), with scenes from the life of Pope Eugenius IV, who held an ecumenical council in Florence in 1441, an attempt to reconcile the differences between the Eastern and Western Churches in face of the mutual Turkish threat; you can recognize Emperor John Palaeologos by his pointy hat, while Ethiopian monks pay homage to Eugenius. Crudely carved on the other side of the right door, at the bottom, Filarete and his workmen may be seen dancing with their tools below an inscription in pidgin Latin. The next set of doors to the left are by Giacomo Manzù (1963), with harrowing scenes of death and martyrdoms and victims torn like paper bags; on the back of these Manzù cast a scene from the Second Ecumenical Vatican Council, Pope John XXIII conversing with a cardinal from Tanzania—a reference to Filarete's doors. The last set of doors, by Luciano Minguzzi (1977), includes a charming hedgehog. The plodding equestrian statue at the left end is of Charlemagne, by Cornacchini, giving the portico two knights in case any of the giant marble saints ever want to play chess. The floor of the portico is by the indefatigable Bernini, embedded with the giant coat of arms of John XXIII by Manzù to commemorate the Second Vatican Council of 1962.

Most people find the **interior** disappointing, again partly because your eyes are confused by its scale; its proportions, as everyone used to say, are so harmonious you don't notice how large it is, but probably no architect who ever lived could have found a solution to making such a vast barn visually stimulating. Up the middle of the nave, bronze markers showing the length of other proud cathedrals prove how each fails miserably to measure up—the fact that they aren't accurate, and make Milan Cathedral some 65ft too small, proves (at least to the Milanese) that the duplicity of the Romans knows no bounds. The round porphyry stone in the pavement near the central door marks the place by the altar of the old basilica where emperors would kneel to be crowned.

✠ The Holy Door

On Christmas Eve 1999, Pope John Paul II will inaugurate the Jubilee according to the long-established ritual: striking the walled-up Holy Door at St Peter's three times with a silver hammer. The masonry, previously undermined, will fall in, and after the debris is cleared (a job given as penance) Pope John Paul will be the first to enter the basilica for the Christmas Eve Mass. On Christmas Day, specially designated cardinals will perform the same ritual at the Holy Doors of S Giovanni Laterano and S Maria Maggiore.

One of the few clues we have to the origins of this undoubtedly ancient custom comes from a 15th-century Spanish pilgrim named Pedro Tapur, who left a written account of his travels. Tapur recounts the legend of a gate called the Porta Tarpea at the Lateran: in pre-Christian times, any criminal who passed through the gate was granted sanctuary. In the 4th century, at the request of Emperor Constantine, Pope Sylvester changed this to a special dispensation for sinners. So many people took advantage of this blessing, however, that eventually the gate was walled up, to be opened only once every hundred years.

Though there is no evidence for it, it is likely that some similar custom continued through the Middle Ages. Pope Celestine V, in 1294, granted a similar privilege to a church he founded at L'Aquila in the Abruzzo, where a Holy Door is still opened and indulgences granted once each year, on 28 August. A Florentine merchant, Giovanni Rucellai, wrote of a Holy Door at the 1450 Jubilee. This was still at St John Lateran, not St Peter's, though otherwise the ceremony seems to have been much the same. The door was opened by Pope Alexander VI in person on Christmas Eve and walled up again at the close of the Jubilee—only back then, the people of Rome and the pilgrims carried off the broken bits of stone and mortar as holy relics. Alexander, the Borgia pope, was a great innovator in papal ritual and ceremony, and in his Jubilee Holy Doors were opened in the major basilicas of the city, as they still are today.

The Pietà

The best work of art is right in front, in the first chapel on the right: Michelangelo's famous *Pietà*, now restored and hard to see behind the glass that protects it from future madmen. Finished in 1499, when he was only 25, the statue helped make Michelangelo's reputation. Its smooth and elegant figures, with the realities of death and grief sublimated on some ethereal plane known only to saints and artists, marked a turning point in religious art—from here, the beautiful, unreal art of the religious Baroque was the logical next step. The *Pietà* is the only work Michelangelo ever signed (on the band of the Virgin's garment); he added it after overhearing a group of tourists from Milan who thought the *Pietà* was the work of a fellow Milanese.

Michelangelo sculpted the *Pietà* for the French ambassador; significantly, none of the art made to order for St Peter's can match it. By the time the basilica was finished, the great artists of the Renaissance were dead, and whatever glories they may have contributed have been replaced by assembly-line Baroque statues and huge Counter-Reformation paintings, in turn replaced by 'more eternal' mosaic copies.

The Right Aisle

Two of the few memorials to real women may be seen in the right aisle: in the arch after the *Pietà* is a **monument to Queen Christina of Sweden**, topped by a large, flattering portrait of the frowzy monarch, who at one point embarrassed her papal sponsors by falling in love with a nun; and in the next chapel, the **cappella di San Sebastiano**, Bernini's **monument to Countess Matilda of Tuscany**, the great benefactress of the temporal papacy who died in 1115, and whose remains were brought here from Mantua in 1635. The pride of the next chapel, the **cappella del Santissimo Sacramento**, is its iron grille by Borromini; on the altar the ciborium by Bernini is a miniature copy of Bramante's Tempietto of S. Pietro in Montorio. In the next arch an allegorical figure of Courage lifts the cover of the sarcophagus of the **monument of Gregory XIII** by Camillo

Rusconi (1723), to reveal an allegory of Gregory's calendar reforms and, underneath, a hobgoblin of a dragon. Beyond, the **cappella Gregoriana** defines the original, pre-Maderno limits of St Peter's; it was designed by Michelangelo. The altar painting of the *Madonna del Soccorso* is an 11th-century relic from the old basilica. In the next arch is the lift up to the roof (*see* below).

The right transept contains three altars, the one on the right dedicated to good King Wenceslas (of Bohemia), the same who 'looked out on the Feast of Stephen'. Around the enormous pier sits the famous bronze **statue of St Peter**, its extended foot worn away by the kisses of the faithful. Its date is a mystery: long believed to belong to the 5th century, made from the bronze of the statue of Capitoline Jove, it was later assumed to be a 13th-century work by Arnolfo di Cambio, though the latest scholarship has reverted to the original date. It may have been part of the tomb of Emperor Honorius, which later became the French monastery of St Martin, just to the left of St Peter's: early Christians, like ancient Romans, often added statues of a personal divine intercessor to help them through the beyond. On 29 June, the feast day of SS. Peter and Paul, the statue is dressed up in full pontifical garb.

The High Altar and the Dome

The **High Altar**, where only the Pope may celebrate mass, is sheltered by Bernini's celebrated **baldacchino** (1633), cast from bronze looted from the Pantheon roof by his Barberini patron, Urban VIII. The canopy is as tall as the Farnese Palace, to give a hint of its scale, and in form resembles the baldacchino of old St Peter's, with its twisted columns and hangings (though now made of bronze). Barberini bees swarm over it as if it were real barley sugar, and on the pedestals supporting the columns, incorporated into coats of arms, are seven female faces expressing labour pains, and lastly a happy baby's face: Urban VIII commissioned the baldacchino as an ex-voto for the safe deliverance of a favourite niece from a dangerous pregnancy. But even the world's biggest canopy shrinks under the world's biggest **dome** (the Pantheon's shallow dome is about 6ft wider, and there are two even bigger ones in Malta, but if inverted this one could hold the most soup). Decorated with a minestrone of religious mosaics spooned on by the tedious Cavaliere d'Arpino, it is a dizzy 352ft to the top. By the time of Michelangelo's death it was completed only so far as the drum, where 7ft-high letters spell out the words of Christ to Peter: 'Tu es Petrus ...' The horseshoe-shaped **confessio**, designed by Maderno and perpetually lit by 95 lamps, contains, behind the grille, a shaft leading down to the tomb of St Peter through which the woollen *pallia* (the strips of cloth that bishops wear around their necks) are lowered to be sanctified. It was when workmen were lowering the floor in the crypt below the Confessio in 1939 that the ancient cemetery was discovered, along with the presumed relics of St Peter (*see* the Ancient Necropolis, below).

The four massive **piers** supporting the dome are graced by mastodonic statues of saints associated with St Peter's most treasured relics. These relics used to be publicly displayed during Holy Week from the piers' upper balconies, each of these adorned with a pair of columns from old St Peter's—six of which were brought from Byzantium by Constantine, while the others are copies made shortly after. Nearest the bronze statue of St Peter is *St*

Longinus (statue by Bernini) whose relic is the lance that Longinus, a Roman soldier, used to pierce the side of Christ; underneath is the entrance to the Vatican Grottoes (*see* below). Also on the right is *St Helen* (whose relic is a piece of the True Cross); across from here is *St Veronica*, whose handkerchief preserves an imprint of Christ's features; and last of all is *St Andrew*, by Duquesnoy, whose relic was his head, but that has recently been returned to the church in Patras, Greece, from which the Despot of Morea grabbed it in the 15th century.

The Tribune

Meant to be seen under the baldacchino from the moment you enter is Bernini's **tribune**, a gaudy 1665 work encasing St Peter's *cathedra*, the chair from which the Apostle was said to have delivered his first sermon to the Romans. Bernini's first training was in the theatre, and this is one of his smash hits, with a multi-media cast of gilt bronze, coloured marbles and stucco, illuminated by a glowing window with a dove emblem that forms an integral part of the composition.

This part of the basilica is usually roped off, but if you have binoculars and are prepared to engage in various bodily contortions, you may just be able to see Bernini's **monument of Urban VIII** (begun in 1628) to the right of Bernini's throne. Here again the sculptor effectively uses different materials and colours: the Pope, jauntily waving from the afterlife, and Death, penning his epitaph, are in dark bronze, while the more worldly figures of Charity and Justice are of white marble. To the left is Guglielmo della Porta's notorious 1575 **monument of Paul III**, flanked by figures of Prudence (modelled on the Pope's mother) and Justice, a portrait of his sister, the lovely Giulia Farnese, who as Alexander VI's mistress did her part in advancing Paul's career. Originally the statue was nude; the story goes that its beauty drove a Spanish student to distraction, until one night he hid in the basilica to make love to it. In the morning he was found dead at its side, and since then it has worn metal draperies.

To the right of the tribune, around the Pier of St Helena, is the **cappella San Michele**, with a mosaic of Guercino's *St Petronilla* (original in the Capitoline museum); behind, on the pier itself, is the **altar of the Navicella** by Lanfranco, inspired by Giotto's mosaic in the portico; directly across from it is Canova's neoclassical **monument of Clement XIII**. Continue around the pier for Michelangelo Slodtz's 1744 *St Bruno*, where the saint is shown gracefully refusing a bishop's mitre.

The Left Aisle

Backtrack across Bernini's tribune to the left aisle; behind the pier of St Veronica is the **cappella della Colonna**, named after a column from the old basilica, painted with a much venerated picture of the Virgin. The chapel contains the **tomb of Leo the Great**, with Algardi's relief of St Leo halting the advance of Attila the Hun (the pope is said to have threatened Attila with a fatal nosebleed if he should enter Rome, but since Attila couldn't understand Latin, we see SS. Peter and Paul translating). In the next arch is Bernini's **monument of Alexander VII**, a late work that juxtaposes the serenely praying pope with Death, popping out of the curtains below, waving a warning hourglass. Across the left transept is the **cappella Clementina**, decorated by Giacomo della Porta and containing the **monument of Pius VII** (1823) by Bertel Thorvaldsen, the only Protestant to contribute to St Peter's.

Beyond, in the arch, is Algardi's **monument of Leo XI**, whose pontificate lasted only 27 days; the relief shows him as a cardinal watching Henry IV of France abjure Protestantism. In the next arch, beyond the ornate **cappella del Coro** is Antonio Pollaiuolo's bronze **monument to Innocent VIII** (1492), the only survivor from the old basilica, with its good-humoured papal effigy of Innocent blessing with a smile and holding the blade of Longinus' spear, given him by Ottoman Sultan Bayazit II, while below another effigy represents Innocent in death. Across is the **monument of St Pius X**, whose tomb is in the next chapel, the **cappella della Presentazione**. Next on the right is Emilio Greco's **monument of John XXIII**. The following arch is dedicated to the last Stuarts: up on the right, the **monument of Clementina Sobieska**, wife of the Old Pretender and grand-daughter of the saviour of Vienna, and here called 'Queen of Great Britain, France, and Ireland,' while on the left, Canova's pyramid-shaped **monument of the Old and Young Pretenders and Henry, Cardinal of York** was paid for by George IV. The **baptistry** contains an ancient font made of Emperor Otto II's sarcophagus lid turned upside-down, with a metal cover by Carlo Fontana.

There's still more: the treasury, grottoes and dome. Just before the left transept and under the monument of Pius VIII is the entrance to **St Peter's treasury** (*open daily 9–6.30; adm*), containing a choice selection of the bits that the Saracens, Normans, Spaniards and Napoleon didn't steal. Near the entrance are two famous relics from the old basilica: the golden cockerel that Leo IV set atop the campanile, whose cock-a-doodle will announce the end of the world, and the beautiful twisted **Colonna Santa**, of Parian marble, traditionally the column on which Christ leaned while disputing with the doctors in the Temple—in the Middle Ages exorcists would place their patients against it to chase out the devil. The bejewelled **Vatican Cross** was given to St Peter's by Justin II in 578, and has portraits of the emperor and empress on the back, who raise their arms as if to say 'Surprise!'; in the same room is the so-called **Dalmatic of Charlemagne**, which tradition claims he wore during his coronation, though it dates from the 11th century (even then, a rare enough example of Byzantine ceremonial dress). Equally intriguing is a 1974 copy of **St Peter's Chair**, the original of the one enclosed in Bernini's Baroque confection, though chances are slim that Peter ever sat in it, as it was donated to the basilica in 875 by Charles the Bald. The upper part is Carolingian, while the lower half, from the 3rd century, is surprisingly decorated with fine ivory reliefs of the Labours of Hercules.

Beyond is a lovely marble tabernacle (1435) by Donatello, saved from the old basilica; it frames a much revered painting of the *Madonna della Febbre*, invoked against malaria. The **tomb of Sixtus IV** by Antonio Pollaiuolo (1493) is a masterpiece of bronze casting, with its fine effigy of the sleeping Pope and the allegories of the Seven Virtues and Ten Sciences that adorn its sides; it can be viewed from the platform above. This is followed by a 14th-century Giottesque fresco of *SS. Peter and Paul,* found in the crypt; a 13th-century bust reliquary of St Luke; a key of St Peter's tomb (one of many copies made; after a time in the sacred keyhole it would become one of the most prized relics a pilgrim could obtain); Sixtus IV's ring; choir antiphonies embellished with beautiful grotesques; the gilded bronze *SS. Peter and Paul* by Torrigiano (most famous in Italy for having broken Michelangelo's nose); a pair of enormous candelabra attributed to Cellini; the jewelled tiara used to crown the ancient statue of St Peter, followed by chalices and other Church paraphernalia studded with precious stones, much of it given to the popes since Napoleon; and lastly, the remarkable **Sarcophagus of Junius Bassus**, prefect of Rome in 359; the reliefs portray both Old and New Testament scenes and baby Bacchuses.

The entrance to the crypt of St Peter's, or **sacred grottoes** is usually by way of the stair by the pier of St Longinus. The grottoes, on the floor level of the old basilica, follow the floor plan of the basilica above, and are lined with tombs: a full house, with a pair of queens, 20 popes and an emperor (*open, except when the Pope is in the basilica, Oct–April 7–5; May–Sept 7–6*).

The horseshoe-shaped **Grotte Nuove**, built 1534–46 under the area of St Peter's altar, are called 'new' because their decoration is more recent. Most beautiful here is the Renaissance **tomb of Paul II**, on which Mino da Fiesole and Giovanni Dalmata laboured for ten years without finishing. Further along, placed in the wall, are lovely marble reliefs from the baldacchino made for Sixtus IV. In the centre of the horseshoe, directly under the High Altar and over the 'Trophy of Gaius' (the 3rd-century shrine built around St Peter's tomb), is the **cappella Clementina** (1605); if the lights are on in the necropolis below, you can see a section of it in a gap to the left of the altar.

The adjoining **Grotte Vecchie** were built at the same time that Maderno extended the nave. The central altar has another exquisite Renaissance work, a relief of *Christ in Majesty* from the tomb of Nicholas V, by Giovanni Dalmata (1450s). In the area under St Peter's right aisle are the simple tombs of John XXIII (always covered with flowers), John Paul I and Paul VI, while those of Christina of Sweden and Charlotte of Cyprus face each other. Canova's large statue of praying **Pius VI**, formerly in the Confessio, was moved to the end of the grottoes in 1980. The Old Pretender, Bonny Prince Charlie, and Henry, Cardinal of York are in the left aisle, as is the English pope, Adrian IV, in a 3rd-century sarcophagus (no one brings *him* pretty flowers—the Romans remember him best for burning Arnold of Brescia). Off the left aisle are a few rooms used to house fragments of the old basilica.

To ascend St Peter's **dome**, one of Rome's biggest thrills and chills (especially if you suffer from vertigo), leave the basilica and join the queue on the far right-hand side (*open Oct–Mar 8–5; April–Sept 8–6; adm; for a few more lire you can take a lift—worthwhile since it's another 200 steps from the roof to the top of the dome*).

The lift leaves you on the roof, a strange world of domes on wavy pavement, where you can measure yourself against the saintly titans who will look over Piazza San Pietro until kingdom come; here, too, is a souvenir shop, post office, coke machine, WCs, and buildings of the *Sanpietrini*, the workmen in charge of maintaining the fabric of the basilica. In the old days the *Sanpietrini* not only worked on the roof, but lived here with their families, producing sons who scoffed at heights and who would later inherit their jobs.

Although recent cupolas cast a shadow on St Peter's superlatives (visitors from New Orleans find it downright puny next to their Superdome) it can still claim to be the largest brick dome in existence. Stairs within the dome lead up to the **first gallery**, for a death-defying view 174ft above the floor of St Peter's that brings home, more than anything, the basilica's scale. A narrower stair, tilted for the curve in the dome, continues up to the **second gallery** 240ft up, but this is closed to the public. An even narrower spiral stair continues the rest of the way up to the terrace under the lantern, from where, on a clear day, all Rome, much of the *campagna*, and the Tyrrhenian Coast lie spread out at your feet. The golden ball high overhead, which looks like a marble from below, is actually big enough to hold 16 people.

The Ancient Necropolis of St Peter's

Open Mon–Sat 9–12 and 2–5; due to lack of space and the delicate condition of the tombs and frescoes only c. 15 people permitted per tour (1½-hrs); try to book as far in advance as possible; adm exp; the tour starts by the Uffizio degli Scavi.

In 1939, when Pius XII ordered the *Sanpietrini* to lower the floor of the sacred grottoes and prepare a tomb for Pius XI, the workmen discovered not only the floor of the Constantinian Basilica, but also below this, signs of an ancient tomb. Although its existence has been documented since Bramante's day, Pius XII was the first pope to consent to an exploration of the area (previous popes had superstitiously feared to disturb the bones or, worse yet, they feared that the Saracens in 846 had stolen St Peter's relics after all). All during the war, the secret excavations continued, uncovering one of the most remarkable sights in all Rome: the Ancient Necropolis of St Peter's, a pristine street of pagan and early Christian tombs built around that of the Apostle.

Apparently the pagan tombs originally overlooked the Vatican Circus, so the dead could enjoy the games even in the afterlife. The guides know their subject well and take you past the delightful, brightly painted tombs lined with niches for urns, described by H.V. Morton as 'little sitting-rooms for the soul'. The burials date from AD 150–300; the Christians, naturally, are near St Peter; one tomb has what is believed to be the earliest Christian mosaic ever found—Christ depicted as the sun god Helios.

Deep under the High Altar the excavations revealed the red walls of a monument-shrine, or *ædicula*, believed to be the so-called 'trophy of Gaius' (built around AD 160, and described by the priest Gaius around the year 200). When constructing St Peter's basilica, Constantine enclosed the 'trophy of Gaius' in marble and porphyry, filled in the surrounding tombs, and laboriously excavated a section of the Vatican hill to ensure that this spot would be under the altar. Physical evidence was found of the Saracens' raid and, in the *ædicula*, a hole which probably contained St Peter's bronze casket. But outside the *ædicula* were found the headless bones of an elderly, strongly built man; graffiti on the wall above invoke the aid of St Peter. After years of consideration, Paul VI announced that these bones were indeed the relics of St Peter. Jammed around are the tombs of Christians anxious to be buried near the Apostle. No one is quite sure how far the street of pagan tombs extends—perhaps to Castel Sant'Angelo.

Vatican City and Gardens

The three-hour guided tours (the only way to get in) begin from in front of the tourist office. Book in advance, showing your ID; tours begin at 10am; daily except Sun and Wed in summer; Sat only in winter; adm exp.

After a short bus ride through the Arco delle Campane, past the 8th-century German cemetery (where you'll be buried for free if you drop dead during the tour) and a plaque marking the original site of the obelisk, you'll see the Vatican railway station, used for bringing in goods to be sold tax free in the Vatican supermarket. It was used only once by a pope, when John XXIII went to Assisi (jet-age John Paul II prefers the heliport near the west wall) and is said to be fitted with a choir loft and organ. Go ahead and laugh, but it was an extremely liberal move to have it built in the first place; popes originally forbade railways in the Papal States for fear that passengers would snog in the tunnels! Next are various office palazzi, the mosaic workshop, and the Ethiopian Seminary, where the Pope sheltered students during Mussolini's imperial adventures. The well-manicured grounds are planted with fine specimens of exotic trees and roses, with beds arranged in 16th-century Italian garden geometry. One section is set aside for something no Polish pope could do without—cabbages. The most beautiful building is Pirro Ligorio and Peruzzi's **Casino of Pius IV** (1558–62), a jewel-like summer pavilion where popes and their cardinals could engage in elegant conversation.

As you leave Piazza San Pietro, note the building to the left of Bernini's colonnade: this is the **Palazzo del Sant'Uffizio**, or Holy Office, or Inquisition. The same kind of perversely reasoned force that it once used to stamp out heresy was employed in 1936–50 to bulldoze two pleasant old lanes of the Borgo and create **Via della Conciliazione**, planned as a triumphal way to St Peter's, and an opportunity to view the famous dome. Critics have always complained that it ruined one of the best surprises in Rome, that of suddenly stumbling upon Bernini's grand piazza. Worst of all, its bossy airs make Via della Conciliazione an uncomfortably sterile no man's land, a perfect runway for the squadrons of jumbo tourist buses descending on St Peter's.

Via della Conciliazione has mediocre cafés, bookshops, and souvenir shops with 3-D winking statues of Jesus, and three Renaissance palazzi salvaged by Mussolini's new 'Ruinantes': the **Palazzo dei Convertendi**, on the left at No.34, where Raphael died of love and exhaustion and an ill-advised bleeding by his surgeons, reassembled here in the 1930s from its original site in Via Scossacavalli; in the next block, No.30, **Palazzo Torlonia**, a 1504 mini-Cancelleria palace by Andrea Bregno, headquarters of Rome's richest banking family; and opposite, at No.33, the **Palazzo dei Penitenzieri**, built in the 1470s and now a hotel.

Turn right after this palace on Via Scossacavalli to Borgo Santo Spirito, site of the church of **Santo Spirito in Sassia**. 'Sassia' as in Saxony: though rebuilt after the Sack of Rome, with a façade by Antonio da Sangallo the Younger, it was founded in the 9th century to serve the Borgo's Anglo-Saxon community. Next to it is the **Ospedale di Santo Spirito in Sassia**, the successor to the Schola Anglorum.

Founded by King Ina of Wessex in 717, it was the largest and best run of the Borgo's national school-hospices. Unfortunately, it was made of wood, and went up like a torch in the great fire of 847 (depicted in Raphael's *Stanze* in the Vatican). Seven years later, King Ethelwolf came with his son, the future Alfred the Great, and rebuilt the Schola, funding it and the pope by a voluntary contribution of his subjects known as Peter's Pence—which soon became a mandatory hearth tax until abolished by Henry VIII (a fortune in Plantagenet-era silver pennies was discovered in 1883, hidden in the House of the Vestal Virgins).

Among the most famous pilgrims to have stayed in the Borgo were Macbeth, who came in 1050 with a guilty conscience, and the half-legendary Tannhäuser, who came in the 13th century and was refused absolution for his love of Venus. But by the time he arrived (walking the whole way with his eyes shut, to deny himself the beauty of Italy), the English had let their Schola decline to such a state that Innocent III had it converted into a hospital (1204). It was rebuilt in 1473 as Rome's main home for foundlings—an improvement on the old practice of leaving unwanted children on the banks of the Tiber. You can still see the wooden revolving table in the façade where infants could be anonymously dropped until the mid-19th century.

The Vatican Museums

The admission (*currently L15,000*) may be the most expensive in Italy, but for that you get 10 museums in one, with the Sistine Chapel and the Raphael rooms thrown in free. Altogether almost 7km of exhibits fill the halls of the Vatican Palace, and unfortunately for you there isn't much dull museum clutter that can be passed over lightly. Seeing this infinite, exasperating hoard properly would be the work of a lifetime. On the bright side, the pope sees to it that his museum is managed more intelligently and thoughtfully than anything run by the Italian state. A choice of colour-coded itineraries, which you may follow according to the amount of time you have to spend, will get you through the labyrinth in 90 minutes, or five hours.

Near the entrance, the first big challenge is a large **Egyptian Museum**—one of Europe's best collections—and then some rooms of antiquities from the Holy Land and Syria, before the **Museo Chiaramonti**, full of Roman statuary (including famous busts of Caesar, Mark Antony and Augustus) and inscriptions. The **Museo Pio Clementino** contains some of the best-known statues of antiquity: the dramatic *Laocoön*, dug up in Nero's Golden House, and the *Apollo Belvedere*. No other ancient works recovered during the Renaissance had a greater influence on sculptors than these two. A 'room of animals' captures the more fanciful side of antiquity, and the 2nd-century 'Baroque' tendency in Roman art comes out clearly in a giant group called 'The Nile', complete with sphinxes and crocodiles—it came from a Roman temple of Isis. The bronze papal fig-leaves that protect the modesty of hundreds of nude statues are a good joke at first—it was the same spirit that put breeches on the saints in Michelangelo's *Last Judgement*, ordered by Pius IV once Michelangelo was safely dead.

The best things in the **Etruscan Museum** (*open Tues*) are Greek, a truly excellent collection of vases imported by discriminating Etruscan nobles that includes the famous picture of *Oedipus and the Sphinx*. Beyond that, there is a hall hung with beautiful high-medieval tapestries from Tournai (15th century), and the long, long **Map Room**, lined with carefully painted town views and maps of every corner of Italy; note the long scene of the 1566 Great Siege of Malta at the entrance. Anywhere else, with no Michelangelos to

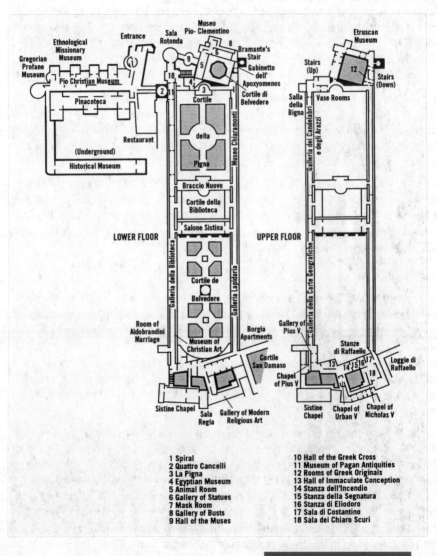

1 Spiral
2 Quattro Cancelli
3 La Pigna
4 Egyptian Museum
5 Animal Room
6 Gallery of Statues
7 Mask Room
8 Gallery of Busts
9 Hall of the Muses

10 Hall of the Greek Cross
11 Museum of Pagan Antiquities
12 Rooms of Greek Originals
13 Hall of Immaculate Conception
14 Stanza dell'Incendio
15 Stanza della Segnatura
16 Stanza di Eliodoro
17 Sala di Costantino
18 Sala dei Chiaro Scuri

The Vatican Museums

offer competition, Raphael's celebrated frescoes in the **Stanze della Segnatura** would be the prime destination on anyone's itinerary.

The *School of Athens* is too well known to require an introduction, but here is a guide to some of the figures: on Aristotle's side, Archimedes and Euclid surrounded by their disciples (Euclid, drawing plane figures on a slate, is a portrait of Bramante); off to the right, Ptolemy and Zoroaster hold the terrestrial and celestial globes. Raphael includes himself among the Aristotelians, standing between Zoroaster and the painter Sodoma. Behind Plato stand Socrates and Alcibiades, and to the left, Zeno and Epicurus. In the foreground, Pythagoras writes while Empedocles and the Arab Averroes look on. Diogenes sprawls philosophically on the steps, while isolated near the front is Heraclitus—really Michelangelo; Raphael put him in at the last minute after seeing the work in progress in the Sistine Chapel.

Across from this apotheosis of philosophy, Raphael painted a Triumph of Theology, the *Dispute of the Holy Sacrament.* The other frescoes include the *Parnassus*, a vision of the ancient Greek and Latin poets, the *Miracle of Bolsena*, the *Expulsion of Heliodorus*, an allegory of the triumphs of the Counter-Reformation papacy, the *Meeting of Leo I and Attila* and, best of all, the solemn, spectacularly lit *Liberation of St Peter.*

Nearby, there is the **Loggia** of Bramante, also with decoration designed by Raphael, though executed by other artists (*only visitable with written permission*), and the **Chapel of Nicholas V**, with frescoes by Fra Angelico. The **Borgia Apartments**, a luxurious suite built for Pope Alexander VI, have walls decorated by Pinturicchio. These run into the **Gallery of Modern Religious Art.**

The Sistine Chapel

To the sophisticated Sixtus IV, building this ungainly barn of a chapel may have seemed a mistake in the first place. When the pushy, despotic Julius II sent Michelangelo up, against his will, to paint the vast ceiling, it might have turned out to be a project as hopeless as the tomb Julius had already commissioned. Michelangelo spent four years of his life on the Sistine Ceiling. No one can say what drove him to turn his surly patron's whim into a masterpiece: the fear of wasting those years, the challenge of an impossible task, or maybe just to spite Julius—he exasperated the pope by making him wait, and refused all demands that he hire some assistants.

Everywhere on the Sistine Ceiling you will note the austere blankness of the backgrounds. Michelangelo always eschewed stage props; one of the tenets of his art was that complex ideas could be expressed in the portrayal of the human body alone. With sculpture, that takes time. Perhaps the inspiration that kept Michelangelo on the ceiling so long was the chance of distilling out of the Book of Genesis and his own genius an entirely new vocabulary of images, Christian and intellectual. Like most Renaissance patrons, Julius had asked for nothing more than virtuoso interior decoration. What he got was the way the Old Testament looks in the deepest recesses of the imagination.

The fascination of the Sistine Ceiling, and the equally compelling **Last Judgement** on the rear wall, done much later (1534–41), is that while we may recognize the individual figures we still have not captured their secret meanings. Hordes of tourists stare up at the heroic Adam, the mysterious *ignudi* in the corners, the Russian masseuse sibyls with their longshoremen's arms, the six-toed prophets, the strange vision of Noah's deluge. They wonder what they're looking at, a question that would take years of inspired wondering to answer. Mostly they direct their attention to the all-too-famous scene of the Creation, with perhaps the only representation of God the Father ever painted that escapes being merely ridiculous. One might suspect that the figure is really some ageing Florentine artist, and that Michelangelo only forgot to paint the brush in his hand.

The restoration of the ceiling and *Last Judgement*, paid for by a Japanese television network, have revealed Michelangelo's true colours—jarring, surprise colours that no interior decorator would ever choose, plenty of sea-green, with splashes of yellow and purple and dramatic shadows. No new paint was applied, only solvents to clear off the grime. Don't overlook the earlier frescoes on the lower walls, great works of art that would have made the Sistine Chapel famous by themselves: scenes from the *Exodus* by Botticelli, Perugino's *Donation of the Keys*, and Signorelli's *Moses Consigning his Staff to Joshua*.

More Miles in the Big Museum

There's still the **Vatican Library** to go, with its endless halls and precious manuscripts tucked neatly away in cabinets. The brightly painted rooms contain thousands of reliquaries and monstrances, medieval ivories, gold-glass medallions from the catacombs, every sort of globe, orrery and astronomical instrument.

If you survive this, the next hurdle is the new and beautifully laid-out **Museo Gregoriano**, with a hoard of classical statuary, mosaics and inscriptions collected by Pope Gregory XVI. Then comes a **Carriage Museum** (*closed for restoration*), the **Pius Christian Museum** of early Christian art and, finally, one of the most interesting of all, though no one has time for it: the **Ethnological Museum**, with wonderful art from every continent, brought home by missionaries over the centuries.

By itself the Vatican **Pinacoteca** would be by far the finest picture gallery in Rome, a representative sampling of Renaissance art from its beginnings, with some fine works of Giotto (*Il Redentore* and the *Martyrdoms of Peter and Paul*) and contemporary Sienese painters, as well as Gentile da Fabbriano, Sano di Pietro and Filippo Lippi.

Don't overlook the tiny but electrically surreal masterpiece of Fra Angelico, the *Story of St Nicolas at Bari*, or the *Angelic Musicians* of Melozzo da Forlì, set next to Melozzo's famous painting of Platina being nominated by Sixtus IV to head the Vatican Library—a rare snapshot of Renaissance humanism. Venetian artists are not well represented, but there is a *Pietà* by Bellini and a *Madonna* by the fastidious Carlo Crivelli. Perhaps the best-known paintings are the *Transfiguration of Christ*, Raphael's last work, and the *St Jerome* of Da Vinci.

Castel Sant'Angelo

Open Tues–Sun 9–7; adm.

Though intended as a resting place for a most serene emperor, this building has seen more blood, treachery and turmoil than any in Rome. Hadrian designed his own mausoleum three years before his death in 138, on an eccentric plan consisting of a huge marble cylinder surmounted by a conical hill planted with cypresses. The marble, the obelisks and the gold and bronze decorations did not survive the 5th-century sacks, but in about 590, during a plague, Pope Gregory the Great saw a vision of St Michael over the mausoleum, ostensibly announcing the end of the plague, but perhaps also mentioning discreetly that here, if anyone cared to use it, was the most valuable fortress in Europe.

There would be no papacy, perhaps, without this castle—at least not in its present form. Hadrian's cylinder is high, steep and almost solid—impregnable even after the invention of artillery. With rebellions of some sort occurring on average every two years before 1400, the popes often had recourse to this place of safety. It last saw action in the sack of 1527, when the miserable Clement VII withstood a siege of several months while his city went up in flames. The popes also used Castel Sant'Angelo as a prison; famous inmates included Giordano Bruno, Benvenuto Cellini and Beatrice Cenci (better known to the English than the Italians, thanks to Shelley's verse drama). Tosca tosses herself off the top at the end of Puccini's opera.

Inside, the spiral ramp leads up to the **Papal Apartments**, decorated as lavishly by 16th-century artists as anything in the Vatican. The **Sala Paolina** has frescoes by Perin del Vaga of events in the history of Rome, and the **Sala di Apollo** is frescoed with grotesques attempting to reproduce the wall decorations of Nero's Golden House. Above everything, a mighty statue of Michael commemorates Gregory's vision. As interesting for its structure as anything on display inside, Castel Sant'Angelo makes a great place to rest after the Vatican. The views from the roof are some of the best in Rome, and there's a café on the 4th floor. The three central arches of the **Ponte Sant'Angelo** were built by Hadrian, although the statues of angels added in 1688 steal the show; at once dubbed Bernini's Breezy Maniacs, they battle a never-ending Baroque hurricane to display the symbols of Christ's Passion.

The Seven Churches of Rome

✝ Besides St Peter's there are three other Patriarchal Basilicas, and three more ancient and revered churches under the care of the pope that have always been a part of the Roman Pilgrimage. San Giovanni in Laterano, Santa Maria Maggiore and San Paolo Fuori le Mura are the basilicas. The others, San Lorenzo, Santa Croce and San Sebastiano, have been important since the earliest days of the Roman Pilgrimage. All are on the edges of the city, away from the political and commercial centre; until the Middle Ages they stood in open countryside, and only recently has the city grown outwards to swallow them again.

San Giovanni in Laterano (St John Lateran)

Bus 16 or 714 from Termini, 85 from Piazza Venezia; Ⓜ *S. Giovanni.*

This Patriarchal Basilica is nothing less than the 'Mother and Head Church of Rome and the World', the first church founded by Constantine, and still the city's cathedral. Lying just within the Aurelian Wall, the site originally belonged to a patrician named Plautinius Lateranus, executed by Nero for plotting against him; the property, however, retained the family name even when it passed to Fausta, the wife of Constantine (*Domus Faustae in Laterano*). Constantine, after 19 years of marriage, had Fausta smothered in a hot bath, but in the meantime he used her palace (the site of the present baptistry) for a church council with Pope Miltiades in 313. It became a cult centre for the new religion, and soon all the surrounding land was donated by Constantine to Rome's Christians; St John's itself was built over the barracks of the emperor's personal guard. When building it, the Christians chose one of the forms they knew best—a basilica—which with its five naves was designed to stand up to the architecture of the pagans. As it contained the *cathedra*, or chair of Rome's bishop, it became the city's *cathedral*. And although nothing remains of the original structure (sacks by Vandals and Normans, two earthquakes and several fires have seen to that) it has all along maintained the same basilican form that inspired countless later churches.

The Lateran was the chief papal residence before Avignon, and throughout the Middle Ages was regarded as the Vatican is today. Popes were crowned here until the 19th century; Charlemagne came here to be baptized in 774, and five Councils of the Church were held here in the Middle Ages. But there have been other moments that the Church would prefer to forget, including the 897 posthumous trial of Pope Formosus. The Romans were notorious for mocking dead popes, but this was an extreme case, especially since the sick charade was acted out in the basilica by Formosus' successor and arch-enemy, Stephen VII, who had the grinning corpse exhumed and dressed in full pontifical regalia. The papal lawyer drilled the mummy with questions. Formosus, though given time to respond, failed to defend himself. Declaring him an usurper, Stephen cut three fingers from his benedicting hand, and tossed the rest of him in the Tiber.

The church building itself has suffered its ups and downs, too. When Boniface VIII declared the first Jubilee in 1300 it was the wonder of the age, and the priests with their long rakes couldn't scrape in the pilgrims' donations fast enough. By 1350, when papal finances demanded another Jubilee year, Petrarch mourned that 'the mother of all churches stands without a roof, exposed to wind and rain'.

It was collapsing again just before the 1650 Jubilee, when Innocent X ordered Borromini to repair the interior; the façade needed to be replaced in the 1730s, and was the subject of a competition, in which Alessandro Galilei eventually triumphed over his 22 competitors with a stretched out version of Maderno's façade for St Peter's, striking for the deep chiaroscuro in its arches. Along the roof a giant Baroque Christ and saints model the latest in marble draperies. The central bronze door originally hung in the Senate House in the Forum; to the right is the Porta Santa, opened only in Holy Years; and to the left stands a whopping great statue of Constantine, carted here from his baths on the Quirinale.

Borromini's solution to reinforcing the basilica's structure was to fill in the spaces between the pillars, creating massive piers with alcoves for more overgrown 18th-century Apostles, glaring down at puny humanity like Roman emperors of old. The intricate, geometric Cosmati floor is matched by the rich ceiling by Daniele da Volterra. Although sheer size is the main effect, there are occasional details worth looking for: Giotto's fresco of *Boniface VIII's Jubilee*, just behind the first pier on the right, and on the next pier a Hungarian-made 1909 memorial to Pope Sylvester II (*see* also S Croce, below), who crowned St Stephen, first king of Hungary, in 1001. The memorial incorporates part of his original tombstone, said to sweat and rattle when a pope is about to die. The other chapels contain plenty of carefree Baroque, with some Jesuit-style cut-out saints.

The **Papal Altar**, with its silver reliquaries said to contain the heads of SS. Paul and Peter, is sheltered by a festive Gothic baldacchino. In the Confessio is the fine bronze tomb slab of Pope Martin V, on whom the Romans drop flowers and coins for good luck. The apse had to be reconstructed in 1885, and the mosaics you see now are a copy of a 13th-century copy by two Iacopos, Torriti and da Camerino, from a much older original; the scene shows a dove descending on the Cross, worshipped by a reindeer, while the four Gospels flow like rivers and the Virgin and saints stand by.

At the end of the left transept is the Altar of the Holy Sacrament (1600), sheltering half of St Peter's communion table, from S. Pudenziana; the bronze columns and lintel are said to have been melted down from the ships' prows of the Forum's Imperial rostra. The right transept holds the tomb of the most powerful medieval pope, Innocent III (d. 1216), who was poisoned in Perugia (some suspect through his slippers, though in the morning he was found in the cathedral stark naked). His remains were brought here in 1891; frescoes tell the story of his life. The 14th-century Cosmatesque tomb of Boniface IX is in the chapel to the right.

The most beautiful thing in the cathedral, however, is its **cloister**, built by the Vassalletti (father and son) between 1215 and 1223. Once Rome was full of such individualistic medieval jewels, well outside the mainstream of Gothic and reviving classicism; this cloister, with its pairs of spiral columns and glittering 13th-century Cosmatesque mosaics, is the most striking survival of this lost chapter in art. All around the cloister walls, fragments from the earlier incarnations of St John's have been assembled, a wistful collection of broken pretty things that includes an interesting tomb of a 13th-century bishop by Arnolfo di Cambio. Entrance to the cloister is in the left aisle (*open daily 9–5; adm*), as well as to the small **Lateran museum,** laden with ecclesiastical finery and pomp—golden vestments, golden reliquaries, and so on; the best piece is a 14th-century gilded silver cross called the Constantiniana, depicting Adam and Eve.

The Lateran's north front has an impressive 1586 façade by Domenico Fontana, incorporating two earlier bell towers in its design. It looks over **Piazza di San Giovanni,** base for the tallest **obelisk** in the world,

1 Statue of Constantine
2 Bronze Door
3 Holy Door
4 Fresco of Boniface VIII's Jubilee
5 Monument of Sylvester II
6 Tomb of Alexander III
7 Corsini Chapel / Tomb of Clement
8 Lancellotti Chapel
9 Papal Altar / Tomb of Martin V
10 Lateran Museum Entrance
11 Entrance to the Cloister
12 Tomb of Innocent III
13 Tomb of Boniface IX
14 Altar of the Holy Sacrament
15 Torriti Mosaics
16 Chapel of St John the Baptist
17 Chapel of SS. Secunda
   e Rufina
18 Chapel of S. Venanzio
19 Chapel of St John
   the Evangelist

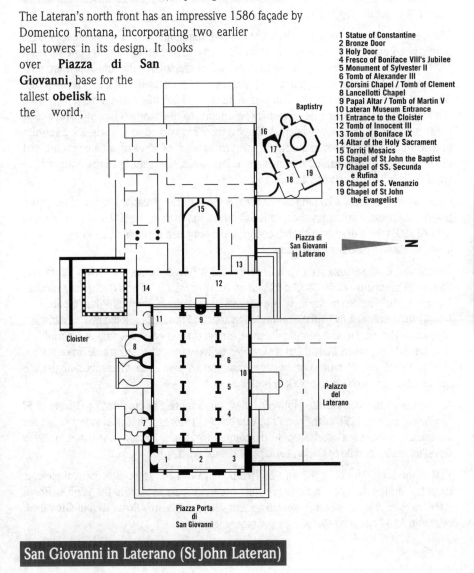

San Giovanni in Laterano (St John Lateran)

just over 100ft of red granite from the Temple of Ammon at Thebes, erected by Thothmes IV in the 15th century BC and stolen by Constantius II in 357 for the Circus Maximus.

In the piazza's southwest corner is the **Baptistry of St John** (*open daily 9–1 and 3–5*), nothing less than the first one in Christendom, built by Constantine in the 320s in an octagonal form copied by baptistries throughout Italy. It was in this holy place that Cola di Rienzo went over the top, even by Roman standards; after a bath in the baptismal font, he spent the night in vigil and emerged in the morning dressed like a Liberace in golden spurs, self-christened as 'Knight Nicolas, Friend of the World'. It feels ancient, but like St Peter's, it magically repels dust.

The green basalt basin, where Rienzo took his presumptuous bath, is surrounded by eight porphyry columns, and there are two famous bronze doors on either side: one set from 1196, etched with scenes of how the Lateran basilica appeared at the time, opens into the **chapel of St John the Evangelist**, with alabaster columns by the altar and an exquisite 5th-century mosaic with birds and flowers in the vault. The other doors, traditionally from the Baths of Caracalla (though they may be original to the baptistry), 'sing' with a low, harmonic sound when slowly opened. The baptistry has two other chapels, **SS. Secunda and Rufina**, with another exquisite 5th-century mosaic, of vines on a blue ground, and the **chapel of S. Venanzio** with mosaics of Dalmatian saints made in the 640s, a time when artistic rigor mortis had already begun to set in.

Opposite the baptistry, adjoining the Basilica, is the **Lateran Palace**, address of the popes before they became voluntary 'Babylonian Captives' in Avignon in 1309. After the massive fire of 1309, which destroyed church and palace, it remained a ruin until 1586 when Sixtus V had it rebuilt by Domenico Fontana.

On the east of the piazza are two holy relics that survived flames, the **Scala Santa** and **Sancta Sanctorum** (*© 06 6988 6433; open in winter 6.15–12 and 3–6.15; in summer closes 6.45*). The Scala Santa is the legendary stair from Pontius Pilate's palace in Jerusalem, descended by Christ after his judgement and brought to Rome by Constantine's mother, St Helena. Devout pilgrims ascend them on their knees—the only way permitted, ever since 1510, when Martin Luther crawled halfway up and heard a little voice saying, 'The just shall live by faith, not by pilgrimage, not by penance,' whereupon he did the unthinkable: he stood up and walked back down.

At the top of the stairs is the Holy of Holies, the **Sancta Sanctorum**, or Chapel of St Lawrence, built in 1278 as the pope's private chapel. Through the locked gate you can see a miraculous 'handless' portrait of Jesus, painted by angels, frescoes attributed to Pietro Cavallini, and a mosaic of Christ, perhaps by the Cosmati.

East of the Scala Santa is a **tribune** erected by Fuga in 1743 to house copies of mosaics from the dining hall, or *Triclinium*, of the medieval palace. Across the lawn is **Porta Asinara**, one of Rome's best-preserved ancient gates, and nearby **Porta di San Giovanni**, rebuilt in 1564 and now site of a huge clothes market.

Three streets southeast of Piazza del Viminale; alternatively, two streets south-west of Termini Station and its metro (take Via Gioberti).

In ancient times a temple of the mother goddess Juno Lucina stood here, and when the 431 Council of Ephesus proclaimed Mary 'the Mother of God', it seemed like the logical place to build her a church, too—the greatest of all Rome's Mary churches, **Santa Maria Maggiore** (*open daily 7–6.30*). The ancient basilica is hidden behind Ferdinando Fuga's elegant, 18th-century shadow-filled façade and its incongruous **campanile**, tallest and fairest in Rome, a brightly decorated relic from the 1380s. The mighty column in front, in Piazza di Santa Maria Maggiore, is a sole survivor from the Forum's Basilica of Maxentius.

Of the four Patriarchal Basilicas, Santa Maria Maggiore has best preserved its medieval appearance. Try to come at least once after nightfall, when the upper floor of Fuga's loggia is illuminated, and you can see the 12th-century mosaics from the medieval façade, telling the legend of the church's founding: on 4 August 352, the Virgin appeared simultaneously to a wealthy Christian and to Pope Liberius, directing them to build a church on the Esquiline. The two found the exact spot Mary wanted by a miraculous snowfall that neatly outlined the shape required. This porch, before Fuga added his façade, was long the favourite place to burn heretical books, as the Church decided such literary sacrifices were particularly pleasing to the Virgin.

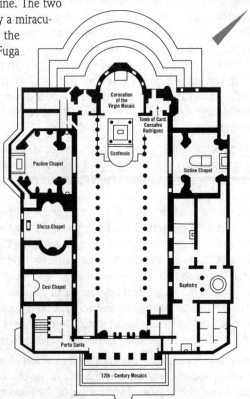

S. Maria Maggiore's elegant basilican **nave** is almost unchanged since its construction by Pope Sixtus III in the 5th century, with the exception of the coffered ceiling by Renaissance architect Giuliano da Sangallo, gilded with the first gold brought back from the New World by Columbus—a gift to Alexander VI from King Ferdinand. Above the columns runs a remarkable cycle of 36 5th-century mosaic panels of Old Testament scenes, while the triumphal arch shows mostly apocryphal scenes of the youth of Christ. They are unfortunately a bit hard to see, unless you have binoculars; try to arrive at noon, when the light is brightest. The floor, of fine Cosmatesque work, dates from the 12th century.

Two enormous chapels were fixed to the Basilica by popes who feared that if they left it to posterity to build them the memorials they deserved, they wouldn't get any. The first, in the right aisle, is the sumptuous **Sistine Chapel** of Sixtus V, designed by Domenico Fontana in 1585 and built, literally, of the coloured marbles of the ancient Septizonium, which the Pope cannibalized into oblivion as part of his policy to convert pagan Rome into Christian Rome.

But in his eagerness to build himself a really special chapel, the Pope inadvertently destroyed one of Christian Rome's most venerated treasures as well: Santa Maria Maggiore's *Presepio*, or Christmas crib, which since the 6th or 7th century stood outside the Basilica, in a grotto simulating Bethlehem's stable. Lined with precious mosaics and containing 13th-century crib figures by the great Arnolfo di Cambio, it was the place where the pope traditionally said Christmas Eve Mass (as Hildebrand did in 1075 when armed thugs suddenly burst in and dragged him off by the hair to the tower of their Ghibelline boss Cencius. When the people learned next morning where their Pope had been taken, they stoned the tower until he was released—whereupon he returned to finish the mass). But Sixtus V ordered Domenico Fontana to move the *Presepio* into his chapel, and despite all the architect's careful preparations (after all, this was the man who moved the Vatican obelisk) it collapsed and broke into bits. Only Arnolfo's charming figures of Joseph, the Magi and animals survive (the Mary and Jesus are 16th-century replacements), and they're locked away in the crypt beneath a wooden canopy shaped like an ideal Renaissance temple and supported by four angels. If you can find a sacristan, you may persuade him to open the gate.

The Borghese pope, Paul V, bears the onus for the hyper-decorated **Pauline Chapel**, across the nave of Sixtus' pile, although to his credit nothing was destroyed to build his precious inanity. An altar of semi-precious stone holds an ancient and highly venerated icon of the Madonna and Child known as the *Salus Populi Romani*, painted by angels. This is the place to come on 5 August, when during mass white petals fall like snow from the dome in memory of the basilica's legendary founding. Fuga designed the porphyry-pillared baldacchino over the altar; below in the Confessio a colossal, ungainly statue of Pius IX kneels in prayer before the basilica's chief relic, five pieces of wood bound with iron said to be nothing less than the genuine manger from Bethlehem. Shimmering above the altar is the magnificent apse mosaic of *The Coronation of the Virgin*, made in 1295 by Iacopo Torriti, who is believed to have reproduced the subject of Sixtus III's original, honouring Mary's new divine status. To the right of the apse is the most beautiful tomb in the church, of 13th-century Cardinal Consalvo Rodriguez, by Giovanni Cosmati.

You can't walk up the magnificent ripple of steps leading to the rear façade of the basilica, even though the restoration of this side of the church has been finished, but you can get a good look at it anyway. The **obelisk** at the bottom, in Piazza dell'Esquilino, came from the Mausoleum of Augustus.

From Piazza Porta San Paolo (Ⓜ San Paolo) take bus 23 or 673 from the top of Via Ostiense, passing through a mile of gas-works and industrial-commercial sprawl.

In the Dark Ages this stretch of the ancient Via Ostiense was one of the marvels of Rome, sheltered by a 1.5km portico, supported by 800 marble columns, built by Pope John VIII in the 870s to shelter pilgrims between Porta S. Paolo and the basilica. A separate walled suburb,'Giovannipoli', grew up around St Paul's.

The colossal portico may as well have been constructed of breadcrumbs for all that has survived; Giovannipoli, pummelled by the Normans in 1084 and every other roughneck coming up the Tiber, was given its *coup de grâce* in an 1823 fire that began when two roofers, horsing around on top of St Paul's, spilled a bucket of hot coals. One fell forgotten in a gutter, and in the night the most beautiful of the four Patriarchal Basilicas and its suburb went up like a torch.

When condemned, St Paul, as a Roman citizen, merited the relatively painless death of decapitation along the road to Ostia. According to an embarrassing tradition, his head bounced three times, bringing forth three springs, now occupied by the Abbazia delle Tre Fontane (in EUR). Paul's head ended up in the Lateran, while over the grave of his trunk Constantine built the first shrine. Theodosius and his children, Honorius and Galla Placidia, erected a basilica over the site, and over the years it was as frequently restored and embellished as it was pillaged. It became the special church of the kings of England, who were honorary canons here until the Reformation; the abbots of St Paul's were automatically made Knights of the Garter.

The nearly total reconstruction in the early 19th century followed the outline of the original basilica, making it the second largest church in Rome. The entrance faces the Tiber, through a massive but pointless courtyard called the Quadriporticus, relieved by four tall palms and the gold of the 19th-century mosaic on the façade that blazes in the setting sun; in the middle a giant marble St Paul, sword in hand, seems ready to thump any would-be art critics. On the right, one of the few things to survive the fire, is the original bronze **Holy Door** with panels inlaid in silver, brought from Constantinople in the 11th century. The long, long nave, lined with a double forest of granite columns, glossy marbles and polished stones, has the cool, solemn majesty of an ice palace, although there are critics who say its shiny newness better evokes the feel of an original basilica than any other. The famous frieze along the nave and aisles has mosaic portraits of all 265 popes, from St Peter on; the first 40 are survivors from the fire. According to Roman tradition, the world will end when there is no room for a new pope's portrait, and as there are only eight spaces left after John Paul II, you may just as well go for the high-calorie *gelato* you passed up yesterday.

The **Triumphal Arch**, adorned with mosaics paid for by Galla Placidia in the 5th century, survived the fire. Art Deco is not what you would expect from those times, but these bear an uncanny resemblance to Roosevelt's public works murals of the early 1930s: a severe-looking Christ in the centre circle, worshipped by winged symbols of the Evangelists, two angels with pointers, and the Elders of the Apocalypse bearing crowns, all posed as if for the last number of a Hollywood musical. Underneath, porphyry columns support another relic of the original church, the ornate 1285 baldacchino by Arnolfo di Cambio, built over the confessio containing the tomb of St Paul.

Whether or not Paul's remains are still there is a matter of debate; his bronze sarcophagus was looted by the Saracens in 846, when they picked up some five tons of gold and silver treasure from St Paul's and St Peter's, all of which went down to Davy Jones' locker off Sicily's coast. If the confessio is open, you can see the inscription PAULO APOSTOLO MART, carved in a stone slab pierced by two holes for the purpose of inserting cloth to be made sacred by the proximity of his relics. Just to the right of the altar is a massive, fantastically medieval paschal candlestick from the 12th century. The mosaics in the apse with a giant Byzantine Christ and smaller saints were made by Venetian artisans in 1220.

The short transepts, covered with precious marbles, are closed by altars of malachite and lapis lazuli donated by Czar Nicholas I, one of many heads-of-state who contributed to the rebuilding; even Mohammed Ali of Egypt sent a precious column or two. Of the chapels, only the one just to the left of the apse survived the flames; designed by Carlo Maderno, it houses a fine 13th-century crucifix and the altar where St Ignatius and his followers took the formal vows that made the Jesuits a religious order. Off the right transept are the lovely **cloisters**, finished in 1208 and similar to those of St John Lateran, with their glittering mosaics and columns that delightfully shun symmetry. The basilica's little **museum** (*© 06 541 0341*) contains a copy of the stone slab over St Paul's tomb along with a souvenir stand and some highly missable art.

San Lorenzo fuori le Mura

Ⓜ *Policlinico or Castro Pretorio (Line B), or bus 9 or 310 from Termini, or Tram 30.*

Lawrence was a 3rd-century deacon with spunk; when commanded by the Roman authorities to hand over the treasures of the Church, he produced all the sick and destitute people he could round up. 'Grill this wise guy,' the Roman police sergeant must have growled, and his minions obeyed—literally. But as they toasted him on the gridiron, Lawrence kept his sense of humour. 'You can turn me over now,' he told his tormentors. 'I'm done on this side.' Even the worst Romans, battened on gladiators' blood, had to admire the courage of such martyrs, which, in no little way, led to their own acceptance of the new religion.

Lawrence's tormented body was interred in the catacombs here, and in the 4th century a cemetery basilica was dedicated to him by Constantine; a second church, dedicated to the Madonna, was built nearby in 440; and in 1216, in response to the increased number of pilgrims visiting the basilica, Pope Honorius III stuck the churches together by chopping off their apses, which gives the basilica its extraordinary form. None of this is apparent from the façade, with its medieval portico rebuilt after the war (when S. Lorenzo had the misfortune to be the only church bombed in Rome), decorated with 13th-century frescoes on the life of St Lawrence and Manzù's tomb of Italy's post-war leader, Alcide de Gasperi.

The nave (*open daily 6.45–12 and 3–6.30; summer daily 3.30–7.30*), formerly the church of the Madonna, has a Cosmatesque pavement, pulpit, paschal candlestick, episcopal throne and other 12th-century furnishings, though the mosaic on the inside of the triumphal arch dates back to the 6th century and shows Pope Pelagius II offering the basilica to Christ.

The long chancel that begins here was once the nave of Pelagius' older, more important basilica of 579, with its beautiful Corinthian columns and embroidered marble windows. SS. Lawrence, Stephen and Justin are buried in the crypt under the altar, while in the chancel is the tomb of Pio Nono (Pius IX, d. 1878). The fine old cloister, beyond the sacristy of Pelagius' basilica, is lined with a hotch-potch of ancient columns and fragments of sarcophagi.

Santa Croce in Gerusalemme

Bus 9 or 16 from Termini, 81 or 810 from Piazza Venezia or Tram 13 or 30 along Viale Carlo Felice; open 7–12.30 and 4–6.30.

According to tradition, Constantine's mother Helen not only found Pilate's stair in Jerusalem, but the True Cross as well, and brought a piece of it back to her palace, which was later converted into S. Croce in Gerusalemme. In Roman legend it is linked to Gerbert (Sylvester II), the pope at the end of the last millennium, which everyone believed would be the end of the world. The election of the Frankish Gerbert, educated in the Muslim schools of Toledo, was a fearful portent; one of the few real scholars of the day and inventor of a hydraulic organ, he was believed to be a wizard. He reputedly owned a prophetic bronze head (like the Templars three centuries later) which told him, among other things, that he would die in 'Jerusalem'. And so it happened, in 1003, while saying mass in this church, he dropped dead.

S. Croce was rebuilt in 1144 (the date of the campanile) and in 1744, when Domenico Gregorini and Pietro Passalacqua added the bold convex rococo façade and oval vestibule. The Cosmati pavement dates from the first rebuilding; the gaudy quattrocento fresco in the apse, of St Helen finding the Cross, is by Antoniazzo Romano; the tomb below, of Charles V's confessor Cardinal Quiñones, is by Jacopo Sansovino; the delicate baldacchino is from the 1600s. Steps from the right aisle lead down into the **chapel of St Helen** (built over St Helen's bedroom), the jewel of S. Croce, with a gorgeous Renaissance vault mosaic of an avuncular Christ designed by Melozzo da Forlì in 1494. The statue of St Helen was converted from a Juno found in Ostia. Off the left aisle is the **cappella della Croce**, built in 1930 to shelter pieces of the True Cross, a larger chunk from the Cross of the Good Thief, and the genuine finger St Thomas stuck in Christ's side.

Via Appia Antica, between the second and third milestones, bus 660. Basilica open daily 8.30–12 and 2.30–5.30.

In the 3rd century, during the persecution of Valerian, the Christians feared even for the safety of their dead martyrs, and brought the relics of SS. Paul and Peter from their original tombs to be temporarily interred here. Under Diocletian's persecutions, a young officer in the imperial household named Sebastian was tied to a tree and pumped full of arrows. He recovered, only to be martyred and laid out in these same catacombs.

Thus rendered twice holy, a basilica was built over their tombs in the 4th century, and was called SS. Apostoli. But 500 years later, long after the bones of Peter and Paul were moved to their respective basilicas, the Romans forgot the origins of the church's name and renamed it for Sebastian.

Always depicted as the most handsome and dashing of saints in art, Sebastian's charms were potent against the plague, but not much good when it came to keeping rot and rain out of his basilica. In 1612 Cardinal Scipio Borghese paid Flaminio Ponzio and Giovanni Vasanzio to raze and rebuild it. Exciting it isn't, but in the chapel on the right are the original set of the footprints in Domine Quo Vadis?, and there's a marble *S. Sebastiano* by Antonio Giorgetti, after a design by Bernini, full of such languid pathos that he seems in love with his own death.

A door to the left of the basilica leads down into the **Catacombs of San Sebastiano**, or, properly, the **cemetery of San Sebastiano 'ad catacumbas'** (*© 06 788 7035; guided tours 8.30–12 and 2.30–5.30; closed Thurs; adm*). As the only catacombs to have remained open through the centuries, these galleries have suffered the most from relic pirates. But they are among the most interesting.

The burial ground was originally pagan, from the time of Trajan, but once the remains of the two apostles were brought here the Christians began to bury their dead nearby and hold funerary banquets to honour Peter and Paul and benefit the poor, a meal known as a *refrigerium*. These took place in the *triclinium* located under the basilica, which the Christians built over the mausoleums of the pagans sometime around the year 250; inscriptions on the walls refer to the Apostles, confirming the tradition that their relics were here, at least for 40 years.

Paintings in the *arcosolia* include a unique manger scene, and there are some charming frescoes in one of the pagan tombs, the **Hypogeum of Clodius Hermes**. The ambulatory of the 4th-century basilica has been converted into a museum, with a model of the complex, inscriptions found in the catacombs, and some fascinating early Christian sarcophagi, especially one belonging to a certain Lot.

Around the City

Piazza Venezia

This traffic-crazed, thoroughly awful piazza, the closest thing Rome has to a centre, takes its name from the **Palazzo Venezia,** built for Pope Paul II in 1455, but long the Embassy of the Venetian Republic. Mussolini made it his residence, leaving a light on all night to make the Italians think he was working. His famous balcony, from which he would declaim to the 'oceanic' crowds in the square (renamed the Forum of the Fascist Empire in those days) still holds its prominent place, a bad memory for the Italians. Nowadays the Palazzo holds a **museum** of Renaissance and Baroque decorative arts (*open Tues–Sun 9–1.30; adm exp*). The palace complex was built around the ancient church of **San Marco,** with a 9th-century mosaic in the apse. Parts of the building are as old as AD 400, and the façade is by the Renaissance architect Benedetto di Maiano.

Long ago the southern edge of this piazza had approaches up to the Monte Capitolino. The hill is still there, though it's now entirely blocked out by the **Altar of the Nation** (also known as the *Vittoriano,* the 'Wedding Cake' or the 'Typewriter'), Risorgimento Italy's own self-inflicted satire and one of the world's apotheoses of kitsch. Its size and its solid marble walls are explained by the 1880s prime minister who commissioned it; he happened to have a marble quarry in his home district of Brescia. Recounting its sculptural allegories would take pages—but of the two big bronze imperial-style *quadrigae* on top, one represents Italian Liberty and the other Italian Unity. In the centre, the modest virtues of Vittorio Emanuele II have earned him a 38ft bronze equestrian statue, perhaps the world's largest. Beneath him, Italy's Unknown Soldier sleeps peacefully with a round-the-clock guard. On the left-hand side of the monument you can see the remains of the republican Roman tomb of C. Publius Bibulus.

East of Piazza Venezia: Capitol, Forum and Colosseum

Monte Capitolino

Behind the *Vittoriano,* two stairways lead to the top of the Capitoline Hill. This is a fateful spot; in 121 BC the great reformer Tiberius Gracchus was murdered here by what today would be called a 'right-wing death squad'. Almost a millennium and a half later Cola di Rienzo was trying to escape Rome in disguise when an enraged mob recognized him by the rings on his fingers and tore him to pieces. Rienzo built the left-hand staircase, and was the first to climb it. It leads to **Santa Maria in Aracoeli,** begun in the 7th century over the temple of Juno Moneta—the ancient Roman Mint was adjacent to it. The Aracoeli, which in Rienzo's time served as a council hall for the Romans, is one of the most revered of churches; legend has it that one of the Sibyls of Tivoli prophesied the coming of Jesus and told Augustus to build a temple here to the 'first born of God'. Inside you can seek out frescoes by Pinturicchio (*San Bernardino of Siena*) and Gozzoli (*St Anthony of Padua*), and a tombstone by Donatello, near the entrance.

The second stairway takes you to the real heart of Rome, Michelangelo's **Piazza del Campidoglio**, passing a rather flattering statue of Rienzo set on a bronze pedestal. Bordering the piazza, a formidable cast of statues includes the Dioscuri, who come from Pompey's Theatre, and Marforio (in the courtyard of the Museo Capitolino, *see* below), a river god once employed as a 'talking statue', decorated with graffiti and placards commenting on current events. The great 2nd-century AD bronze equestrian statue of the benign and philosophical emperor **Marcus Aurelius** that stood on the plinth in the middle of the piazza from the 16th century until 1981, has been fully restored and regilded and is now in the Musei Capitolini, fortunately enough, since it was an old Roman saying that the world would end when all the gold flaked off. The Christians of old only refrained from melting him down for cash because they believed he was not Marcus Aurelius, but Constantine. A faithful copy now stands in the piazza.

The Musei Capitolini

Michelangelo's original plans may have been adapted and tinkered with by later architects, but nevertheless his plan for the Campidoglio has come out as one of the triumphs of Renaissance design. The centrepiece, the **Palazzo Senatorio**, Rome's city hall, with its distinctive stairway and bell tower, is built over the ruins of the Roman tabularium, the state archive. At the base of the stair, note the statue of Minerva, in her aspect as the allegorical goddess Roma.

Flanking it, Michelangelo redesigned the façade of the **Palazzo dei Conservatori** (on the right), and projected the matching building across the square, the **Palazzo Nuovo**, built in

the early 18th century. Together they make up the **Capitoline Museums**. Founded by Pope Clement XII in 1734, the oldest true museum in the world, the Capitolini (*currently closed for restoration; due to reopen by 2000*) displays both the heights and depths of ancient society and culture. For the heights there are the reliefs from the triumphal arch of Marcus Aurelius—first-class work in scenes of the emperor's clemency and piety, and his triumphal receptions in Rome. Marcus always looks a little worried in these, perhaps considering his good-for-nothing son Commodus, and the empire he would inherit, sinking into corruption and excess. What was

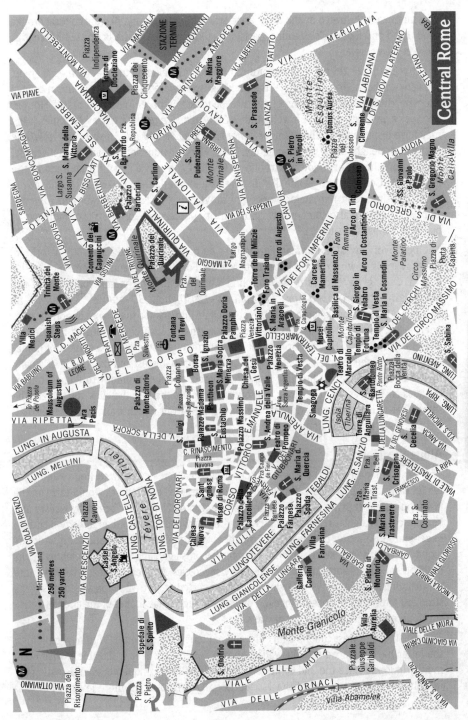

Central Rome

107

to come is well illustrated by the degenerate art of the 4th century, like the colossal bronze head, hand and foot of Constantine, parts of a colossal statue in the Basilica of Maxentius (now in the courtyard).

In between these extremes come roomfuls of statuary, including the *Capitoline She-Wolf*, the very symbol of Rome (note that the suckling twins were added to the Etruscan bronze she-wolf during the Renaissance); statues of most of the emperors, busts of Homer, Sophocles and Pythagoras; the voluptuous *Capitoline Venus*; a big baby Hercules (who may have inspired Donatello's famous *Amor* in Florence); and the *Muse Polyhymnia*, one of the most delightful statues of antiquity. Later works include lots of papal paraphernalia, a statue of Charles of Anjou by Arnolfo di Cambio and—in a small **Pinacoteca** in the Palazzo dei Conservatori—some dignified Velàzquez gentlemen, looking scornfully at the other paintings, and two major works by Caravaggio, the *Fortune Teller* and *John the Baptist*. There are also some lovely 18th-century porcelains—orchestras of monkeys in powdered wigs, and such.

The best overview of the Roman Forum is to be had from behind Palazzo Senatorio. A stairway leads down from the left side to Via dei Fori Imperiali and the entrance to the Forum. On the way, beneath the church of San Giuseppe Falegnami, you can visit the **Mamertine Prison** (*open April–Sept daily 9–12.30 and 2.30–6; Oct–Mar daily 9–12 and 2–5*), the small calaboose used by the ancient Romans for their most important prisoners—the Cataline conspirators, Vercingetorix (the Gaulish chief captured by Caesar), and finally St Peter. The southern end of the Capitol, one of the quietest corners of Rome, was the site of the temple of Jupiter Optimus Maximus (Greatest and Best), built originally by the Etruscan kings. At the time it was the largest in Italy, testimony to Rome's importance as far back as 450 BC. Along the southern edge of the hill, the cliffs you see are the somewhat reduced remains of the **Tarpeian Rock**, from which traitors and other malefactors were thrown in Rome's early days.

Along the Tiber

The early emperors did their best to import classical Greek drama to Rome, and for a while, with the poets of the Latin New Comedy, it seemed the Romans would carry on the tradition. Great theatres were built like the **Teatro di Marcello**, begun by Caesar and completed by Augustus. By the 2nd century AD, however, theatre had already begun to degenerate into music hall, lewd performances with naked actresses and grisly murders (condemned prisoners were sometimes butchered on stage), and shows by celebrity actors probably much like some of today's unseemly spectacles. Marcellus' theatre survived into the Middle Ages, when the Orsini family converted it into their palace-fortress, the strongest after the Castel Sant'Angelo. You can still see the tall arches of the circumference surmounted by the rough medieval walls.

The streets to the west contain a mix of some of Rome's oldest houses with new buildings; the latter have replaced the old walled **ghetto**. There has been a sizeable Jewish community in Rome since the 2nd century BC, when Israel was conquered; after defeating the Jewish rebellion at the end of the 1st century AD, Titus brought more Jews to Rome as slaves. The Jews helped finance the career of Julius Caesar, who would prove to be their greatest benefactor. For centuries they lived near this bend in the river and in Trastevere. Paul IV took time off from burning books and heretics to wall them into the tiny ghetto in 1555; at the same time he forced them to wear orange hats, attend Mass on Sunday, and limited them to the rag and old-iron trades. Tearing down the ghetto walls was one of the first acts of the Italian kingdom after the entry into Rome in 1870. The exotic, eclectic main **synagogue** was built in 1904; inside, there is a small **museum of the Jewish Community** (*open Mon–Thurs 9.30–2 and 3–5, Fri 9.30–2, Sun 9.30–12; adm*).

Opposite the synagogue, the **Isola Tiberina** is joined to both sides of the river by surviving ancient bridges. In imperial times the island was sacred to Aesculapius, god of healing; a legend records how some serpents brought from the god's shrine in Greece escaped and swam to the spot, choosing the site by divine guidance. Now, as in ancient times, most of the lovely island is taken up by a hospital, the Ospedale Fatebenefratelli; in place of the Temple of Aesculapius there is also the church of **San Bartolomeo**, most recently rebuilt in the 1690s.

The **Velabrum**, in the earliest days of Rome, was a cattle market (interestingly, in the Middle Ages, the Roman Forum itself was used for the same purpose). In this area, east of the Isola Tiberina, is **San Giorgio in Velabro**, in parts as old as the 7th century; there is a Cosmatesque altar, and early-Christian fragments on the left wall. The lovely portico has been completely restored after a mafia bombing in 1993. Of the two ancient arches outside, the **Arch of the Argentarii** was erected by the moneychangers in honour of Septimius Severus; the larger, and unfinished, four-sided **Janus Quadrifons**, dates from the time of Constantine.

Piazza Bocca della Verità

Tourists almost always overlook this beautiful corner along the Tiber, but here you can see two well-preserved Roman temples. Both go under false names: the round **Temple of Vesta**, used as an Armenian church in the Middle Ages, and the **Temple of Fortuna Virilis**—it now seems almost certain that they were actually dedicated to Hercules Victor and Portunus (the god of harbours) respectively. Some bits of an exotic Roman cornice are built into the brick building opposite, part of the **House of the Crescenzi**, a powerful family in the 9th century, descended from Theodora Senatrix. Look over the side of the Tiber embankment here and you can see the outlet of the **Cloaca Maxima**, the sewer begun by King Tarquin; big enough to drive two carriages through, it is still in use today.

Just upstream, past the Ponte Palatino, a single arch decorated with dragons is all that remains of the *Pons Aemilius*. Originally built in the 2nd century BC, it collapsed twice and was last restored in 1575 by Gregory XIII, only to fall down again 20 years later. Now it is known as the 'broken bridge', or **Ponte Rotto.**

Across from the temples, the handsome medieval church with the lofty campanile is **Santa Maria in Cosmedin**, built over an altar of Hercules in the 6th century and given to Byzantine Greeks escaping from the Iconoclast emperors in the 8th. The name (like 'cosmetic') means 'decorated', but little of the original art has survived; most of what you see is from the 12th century, including some fine Cosmatesque work inside. In the portico, an ancient, ghostly image in stone built into the walls has come down in legend as the **Bocca della Verità**—the Mouth of Truth. Medieval Romans would swear oaths and close business deals here; if you tell a lie with your hand in the image's mouth he will most assuredly bite your fingers off. Try it.

The Heart of Ancient Rome

Long-standing plans to turn this area into an archaeological park are finally being realized. At the time of writing the area alongside Via dei Fori Imperiali is under excavation; it remains unclear what will be accessible to the public by 2000.

In the 1930s Mussolini built a grand boulevard between the Vittoriano and the Colosseum to ease traffic congestion and show off the ancient sites. He called it the Via del Impero, coinciding with his aspirations of returning Rome to greatness through a new empire in Africa. After Mussolini's demise the road was re-christened Via dei Fori Imperiali, after the Imperial Fora which it partly covers. The Imperial Fora of Augustus, Nerva and Trajan were built to relieve congestion in the original Roman Forum. Trajan's Forum, built with the spoils of his conquest of Dacia (modern Romania) was perhaps the grandest architectural and planning conception ever built in Rome, a broad square surrounded by colonnades, with a huge basilica flanked by two libraries and a covered market outside (the world's first shopping mall). A large part of Trajan's Market still stands, with entrances on Via IV Novembre and down the stairs just to the side of Trajan's Column (*open Tues–Sun 9–one hour before sunset; adm*).

Behind it, you can see Rome's own leaning tower, the 12th-century **Torre delle Milizie**. All that remains of Trajan's great square is the paving and its centrepiece, the **Trajan Column**. The spiralling bands of reliefs, illustrating the Dacian Wars, reach to the top, some 96ft high, and rank with the greatest works of Roman art. Behind the column, **Santa Maria di Loreto** is a somewhat garish High Renaissance bauble, built by Bramante and Antonio da Sangallo the Younger. The Romans liked the church so much that in the 1730s they built another one just like it next door, the **Santissimo Nome di Maria**. Scanty remains of the **Forum of Caesar** and the **Forum of Augustus** can be seen along the boulevard to the south.

The Roman Forum

For a place that was the centre of the Mediterranean world, there is surprisingly little to see; centuries of use as a quarry have seen to that. The word *forum* originally meant 'outside' (like the Italian *fuori*), a market-place outside the original Rome that became the centre of both government and business as the city expanded. The entrances are on Via dei Fori Imperiali at Via Cavour, and at the end of the ramp that approaches the Forum from the Colosseum side (*open daily 9–one hour before sunset*).

The **Via Sacra**, ancient Rome's most important street, runs the length of the Forum. At the end of it beneath the Capitol you will be facing the **Arch of Septimius Severus** (AD 203), with reliefs of some rather trivial victories over the Arabs and Parthians; conservative

Romans of the time must have strongly resented this upstart African emperor planting his monument in such an important spot. The arch also commemorated Septimius' two sons, Geta and Caracalla; when the nasty Caracalla did his brother in, he had his name effaced from it. In front of it, the **Lapis Niger**, a mysterious stone with an underground chamber beneath it, is the legendary tomb of Romulus. The inscription down below—a threat against the profaning of this sacred spot—is one of the oldest ever found in the Latin language. The famous Golden Milestone also stood here, the 'umbilicus' of Rome and the point from which all distances in the Empire were measured. To the right is the **Curia** (the Senate House), heavily restored after centuries' use as a church (the good Baroque church behind it is **SS. Luca e Martina**, built by Pietro di Cortona in the 1660s).

To the left of the arch the remains of a raised stone area were the **Rostra**, the speakers' platform under the republic, decorated with ships' prows (*rostra*) taken in a sea battle in about 320 BC. Of the great temples on the Capitol slope only a few columns remain; from left to right, the **Temple of Saturn**, which served as Rome's treasury, the **Temple of Vespasian** (three standing columns) and the **Temple of Concord**, built by Tiberius to honour the peace—so to speak—that the emperors had enforced between patricians and plebeians.

Behind the Rostra, in the open area once decorated with statues and monuments, the simple standing **column** was placed in honour of Nikephoros Phocas, Byzantine Emperor in 608—the last monument ever erected in the Forum; the Romans had to steal the column from a ruined building. Just behind it a small pool once marked the spot of one of ancient Rome's favourite legends. In 362 BC, according to Livy, an abyss suddenly opened across the Forum, and the sibyls predicted that it would not close unless the 'things that Rome held most precious' were thrown in. A consul, Marcus Curtius, took this as meaning a Roman citizen and soldier. He leapt in fully armed, horse and all, and the crack closed over him.

This section of the Forum was bordered by two imposing buildings, the **Basilica Aemilia** to the north and the **Basilica Julia** to the south, built by Caesar with the spoils of the Gallic Wars. The **Temple of Caesar** closes the east end, built by Augustus as a visual symbol of the new imperial mythology.

The adjacent **Temple of the Dioscuri** makes a good example of how temples were used in ancient times. This one was a meeting hall for men of the equestrian class (the knights, though they were really more likely to be businessmen); they had safe-deposit boxes in the basement, where the standard weights and measures of the empire were kept. Between them, the round pedestal was the foundation of the small **Temple of Vesta**, where the sacred hearth-fire was kept burning by the Vestal Virgins; ruins of their extensive apartments can be seen next door.

Two more Christian churches stand in this part of the Forum. **SS. Cosma e Damiano** was built on to the Temple of Antoninus Pius and Faustina in the 6th century; most of the columns survive, with a fine sculptural frieze of griffons on top. **Santa Francesca Romana** is built over a corner of Rome's largest temple, that of Venus and Rome. Built by Hadrian, this was a curious, double-ended shrine to the state cult; one side devoted to the Goddess Roma and the other to Venus—in Roman mythology she was the ancestress of the Caesars. The church entrance is outside the Forum, but the adjoining convent, inside the monumental area, houses the **Antiquarium Forense**, with Iron-Age burial urns and other paraphernalia from the Forum excavations. Between the two churches the mastodonic **Basilica of Maxentius**, finished by Constantine, remains the largest ruin of the Forum, its clumsy arches providing an illustration of the ungainly but technically sophisticated 4th century.

Near the exit, the **Arch of Titus** commemorates the victories of Titus and his father Vespasian over the rebellious Jews (AD 60–80), one of the fiercest struggles Rome ever had to fight. The reliefs show the booty being carted through Rome in the triumphal parade—including the famous seven-branched golden candlestick from the holy of holies in the Temple at Jerusalem. South of the arch a path leads up to the **Palatine Hill** (*open daily 9–one hour before sunset; adm; combined ticket with Colosseum available*). Here, overlooking the little corner of the world that gave our language words like *senate, committee, rostrum, republic, plebiscite* and *magistrate*, you can leave democracy behind and visit the etymological birthplace of *palace*. The ruins of the imperial *Palatium* once covered the entire hill. As with the Forum, almost all the stone has been cannibalized, and there's little to see of what was once a complex half a mile long, contributed to by a dozen emperors.

There are good views across the Circus Maximus from just above what was once the portico from which the emperor could watch the races. Don't miss the chance to take a stroll through the gardens planted by the Farnese family over what were the imperial servants' quarters—one of the most peaceful spots in the city. The one modern building on the Palatino houses the **Antiquarium**, a good little collection of relics found within a stone's throw of the building.

The Colosseum

Its real name was the Flavian Amphitheatre, after the family of emperors who built it, beginning with Vespasian in AD 72; Colosseum refers to the *Colossus*, a huge gilded statue of Nero (erected by himself, of course) that stood in the square in front. There doesn't seem to be much evidence that Christians were literally thrown to lions here—there were other places for that—but what did go on was perhaps the grossest and best-organized perversity in all history. Gladiatorial contests began under the republic, designed to make Romans better soldiers by rendering them indifferent to the sight of death. Later emperors introduced new displays to relieve the monotony—men versus animals, lions versus elephants, women versus dwarfs, sea-battles (the arena could be flooded at a moment's notice), public tortures of condemned criminals, and even genuine athletics, a Greek import the Romans never much cared for. In the first hundred days of the Colosseum's opening, 5000 animals were slaughtered. The native elephant and lion of North Africa and Arabia are extinct thanks to such shenanigans.

However hideous its purpose, the Colosseum ranks with the greatest works of Roman architecture and engineering; all modern stadia have its basic plan. One surprising feature was a removable awning that covered the stands. Sailors from Cape Misenum were kept to operate it; they also manned the galleys in the mock sea-battles. Originally there were statues in every arch and a ring of bronze shields around the cornice. The concrete stands have eroded away, showing the brick structure underneath. Renaissance and Baroque popes hauled away half the travertine exterior—enough to build the Palazzo Venezia, the Palazzo Barberini, a few other palaces and bridges and part of St Peter's. Almost all of the construction work under Vespasian and Titus was performed by Jewish slaves, brought here for the purpose after the suppression of their revolt (*open daily 9–one hour before sunset; adm; combined ticket with Palatine Hill available*).

Just outside the Colosseum, the **Arch of Constantine** marks the end of the ancient Triumphal Way (now Via di San Gregorio) where victorious emperors and their troops would parade their captives and booty. The arch, with a coy inscription mentioning Constantine's 'divine inspiration' (the Romans weren't sure whether it was yet respectable to mention Christianity), is covered with reliefs stolen from older arches and public buildings—a sad commentary on the state of art in Constantine's day.

Domus Aurea (Golden House) and the Monte Esquilino

Domus Aurea open for visits by reservation only, call ✆ 06 3974 9907 (daily 9–7); tours are in Italian, and there is an acoustiguide tour in English.

When Nero decided he needed a new palace, money was no object. Taking advantage of the great fire of AD 64 (which he apparently did *not* start), he had a huge section of Rome (temporarily renamed Neropolis) cleared to make a rural estate in the middle of town. The **Domus Aurea** was probably the most sumptuous palace ever built in Rome, decorated in an age when Roman art was at its height, but Nero never lived to see it finished—he committed suicide during an army coup by Spanish legions. When the dust settled, the new Emperor Vespasian realized that this flagrant symbol of imperial decadence had to go. He demolished it, and Titus and Trajan later erected great bath complexes on its foundations; Nero's gardens and fishponds became the site of the Colosseum. In the 1500s some beautifully decorated rooms of the Domus Aurea were discovered underground, saved for use as the basement of Titus' baths. Raphael and other artists studied them closely and incorporated some of the spirit of the fresco decoration into the grand manner of the High Renaissance (our word 'grotesque', originally referring to the leering faces and floral designs of this time, comes from the finds in this 'grotto'). The Domus Aurea was reopened to the public in 1999.

The **Monte Esquilino** is better known today as the *Colle Oppio*. Much of it is covered with parks; besides the Domus Aurea there are very substantial ruins of the **Terme di Traiano**, still unexcavated. On the northern slope of the hill, **San Pietro in Vincoli** takes its name from relics supposed to be the chains Peter was locked in before Nero had him crucified; they are kept over the main altar. The other attraction of this church is the famous, ill-fated **Tomb of Julius II** which tortured Michelangelo for so many years. Of the original project, planned as a sort of tabernacle with 40 individual statues, the artist completed only the powerful figure of *Moses*, perhaps the closest anyone has ever come to capturing prophetic vision in stone, even if he bears a striking resemblance to Charlton Heston. All the other statues on the tomb are the work of Michelangelo's students.

San Clemente

This church, a little way to the east of the Colosseum on Via San Giovanni in Laterano, is one of the more fascinating remnants of Rome's many-layered history. One of the first substantial building projects of the Christians in Rome, the original basilica (*c.* 375) burned along with the rest of the quarter during a sacking by the Normans in 1084. It was rebuilt soon afterwards with a new Cosmatesque pavement, and the 6th-century choir screen—a rare example of sculpture from that ungifted time—saved from the original church. The 12th-century mosaic in the apse represents the *Triumph of the Cross*, and the chapel at the entrance contains a beautiful series of quattrocento frescoes by Masolino. From a vestibule, tickets are sold to the **Lower Church** (*open daily 9–12 and 3.30–6.30; adm*). This is the lower half of the original San Clemente, and there are remarkable, though deteriorated, frescoes from the 9th and 11th centuries. The plaque from Bulgaria, mentioned on p.60, commemorates SS. Cyril and Methodius, who went from this church to spread the Gospel among the Slavs; they translated the Bible into Old Slavonic, and invented the first Slavic alphabet (Cyrillic) to do it.

From here, steps lead down to the lowest stratum, 1st and 2nd century AD buildings divided by an alley; this includes the **Mithraeum**, the best-preserved temple of its kind after the one in Capua. The larger, neighbouring building was filled with rubble to serve as a foundation for the basilica, and the apse was later added over the Mithraeum. Father Mulhooly of Boston started excavating in the 1860s, and later excavations have revealed a Mithraic antechamber with a fine stuccoed ceiling, a Mithraic school with an early fresco, and the temple proper, a small cavern-like hall with benches for the initiates to share a ritual supper.

Mithraism was a mystery religion, full of secrets closely held by the initiates (all male, and largely soldiers) and it is difficult to say what else went on down here. Two altars were found, each with the usual image of the Persian-import god Mithras despatching a white bull, including a snake, a scorpion and a crow, and astrological symbolism. Underneath all this, there is yet a fourth building level, some foundations from the republican era. At the end of the 1st-century building you can look down into an ancient sewer or underground stream, one of a thousand entrances to the surreal sub-Roma of endless subterranean caves, buildings, rivers and lakes, mostly unexplored and unexplorable. A century ago a schoolboy fell in the water here; they found him, barely alive, in open country several kilometres from the city.

Corso Vittorio Emanuele

This street, chopped through the medieval centre in the 1880s, from the river to the Piazza Venezia, still hasn't quite been assimilated into its surroundings; nevertheless, this ragged, smoky traffic tunnel will come in handy when you find yourself lost in the tortuous, meandering streets of Rome's oldest quarter.

St Philip Neri, the gifted, irascible holy man who is patron saint of Rome, built the **Chiesa Nuova** near the eastern end in 1584. Philip was quite a character, with something of the Zen Buddhist in him. He forbade his followers any sort of philosophical speculation, but made them sing and recite poetry; two of his favourite pastimes were insulting popes and embarrassing initiates—making them walk through Rome with a foxtail sewn to the back of their coat to learn humility.

As was common in those times, sincere faith and humility were eventually translated into flagrant Baroque. The Chiesa Nuova is one of the largest and fanciest of the species. Its altarpiece is a *Madonna with Angels* by Rubens. Even more flagrant, outside the church you can see the curved arch-Baroque façade of the **Philippine Oratory** by Borromini. The form of music called the *oratorio* takes its name from this chapel, a tribute to St Philip's role in promoting sacred music.

The biggest palace on the street, attributed to Bramante, is the **Palazzo della Cancelleria**, once the seat of the papal municipal government. One of the earliest and best of the palaces, the delicate **Piccola Farnesina** by Antonio da Sangallo the Younger, houses a little museum, a collection of ancient sculpture called the **Museo Barracco** (*open Tues–Sat 9–7, Sun 9–1.30; adm*).

The grand Baroque church of **Sant'Andrea della Valle**, with the city's second-tallest dome, was for the most part designed by Maderno, one of the architects of St Peter's. The curving façade across the street belongs to **Palazzo Massimo alle Colonne**, the masterpiece of the Renaissance architect Baldassare Peruzzi; he transplanted something of the Florentine style of monumental palaces, adding some light-hearted proto-Baroque decoration.

The centre of the ghastly square called Largo Argentina is occupied by the remains of several republican-era temples, unearthed far below ground level. Next comes the church of the **Gesù** (1568–84), just west of Piazza Venezia, a landmark for a new era and the new aesthetic of cinquecento Rome. The transitional, pre-Baroque fashion was often referred to as the 'Jesuit style', and here in the Jesuits' head church architects Vignola and della Porta laid down Baroque's first law: an intimation of paradise through decorative excess. It hasn't aged well, though at the time it must have seemed to most Romans a perfect marriage of Renaissance art and a reformed, revitalized faith.

St Ignatius, the Jesuits' founder, is buried in the left transept right under the altar, Spanish-style; the globe incorporated in the sculpted Trinity overhead is the biggest piece of lapis lazuli in the world.

Campo de' Fiori

Few cities can put on such a variety of faces to beguile the visitor; depending on where you spend your time in Rome, you may come away with the impression of a city that is one great Baroque stage set, a city of grimy early 1900s palazzi and bad traffic, or a city full of nothing but ruins and parks. Around **Campo de' Fiori**, one of the spots dearest to the hearts of Romans themselves, you may think yourself in the middle of some scruffy southern Italian village. Rome's market square, disorderly, cramped and chaotic, is easily the liveliest corner of the city, full of market barrows, buskers, teenage Bohemians and the folkloresque types who have lived here all their lives—the least decorous and worst-dressed crowd in Rome. During papal rule the old square was also used for executions—most notoriously the burning of Giordano Bruno in 1600. This well-travelled philosopher was the first to take Copernican astronomy to its logical extremes—an infinite universe with no centre, no room for Heaven, and nothing eternal but change. The Church had few enemies more dangerous. Italy never forgot him; the statue of Bruno in Campo de' Fiori went up only a few years after the end of papal rule.

Just east of the square, the heap of buildings around Piazzetta di Grottapinta is built over the cavea of **Teatro di Pompeo**, ancient Rome's biggest. This complex included a *curia*, the place where Julius Caesar was assassinated in 44 BC. Walk south from Campo de' Fiori and you will be thrown back from cosy medievalism into the heart of the High Renaissance with the **Palazzo Farnese**, one of the definitive works of that Olympian style. The younger Sangallo began it in 1514, and Michelangelo contributed to the façades and interiors. The building now serves as the French Embassy. The façade has been restored to its original splendour. The frescoed *piano nobile* can be visited by written request (write at least a month in advance to the Servizio Culturale dell'Ambasciata Francese, Palazzo Farnese, Rome, ✆ 06 6860 1443, ✉ 06 6860 1331).

Most of the palaces that fill up this neighbourhood have one thing in common—they were made possible by someone's accession to the papacy, the biggest jackpot available to any aspiring Italian family. Built on the pennies of the faithful, they provide the most outrageous illustration of Church corruption at the dawn of the Reformation. Alessandro Farnese, who as Pope Paul III was a clever and effective pope—though perhaps the greatest nepotist ever to decorate St Peter's throne—managed to build this palace 20 years before his election, with the income from his 16 absentee bishoprics.

Palazzo Spada, just to the east along Via Capo di Ferro, was the home of a mere cardinal, but its florid stucco façade (1540) almost upstages the Farnese. Inside, the **Galleria Spada** (*open Tues–Sat 9–7, Sun 9–1; adm*) is one of Rome's great collections of 16th- and 17th-century painting. Guido Reni, Guercino and other favourites are well represented. Don't miss the courtyard, which has decoration similar to the façade, and a glass window with a view through the library to one of Rome's little Baroque treasures: the *trompe l'oeil* corridor, designed by Borromini to appear four times its actual length (the statue at the end of the path is actually less than a yard in height). To the south, close to the Tiber, **Via Giulia** was laid out by Pope Julius II: a pretty thoroughfare lined with churches and palazzi from that time. Many (successful) artists have lived here, including Raphael.

Piazza Navona

In 1477 the area now covered by one of Rome's most beautiful piazzas was a field full of huts and vineyards, tucked inside the imposing ruins of the Stadium of Domitian. A redevelopment of the area covered the long grandstands with new houses, but the decoration had to wait for the Age of Baroque. In 1644, with the election of Innocent X, it was the Pamphili family that won the papal sweepstakes. Innocent, a great grafter and such a villainous pope that when he died no one—not even his newly wealthy relatives—would pay for a proper burial, built the ornate **Palazzo Pamphili** (now the Brazilian Embassy) and hired Borromini to complete the gaudy church of **Sant'Agnese in Agone**, begun by Carlo and Girolamo Rainaldi.

Borromini's arch-rival, Bernini, got the commission for the piazza's famous fountains; the Romans still tell stories of how the two artists carried on. Borromini started a rumour that the tall obelisk atop the central **Fountain of the Four Rivers** was about to topple; when the alarmed papal commissioners arrived to confront Bernini with the news, he tied a piece of twine around it, secured the other end to a lamppost, and laughed all the way home. The fountain is Bernini's masterpiece, Baroque at its flashiest and most lovable. Among the travertine grottoes and fantastical flora and fauna under the obelisk, the four colossal figures represent the Ganges, Danube, Rio de la Plata and Nile (with the veiled head because its source was unknown).

Bernini also designed the smaller **Fontana del Moro**, at the southern end. The third fountain, that of *Neptune*, was an empty basin until the 19th century, when the statues by Giacomo della Porta were added to make the square seem more symmetrical. Off the southern end of the piazza, at the back of Palazzo Braschi, **Pasquino** is the original Roman 'talking statue', embellished with placards and graffiti ('pasquinades') since the 1500s—one of his favourite subjects in those days was the insatiable pigginess of families like the Farnese; serious religious issues were usually too hot to touch, even for a statue.

Piazza Navona seems mildly schizoid these days, unable to become entirely part of high-fashion, tourist-itinerary Rome, yet no longer as comfortable and unpretentious as the rest of the neighbourhood. One symptom will be readily apparent should you step into any of the old cosy-looking cafés and restaurants around the piazza: they're as expensive as in any part of Rome. The best time to come to Piazza Navona is at night when the fountain is illuminated—or, if you can, for the noisy, traditional toy fair of the **Befana**, set up between just before Christmas and Epiphany. **Palazzo Altemps** on Piazza Sant'Apollinare, now contains half of the excellent **Museo Nazionale Romano** (*see* p.126).

Some of the churches in the neighbourhood are worth a look, such as **Santa Maria della Pace** (*closed for restoration*), with Raphael's series of *Sibyls and Prophets* on the vaulting and a cloister by Bramante. **San Luigi dei Francesi** (*open daily 7.30–12.30 and 3.30–6.30; closed Thurs pm*), the French church in Rome, contains the great *Life of St Matthew* by Caravaggio in a chapel on the left aisle. **Sant'Agostino**, just a couple of blocks away, contains another Caravaggio—the *Madonna of the Pilgrims*—in the first chapel on the left (bring L500 coins for the lights in both churches). Towards the Pantheon, **Sant'Ivo alla Sapienza** once served the English community in Rome. Borromini built them one of his most singular buildings (1660), with its dome and spiralling cupola (*open Sun 10–12*).

The Pantheon

When we consider the fate of so many other great buildings of ancient Rome we begin to understand what a slim chance it was that allowed this one to come down to us. The first Pantheon was built in 27 BC by Agrippa, Emperor Augustus' son-in-law and right-hand man, but was destroyed by fire and replaced by the present temple in 119–128 by the Emperor Hadrian, though curiously retaining Agrippa's original inscription on the pediment. Its history has been precarious ever since. In 609 the empty Pantheon was consecrated to Christianity as 'St Mary of the Martyrs'.

Becoming a church is probably what saved it, though the Byzantines hauled away the gilded bronze roof tiles soon after, and for a while in the Middle Ages the portico saw use as a fish market. The Pantheon's greatest enemy, however, was Gian Lorenzo Bernini. He not only 'improved' it with a pair of Baroque belfries over the porch (demolished in 1887), but he had Pope Urban VIII take down the bronze covering on the inside of the dome to melt down for his *baldacchino* over the altar at St Peter's. Supposedly there was enough left over to make the pope 60 cannons.

You may notice the building seems perilously unsound. There is no way a simple vertical wall can support such a heavy, shallow dome (steep domes push downwards, shallow ones outwards). Obviously the walls will tumble at any moment. That is a little joke the Roman architects are playing, for here they are showing off as shamelessly as in the Colosseum, or the aqueduct with four storeys of arches that used to run *up* to the Palatine Hill. The wall that looks so fragile is really 23ft thick and the dome on top isn't a dome at all; the real hemispherical dome lies underneath, resting easily on the walls inside. The ridges you see on the upper dome are courses of cantilevered bricks, effectively almost weightless. The real surprise, however, lies behind the enormous original bronze doors, an interior of precious marbles and finely sculpted details, the grandest and best-preserved building to have survived from the ancient world (*open Mon–Sat 9–6.30, Sun 9–1*). The movie directors who made all those Roman epics in the 1950s and '60s certainly took many of their settings from this High Imperial creation, just as architects from the early Middle Ages onwards have tried to equal it.

Brunelleschi learned enough from it to build his dome in Florence, and a visit here will show you at a glance what Michelangelo and his contemporaries were trying so hard to outdo. The coffered dome, the biggest cast concrete construction ever made before the 20th century, is the crowning audacity, even without its bronze plate. At 141ft in diameter it is probably the largest in the world (a little-known fact—but St Peter's dome is 6ft less, though much taller). Standing in the centre and looking at the clouds through the 28ft *oculus*, the hole at the top, is an odd sensation you can experience nowhere else.

Inside, the niches around the perimeter held statues of the Pantheon's 12 gods, plus those of Augustus and Hadrian; in the centre, illuminated by a direct sunbeam at midsummer noon, stood Jove. All these are gone, of course, and the interior decoration is limited to an *Annunciation*, attributed to Melozzo da Forlì, and the tombs of eminent Italians such as Raphael and kings Vittorio Emanuele II and Umberto I. The Pantheon simply stands open, with no admission charges, probably fulfilling the same purpose as in Hadrian's day—no purpose at all, save that of an unequalled monument to art and the builder's skill.

Just behind the Pantheon the big church of **Santa Maria Sopra Minerva** is interesting for being one of the few medieval churches of Rome (*c.* 1280) to escape the Baroque treatment; its Gothic was preserved in restoration work in the 1840s. Two Medici popes, Leo X and Clement VII, are buried here, as is Fra Angelico. Santa Maria's Florentine connection began with the Dominican monks who designed it; they also did Florence's Santa Maria Novella. A work of Michelangelo, *Christ with the Cross*, can be seen near the high altar; the Carafa Chapel off the right aisle, where you can pay your respects to Pope Paul IV, has a series of frescoes (1489) on the *Life of St Thomas* by Filippino Lippi, his best work outside Florence.

Trastevere

So often just being on the wrong side of the river encourages a city district to cultivate its differences and its eccentricities. Trastevere isn't really a Left Bank—more of a pocket-sized Brooklyn, and as in Brooklyn those differences and eccentricities often turn out to be the old habits of the whole city, preserved in an out-of-the-way corner.

The people of Trastevere are more Roman than the Romans. Indeed, they claim to be the real descendants of the Romans of old; one story traces their ancestry back to the sailors who worked the great awning at the Colosseum. Such places have a hard time surviving these days, especially when they are as trendy as Trastevere is right now. But even though such things as Trastevere's famous school of dialect poets may be mostly a memory, the quarter remains the liveliest and most entertaining in Rome. The young crowd that Trastevere attracts now provides much of the local colour, their colourful trendy clothes somehow a perfect match for the medieval alleys.

Just over Ponte Garibaldi is Piazza Sonnino, with the **Torre degli Anguillara**, an uncommon survival of the defence towers that once loomed over medieval Rome, and the 12th-century church of **San Crisogano**, with mosaics by Pietro Cavallini (master of the Roman 13th-century school), built over the remains of an earlier church. Near the bridge, the dapper statue in the top hat is Giuseppe Gioacchino Belli, one of Trastevere's 19th-century dialect poets.

Turn left on to one of the narrow streets off Viale di Trastevere and make your way to the church of **Santa Cecilia in Trastevere**, founded over the house of the 2nd-century martyr whom centuries of hagiography have turned into one of the most agreeable of saints, the inventor of the organ and patroness of music. Cecilia was disinterred in 1599, and her body was found entirely uncorrupted. Clement VIII commissioned Maderno to sculpt an exact copy from sketches made before her body dissolved into thin air; this charming work can be seen near the altar, beneath an altarpiece by Giuliano Romano. Nearby there is a *Tabernacle* by Arnolfo di Cambio similar to the one in St Paul's, and 9th-century mosaics in the apse.

The church has other treasures: Renaissance tombs,; frescoes by the school of Pinturicchio in a chapel on the right, and a **crypt** (*adm*) built in the underlying Roman constructions, thought to be Cecilia's home. Up in the **singing gallery** (*open Tues and Thurs 10.30–11.30; adm*) are the remains of the original church wall decoration—a wonderful fresco of the *Last Judgement* by Cavallini.

Across Viale di Trastevere—an intrusive modern boulevard that slices the district in two—lies the heart of old Trastevere, around **Piazza Santa Maria in Trastevere** and its church. Most of this building dates from the 1140s, though the original church, begun perhaps in 222, may be the first anywhere dedicated to the Virgin Mary. The medieval building is a treasure-house of Roman mosaics, starting with the frieze with the Virgin breast-feeding Christ flanked by ten female figures on the façade, and continuing with the remarkable series from the *Life of Mary* by Cavallini in the apse, a bit of the early Renaissance 100 years ahead of schedule (*c.* 1290). Above them are earlier, more glittering mosaics from the 1140s.

The piazza, and the streets around it, have been for decades one of the most popular spots in Rome for restaurants; tables are spread out wherever there's room, and there will always be a crowd in the evening.

North of Piazza Venezia: Around Via del Corso

The Campus Martius, the open plain between Rome's hills and the Tiber, was the training ground for soldiers in the early days of the republic. Eventually the city swallowed it up and the old path towards the Via Flaminia became an important thoroughfare, *Via Lata* (Broadway!). Not entirely by coincidence, the popes of the 14th and 15th centuries laid out a new boulevard almost in the same place. Via del Corso, or simply the Corso, has been the main axis of Roman society ever since. Goethe left a fascinating account of the Carnival festivities of Rome's benignly decadent 18th century, climaxing in the horse races that gave the street its name.

Much of its length is taken up by the overdone palaces of the age, such as the Palazzo Doria (1780), where the **Galleria Doria Pamphili** (*open Fri–Wed 10–5; visits to the apartments at 10.30 and 12.30; adm*), still owned by the Pamphili, has a fine painting collection—with Velàsquez' *Portrait of Innocent X*, Caravaggio's *Flight into Egypt*, and works by Rubens, Titian, Brueghel and more. Guided tours of the apartments (in English by request) give an idea of the lifestyle a family expected when one of their members hit the papal jackpot.

Continuing northwards, the palaces have come down in the world somewhat, tired-looking blocks that now house banks and offices. Look on the side-streets for some hidden attractions: **Sant'Ignazio**, on Via del Seminario, is another Jesuit church with spectacular *trompe l'oeil* frescoes on the ceiling; a block north, columns of the ancient **Temple of Hadrian** are incorporated into the north side of the city's tiny Stock Exchange.

Piazza Colonna takes its name from the column of Marcus Aurelius, whose military victories are remembered in a column (just like those of Trajan); atop stands a statue of St Paul. The obelisk in adjacent Piazza di Montecitorio once marked the hours on a gigantic sundial in Emperor Augustus' garden; **Palazzo Montecitorio**, begun by Bernini, now houses the Italian Chamber of Deputies.

A little way east of Piazza Colonna is the **Trevi Fountain,** into which you can throw your coins to guarantee your return trip to Rome. The fountain, completed in 1762, was originally planned to commemorate the restoration of Agrippa's aqueduct by Nicholas V in 1453. The source was called the 'Virgin Water' after Virgo, a young girl who had showed thirsty Roman soldiers the hidden spring. It makes a grand sight—enough to make you want to come back; not many fountains have an entire palace for a stage backdrop. The big fellow in the centre is Oceanus, drawn by horses and tritons through cascades of travertine and blue water. Across from the fountain, little **SS. Vicenzo and Anastasio** has the distinction of caring for the pickled hearts and entrails of dozens of popes; an odd custom. They're kept down in the crypt.

Further north, the Corso reaches close to the Tiber and the dilapidated and overgrown **Mausoleum of Augustus**, a cylinder of shabby brick once covered in marble and golden statues. All the Julian emperors except Nero were interred here, in the middle of what were Augustus' enormous gardens. After the centuries had despoiled the tomb of its riches the Colonna family turned the hulk into a fortress. Further indignities were in store. Until 1823, when the pope forbade them, bullfights were popular in Rome, and a Spanish entrepreneur found the circular enclosure perfect for the *toreros*. After that the tomb was used as a circus, before Mussolini, wishing to afford the founders of Imperial Rome due respect (and perhaps intending to be buried there himself), declared it a national monument and had trees planted around it. Even so, no one quite seems to know what to do with it; it sits locked and empty.

Across the street, Augustus' **Ara Pacis** (Altar of Peace; *open Tues–Sat 9–5, Sun 9–1; adm*) has had a better fate. Bits and pieces of the beautiful sculpted reliefs, dug up in 1937, were joined with casts of others from museums around Europe to recreate the small building almost in its entirety. One of antiquity's noblest (and least pretentious) conceptions now sits under a glass pavilion; among the mythological reliefs, note the side facing the river, with the emperor and his family dedicating a sacrifice.

Piazza di Spagna

The shuffling crowds of tourists who congregate here at all hours of the day are not a recent phenomenon; this supremely sophisticated piazza has been a favourite with foreigners ever since it was laid out in the early 16th century. The Spaniards came first, as their embassy to the popes was established here in 1646, giving the square and the steps their name. Later, the English Romantic poets made it their headquarters in Italy; typical mementoes—locks of hair, fond remembrances, death masks—are awaiting your inspired contemplation at the Keats-Shelley Memorial House at No.26 (*open April–Sept Mon–Fri 9–1 and 3–6; Oct–Mar Mon–Fri 9–1 and 2.30–5.30; adm*). Almost every artist, writer or musician of the last century spent some time here, but today the piazza often finds itself bursting at the seams with refreshingly Philistine gawkers and wayward youth from all over the world, caught between the charms of McDonald's (the first one built in Rome) and the fancy shops around nearby Via Condotti.

All these visitors need somewhere to sit, and the popes obliged them in 1725 with the construction of the **Spanish Steps**, an exceptionally beautiful and exceptionally Baroque ornament. The youth who loll about here are taking the place of the hopeful artists' models of the more picturesque centuries, who once crowded the steps, striking poses of antique heroes and Madonnas, waiting for some easy money. At the top of the stairs the simple but equally effective church of **Trinità dei Monti** by Carlo Maderno (early 16th century) was paid for by the King of France. At the southern end of Piazza di Spagna, a Borromini palace housed the papal office called the *Propaganda Fide*, whose job was just what the name implies. The column in front (1856) celebrates the proclamation of the Dogma of the Immaculate Conception. Via del Babuino, a street named after a siren on a fountain so ugly that Romans called her the 'baboon', connects Piazza di Spagna with Piazza del Popolo. Besides its very impressive antique shops, the street carries on the English connection, with All Saints' Church, a sleepy neo-pub and an English bookshop just off it.

Piazza del Popolo

If you have a choice of how you enter Rome, this is the way to do it, through the gate in the old Aurelian Wall and into one of the most successful of all Roman piazzas, copied on a smaller scale all over Italy. No city has a better introduction, and the three diverging boulevards direct you with thoughtful efficiency towards your destination. Valadier, the pope's architect after the Napoleonic occupation, gave the piazza the form it has today, but the big obelisk of Pharaoh Ramses II, punctuating the view down the boulevards, arrived in the 1580s. It is 3200 years old but, like all obelisks, it looks mysteriously brand-new; Augustus brought it to Rome from Heliopolis and planted it in the Circus Maximus; it was transferred here by Pope Sixtus V. The two domed churches designed by Rainaldi, set like bookends at the entrance to the three boulevards, are from the 1670s, part of the original plan for the piazza to which Bernini and Fontana may have contributed.

Nero's ashes were interred in a mausoleum here, at the foot of the Monte Pincio. The site was planted with walnut trees and soon everyone in Rome knew that Nero's ghost haunted the grove, sending out demons—in the forms of flocks of ravens that nested there—to perform deeds of evil. In about 1100 Pope Paschal II destroyed the grove and scattered the ashes; to complete the exorcism he built a church on the site, **Santa Maria del Popolo**. Rebuilt in the 1470s, it contains some of the best painting in Rome: Caravaggio's stunning *Crucifixion of St Peter* and *Conversion of St. Paul* (in the left transept), and frescoes by Pinturicchio near the altar. Raphael designed the Chigi Chapel, off the left aisle, including its mosaics.

Villa Borghese

From Piazza del Popolo a winding ramp leads up to Rome's great complex of parks. Just by coincidence this was mostly parkland in ancient times. The **Monte Pincio** once formed part of Augustus' imperial gardens, and the adjacent **Villa Medici** occupies the site of the Villa of Lucullus, the 2nd-century BC philosopher and general who conquered northern Anatolia and first brought cherries to Europe. Now the home of the French Academy, the Villa Medici was a posh jail of sorts for Galileo during his Inquisitorial trials. The Pincio, redesigned by Valadier as a lovely formal garden, offers rare views over Rome. It is separated from the **Villa Borghese** proper by the Aurelian Wall and the modern sunken highway that borders it; its name, Viale del Muro Torto, means crooked wall, and refers to a section that collapsed in the 6th century and was left as it was because it was believed to be protected by St Peter.

Exploring the vast spaces of Villa Borghese, you will come across charming vales, woods and a pond (rowing boats for rent), an imitation Roman temple or two, rococo avenues where the bewigged dandies and powdered tarts of the 1700s came to promenade, bits of ancient aqueduct and a dated **zoo** (*open daily 8–2 hours before sunset; adm*). On the northern edge of the park is a ponderous boulevard called **Viale delle Belle Arti**, a setting for academies set up by foreign governments to stimulate cultural exchange. The **Galleria Nazionale d'Arte Moderna** (*open Tues–Sun 9–7; adm exp*) makes its home here in one of Rome's most inexcusable buildings (1913), but the collection includes some great works of Modigliani and the Futurists, as well as a fair sampling of 19th- and 20th-century artists from the rest of Europe.

From there, gingerly skirting the Romanian Academy, you come to the **Museo Nazionale di Villa Giulia** (*open Tues–Sun 9–7, Sun 9–2; adm*). If you cannot make it to Tarquinia, this is the place to get to know the Etruscans. Some of their best art has been collected here, as well as laboriously reconstructed terracotta façades to give you some idea of how an Etruscan temple looked. As usual, the compelling attraction is the Etruscans' effortless, endearing talent for portraiture: expressive faces that bridge the gap between the centuries can be seen in terracotta ex-votos (some of children), sarcophagi and even architectural decoration. Serious art is often more stylized; fine examples are the charming couple on the *Sarcophago dei Sposi* from Cerveteri, and the roof statues from the Temple of Portonaccio at Veii—these by Vulca, the only Etruscan artist whose name has survived along with his work. The museum building and its courts and gardens are attractions in themselves; Julius III had Vignola and Ammannati build this quirky Mannerist villa in 1553, and Vasari and Michelangelo may also have helped.

The fantastic trove of ancient relics and late-Renaissance and Baroque painting and sculpture—including masterpieces by Bernini and Caravaggio—at the **Museo e Galleria Borghese** (*open Tues–Sun 9–7; adm; tickets should be reserved in advance, but some are occasionally available at the box office at the last minute, call © 06 328 101, Mon–Fri 9.30–6*) is testimony to the legendary greed and avarice of Cardinal Scipione Borghese, nephew of Pope Paul IV. He amassed, by any means available, one of the great private collections of the 17th century and built a magnificently decorated palace on the family's property to hold it all. The display today is all the more impressive because a descendant of the Cardinal 'sold' many pieces to his brother-in-law, Napoleon Bonaparte, who put them in the Louvre.

The **Museo Borghese** (ground floor) offers an intriguing mix of great art and Roman preciosity. Often the two go hand-in-hand, as with the sensuously charged showpieces of Bernini: *Apollo and Daphne, The Rape of Proserpina* and especially his *David*, which the artist modestly chiselled in his own image. Canova, the hot item among sculptors in Napoleon's day, contributes a titillatingly languorous statue of Pauline Borghese (Napoleon's sister) as the *Conquering Venus*. Even the ancient world joins in the fun, with such works as the famous Hellenistic *Sleeping Hermaphrodite*. Also downstairs are several Caravaggios, including the *Madonna of the Palafrenieri, David with the head of Goliath* and *St Jerome*.

No less impressive are the paintings in the **Galleria** upstairs (entrance through the café in the basement), representing many of the finest 16th- and 17th-century painters: Titian's *Sacred and Profane Love, St Sebastian* and *Christ Scourged*, two Bernini self-portraits, Raphael's *Deposition*, Correggio's *Danae* and Rubens' *Deposition*.

Via Veneto and the Quirinale

This chain of gardens was once much bigger, but at the end of the last century many of the old villas were lost to the inevitable expansion of the city. Perhaps the greatest loss was the Villa Ludovisi, praised by many as the most beautiful of all Rome's parks. Now the choice 'Ludovisi' quarter, it has given the city one of its most famous streets, Via Veneto, the long winding boulevard of grand hotels, cafés and boutiques that stretches down from Villa Borghese to Piazza Barberini. A promenade for the smart set in the 1950s, it wears something of the forlorn air of a jilted beau now that fashion has moved on.

Pull yourself away from the passing show on the boulevard to take in the unique spectacle provided by the **Convento dei Cappuccini** at the southern end of the street, just up from Piazza Barberini (*entrance halfway up the stairs of Santa Maria della Concezione; open Fri–Wed 9–12 and 3–6; adm*). Unique, that is, outside Palermo, for, much like the Capuchin convent there, the Roman brethren have created a loving tribute to our friend Death. In the cellars 4000 dead monks team up for an unforgettable *Danse Macabre* of bones and grinning skulls, carefully arranged by serious-minded Capuchins long ago to remind us of something we know only too well.

On the other side of Piazza Barberini, up a gloomy Baroque avenue called Via delle Quattro Fontane, you'll find the **Palazzo Barberini**, one of the showier places in Rome, decorated everywhere with the bees from the family arms. Maderno, Borromini and Bernini all worked on it, with financing made possible by the election of a Barberini as Pope Urban VIII in 1623. Currently it houses the **National Museum of Ancient Art** (*open Tues–Sat 9– 7; adm*)—a misleading title, since this is a gallery devoted to Italian works of the 12th–18th centuries. Often the original decoration steals the show from the pictures: Bernini's Great Hall, for example, with a ceiling fresco by Pietro da Cortona, the *Triumph of Divine Providence*, or the ceiling in Room 7, with a fresco by Andrea Sacchi where the enthroned Virgin looking down on the round earth seems like a Baroque attempt to create a new Catholic astronomy. Works present include a Bernini self-portrait, Raphael's famous portrait of his beloved mistress *La Fornarina*, the 'baker's girl', more portraits by the Genoese artist Baciccio, lots of Caravaggios, Lippi's *Madonna* and two rather sedate pictures by El Greco. A large section of 15th-century artists not from Tuscany proves that not all the action was happening in Florence.

San Carlino (*currently closed for restoration*), on the corner of Via delle Quattro Fontane and Via Quirinale, is one of Borromini's best works—and his first one (1638), a purposely eccentric little flight of fancy built exactly the size of one of the four massive pillars that hold up the dome in St Peter's. Follow **Via Quirinale** and you'll reach the summit of that hill, covered with villas and gardens in ancient times, and abandoned in the Middle Ages. Then even the name Quirinale had been forgotten, and the Romans called the place 'Montecavallo' after the two big horses' heads projecting above the ground. During the reign of Sixtus V they were excavated to reveal monumental Roman statues of the **Dioscuri** (Castor and Pollux), probably copied from Phidias or Praxiteles. Together with a huge basin found in the Forum, they make a centrepiece for Piazza di Quirinale. Behind it, stretching for a dreary half-kilometre along the street is the **Palazzo del Quirinale** (*open 8.30–12.30 on the second and fourth Sun of each month; closed mid-July through mid-Sept; adm exp*), built in 1574 to symbolize the political domination of the popes, later occupied by the kings of Italy, and now the official residence of the country's president.

Via XX Settembre, the important thoroughfare coming off the Monte Quirinale, passes the Aurelian Wall at **Porta Pia**, redesigned by Michelangelo. Here it changes its name to Via Nomentana, a boulevard lined with villas which have not yet been swallowed up by creeping urbanization. A kilometre east, stop at the thoroughly charming complex of

Sant'Agnese Fuori le Mura (Outside the Walls) (*open Mon 9–12, Tues–Sat 9–12 and 4–6, Sun 4–6*), including a 4th-century church with a beautiful early mosaic of St Agnes in the apse, and 15 ancient marble columns. Along the stairway descending to the church, Early-Christian reliefs and inscriptions have been arranged as in a museum; inside the church is the entrance to the small, aristocratic **catacombs** (3rd-century), absorbing parts of earlier pagan catacombs (*guided tours arranged Wed–Sun during church hours; adm*).

Around the back, through gardens where the neighbourhood children play, stands one of Rome's least known but most remarkable churches. **Santa Costanza** was built as a mausoleum for Constantia, the daughter of Emperor Constantine. In this domed, circular building—one of the finest late-Roman works—more than anywhere else, you can see the great religious turning point of the 4th century come alive; among the exquisite mosaics (regrettably not all have survived) are scenes of a grape harvest, and motifs that would be familiar to any ancient devotee of Dionysus or Bacchus. In the two side chapels are later mosaics of Christ and the Apostles.

Peripheral Attractions

Around Stazione Termini: Terme di Diocleziano (Baths of Diocletian) and the Museo Nazionale Romano

Rome's great big station takes its name from the nearby **Terme di Diocleziano**, just on the other side of Piazza dei Cinquecento. Until the popes dismantled it for building stone this was by far Rome's biggest ruin; its outer wall followed the present-day lines of Via XX Settembre, Via Volturno and Piazza dei Cinquecento, and the big semi-circular **Piazza della Repubblica**, with its mouldering, grandiose 1890s palazzi and huge fountain, occupies the site of the baths' exercise ground, or *palaestra*. All together the complex covered some 11 hectares.

Michelangelo, not on one of his better days, converted a section of the lofty, vaulted central bathhouse into the church of **SS. Maria degli Angeli**, conserving some of the building's original form, and added a broad new cloister. The cloister and adjacent building are now empty– the **Museo Nazionale Romano**, the greatest Italian collection of antiquities after the museum in Naples, has been relocated to two recently renovated *palazzi*– **Palazzo Massimo alle Terme** (*open Tues–Sun 9–7; adm*), right across the street, and **Palazzo Altemps**, near Piazza Navona (*see* p.117). A block north of the baths, Piazza San Bernardo has two interesting churches: **San Bernardo**, built out of a circular library that once occupied a corner of the baths' walls, and **Santa Maria della Vittoria**, home to one of the essential works of Baroque sculpture, the disconcertingly erotic *St Teresa in Ecstasy* by Bernini (in a chapel off the left aisle).

Almost directly under the tracks going into Stazione Termini, the **Underground Basilica**, only discovered in 1916, was not covered up by the centuries—it was built that way for a secret, possibly illegal, religious sect in the 1st century AD. Its stucco reliefs are strange; scholars can't guess anything about the cult's beliefs, but venture to call it 'neo-

Pythagorian' (*contact the Soprintendenza Archeologica di Roma, Piazza Santa Maria Nova 53, © 06 699 0110, well in advance, for permission to visit*).

Monte Celio

South of the Colosseum you can see nothing but trees, but on every inch of this vast tract of parkland, ancient neighbourhoods wait just a few feet beneath the surface. Modern Rome never expanded in this direction, and almost the whole of it has been preserved as open space. It's a fascinating place to walk around, if you can avoid the traffic thundering down the big boulevards towards the southern suburbs. The Monte Celio is only a small part of it, but it is one of the least known and most delightful corners of Rome. Have a picnic in the **Villa Celimontana** behind Piazza della Navicella and you may have squirrels for company.

Some of Rome's most ancient churches repose in quiet settings here, all worth a look inside if they are open: **Santo Stefano Rotondo**, the oldest circular church in Italy, was built around 470 over the ruins of a market-place of Nero's time; across the street more mosaics from the age of Paschal I (*c.* 820) can be seen in **Santa Maria in Domnica**, standing in **Piazza della Navicella**, with a fountain made in the form of an ancient Roman ship. Take the narrow road (just downhill from the church) that cuts down into the hill to **SS. Giovanni e Paolo**, built in the 4th century in the top floor of three Roman houses (*closed for restoration*). Down the western slope you reach **San Gregorio Magno**, begun by Pope Gregory the Great in 590. St Augustine lived here before being sent by Gregory to convert the Angles and Saxons of Britain. Adjacent to the church are several chapels (*adm*) with remarkable frescoes by Guido Reni, Domenichino and Pomarancio.

Circus Maximus and Terme di Caracalla (Caracalla's Baths)

Piazza Porta Capena, at the foot of the Monte Celio, has an odd decoration, an obelisk erected by Mussolini to commemorate his conquest of Ethiopia—he stole it from the Ethiopian city of Axum, although at long last it is scheduled to be returned to its rightful owners. The piazza itself is a vortex of Mussolinian pretensions; the dictator built himself a new Triumphal Way (now Via San Gregorio) along the route of the original one, to celebrate his piddling triumphs in Roman imperial style. An enormous building that was to house the Ministry of Africa to administer Mussolini's colonies found a more agreeable use after the war—as home of the United Nations Food and Agricultural Organization (FAO). To the west, a broad green lawn is all that's left of the **Circus Maximus**. Archaeologists have estimated that as many as 300,000 Romans could squeeze in here and place their bets on the chariot races. Founded by King Tarquin and completed by Trajan, the stadium proved simply too convenient a quarry; the banked, horseshoe-shaped depression, however, still follows the line of the grandstands.

The **Terme di Caracalla** (AD 206–220; *open Tues–Sat 9–2hrs before sunset, Sun and Mon 9–1; adm*), in a large park south of Porta Capena, rank with those of Diocletian as the largest and most lavish. Roughly 1000ft square, with libraries and exercise courts, the baths probably boasted more gold, marble and art than any building complex in Rome; here the Farnese family dug up such masterpieces as the *Hercules* and the *Farnese Bull*, now in the Naples Museum. In the 1700s these baths were one of the obligatory sights of the Grand Tour; their lofty, broken arches and vaults appealed to the Romantic love of ruins like no others. Much of the central building survives, with its hot and cold rooms, great hall and swimming pool, all decorated with mosaics. A large tunnel connects the baths with the area around Palazzo Venezia, a mile away; its purpose was to transport the vast amounts of wood needed to keep the baths hot. Mussolini initiated the custom (now under threat due to the frailty of the ruins) of holding summer operas here; he liked to drive his roadster through the tunnel and pop out dramatically on stage at the beginning of the festivities.

Behind the baths a stretch of the Antonine Aqueduct that supplied it can still be seen. On the other side, facing Via Terme di Caracalla, **SS. Nereo e Achilleo** (*open daily 10–12 and 4–6; ring for custodian*) has more mosaics from the time of Leo III (*c.* 800), a Cosmatesque floor and choir and some gruesome 16th-century frescoes of the martyrdoms of the saints.

The Via Appia: Rome's Catacombs

Rome's 'Queen of Roads', the path of trade and conquest to Campania, Brindisi and the East, was begun in 312 BC by Consul Appius Claudius. Like most of the consular roads outside Rome, over the centuries it became lined with cemeteries and the elaborate mausolea of the wealthy: ancient Roman practice, inherited from the Etruscans, prohibited any burials within the *pomerium*, the sacred ground of the city itself. Later the early Christians built extensive catacombs here—the word itself comes from the location, *ad catacumbas*, referring to the dip in the Via Appia near the suburban Circus of Maxentius. The Via Appia Antica (as distinguished from the modern Via Appia Nuova) makes a pleasant excursion outside the city, especially on Sundays when the road is closed to traffic all the way back to Piazza Venezia.

The road passes under the Aurelian Wall at **Porta San Sebastiano**, one of the best-preserved of the old gates. It houses the **Museum of the Walls** (*open Tues–Sun 9–one hour before sunset; adm*), admission to which also gives you access to a well-preserved section of the 4th-century wall alongside it. Continuing along the road, after about ½km, with some ruins of tombs along the way, there is the famous church of **Domine Quo Vadis**, on the spot where Peter, fleeing from the dangers of Rome, met Christ coming the other way. 'Where goest thou, Lord?' Peter asked. 'I am going to be crucified once more,' was the reply. As the vision departed the shamed Apostle turned back, to face his own crucifixion in Rome.

Another kilometre or so takes you to the **Catacombe di San Calisto**, off on a side road to the right (*open 8.30–12 and 2.30–5; closed Wed and Nov; guided tours only; adm*). Here the biggest attraction is the 'Crypt of the Popes', burial places of 3rd- and 4th-century pontiffs with some well-executed frescoes and inscriptions. A word about catacombs: popular romance and modern cinema notwithstanding, these were never places of refuge from persecution, but simply burial grounds. The word 'catacombs' was only used after the 5th century; before that the Christians simply called them 'cemeteries'. The burrowing instinct is harder to explain. Few other places have ancient catacombs (Naples, Syracuse, Malta and the Greek island of Milos are among them). One of the requirements seems to be tufa, or some other stone that can be easily excavated. Even so, the work involved was tremendous, and not explainable by any reasons of necessity. Christians were still digging them after they had become a power in Rome, in Constantine's time. No one knows for certain what sort of funeral rites were celebrated in them.

Most catacombs began small, as private family cemeteries; over generations some grew into enormous termitaries extending for miles. Inside, most of the tombs you see will be simple *loculi*, walled-up niches with only a symbol or short inscription. Others, especially the tombs of popes or the wealthy, may have paintings of scriptural scenes, usually poor work that reflects more on the dire state of the late-Roman imagination than on the Christians.

You can detour from here another ½km west to the **Catacombe di Santa Domitilla** (*open 8.30–12 and 2.30–5; closed Tues and Jan; guided tours only; adm*). She was a member of a senatorial family and, interestingly, the catacombs seem to incorporate parts of earlier pagan *hypogea*, including a cemetery of the Imperial Flavian family; the paintings include an unusual *Last Supper* scene, portraying a young and beardless Jesus and Apostles in Roman dress. There is an adjacent basilica, built about the tombs of SS. Nereus and Achilleus, on Via delle Sette Chiese.

Not far away is a monument to martyrs of a very different sort, the **Mausoleum of the Fosse Ardeatine** (*open daily 9–5*) dedicated to the three hundred and thirty-five Romans massacred by the Nazis on this spot in 1944 in retaliation for a partisan attack. Back on the Via Appia Antica, there are several catacombs near the corner of Via Appia Pignatelli, including a Jewish one, but the largest are the **Catacombe di San Sebastiano** (*open 8.30–12 and 2.30–5; closed Thurs and Nov; guided tours only; adm*).

This complex, too, began as a pagan cemetery and has intriguing paintings and incised symbols throughout. The place had some special significance for the early Christians, and it has been conjectured that Peter and Paul were originally buried here, before their removal to the basilicas in Constantine's time.

Further south, by now in fairly open country, there are the ruins of the Circus of Maxentius (*open Tues–Sun 9–one hour before sunset*), built in the early 4th century, and then the imposing, cylindrical **tomb of Cecilia Metella** (*open Tues–Fri 9–one hour before sunset, Sat and Sun 9–1*), from the time of Augustus. In the Middle Ages the Caetani family turned the tomb into a family fortress, guarding the road to the south; at other times, before and since, it was a famous rendezvous for *banditti.* The road continues, flanked by tombs and stately parasol pines, with stretches of the original paving, for 16km beyond the walls of Rome.

Monte Aventino

Every now and then, when left-wing parties walk out of negotiations, Italian newspapers may call it an 'Aventine Secession', an off-the-cuff reference to events in Rome 2500 years ago. Under the Republic, the Monte Aventino was the most solidly plebeian quarter of the city. On several occasions, when legislation proposed by the senate and consuls seriously threatened the rights or interests of the people, they retired *en masse* to the Aventino and stayed there until the plan was dropped. Rome's unionists today often keep the city tied up in knots, but most are probably unaware that their ancestors had the honour of inventing the general strike.

The Aventino had another distinction in those times. In its uninhabited regions—the steep, cave-ridden slopes towards the south—Greek immigrants and returning soldiers introduced the midnight rituals of Dionysus and Bacchus. Though secret, such goings-on soon came to the attention of the senate, which rightly saw the orgies as a danger to the state and banned them in 146 BC. They must not have died out completely, however, and in the Middle Ages the Aventino had a reputation as a haunt of witches. The early Christian community also prospered here, and their churches are the oldest relics on the Aventino today.

Coming up from the Circus Maximus along Via Santa Sabina, **Santa Sabina** is a simple, rare example of a 5th-century basilica, with an atrium at its entrance like a Roman secular basilica, and an original door of cypress carved with scriptural scenes. This has been the head church of the Dominicans ever since a 13th-century pope gave it to St Dominic. Both Santa Sabina and the church of **Sant'Alessio**, down the street, have good Cosmatesque cloisters. At the end of this street, one of the oddities only Rome can offer stands on its quiet square, oblivious of the centuries: the **Prioria delle Cavaliere di Malta**, a fancy Rococo complex designed by Giambattista Piranesi. The Knights of Malta—or more properly, the Knights Hospitallers of St John—no longer wait for the popes to unleash them against Saracen and Turk. Mostly this social club for nobles bestirs itself to assist hospitals, its original job during the Crusades. The order's ambassadors to Italy and the Vatican still live here. You can't go inside, but the gate is the most visited in Rome for the intriguing view from the keyhole.

Elsewhere on the Aventino, **Santa Prisca** has beginnings typical of an early-Roman church; its crypt, the original church, was allegedly converted from the house of the martyr Prisca, host to St Peter; the Apostle must have often presided over Mass here. **San Saba**, on Via San Saba, was founded in the 7th century by monks fleeing the Arabs in Jordan and Syria, with a 1205 rebuilding, including some Cosmatesque details, a superb mosaic floor and a crypt with 7th–11th-century frescoes.

Rome's Pyramid and Monte Testaccio

Porta San Paolo stands in one of the best-preserved sections of the Aurelian Wall. The gate itself looks just as it did 1700 years ago, when it was the *Porta Ostiense*; its name was changed because Paul passed through it on the way to his execution. Near the gate is something unique: the 92ft **Pyramid of Caius Cestius** (AD 12) may seem a strange self-tribute for a Roman, but at least Cestius, who had served in Egypt, paid for the tomb himself.

Behind it, inside the walls, the lovely **Protestant Cemetery** (*open daily 8–dusk*) is a popular point of Romantic pilgrimage. The graves of Shelley and Keats are there, recently joined by 400 British soldiers who died during the march on Rome in 1944. Just to the west is the youngest of Rome's hills, **Monte Testaccio**, made up almost entirely of pot-shards. In ancient times, wine, oil, olives, and nearly everything else was shipped in big *amphorae*; here, in what was Rome's port warehouse district, all the broken, discarded ones accumulated in one place. The hill, now grassed over, is 115ft at its highest point—there is a big cross on top—and it covers a large area. The vast cellars the Romans left beneath it are now used as workshops, wine cellars and nightclubs that make Testaccio a swinging area after dark.

Rome ✉ *00100*   **Where to Stay**

For a city that has been entertaining visitors for the last 2000 years, Rome has not acquired any special flair for accommodating them. Perhaps it is just the uninterrupted flow of the curious and faithful that keeps prices higher and service and quality lower than elsewhere in Italy. From Belle Epoque palaces on Via Veneto to grimy hovels on the wrong side of Stazione Termini, there will always be something for you to come home to after a hard day's sight-seeing, although places with a history, a view or quiet gardens are rare. Exceptions exist, but this is probably not the place to make the big splurge: check into some comfortable spot in the area that suits your fancy.

In the 1890s, when the Stazione Termini district was the choicest part of Rome, the streets around the station spawned hundreds of hotels, some quite elegant. Today much of the city's accommodation is still here. Unfortunately it has gone the way of all such 19th-century toadstool neighbourhoods: overbuilt, dingy and down-at-heel, and not at all the place to savour Rome. It's also inconvenient for most of the sights.

Rooms can be difficult to find on short notice, but the free **Hotel Reservation Service**, ✆ 06 699 1000, will do the looking for you. The private **Enjoy Rome** (*see* 'Tourist Information' p.73) will also make commission-free hotel bookings, and **Bed and Breakfast Italy**, ✆ 06 564 0716, and the **Bed and Breakfast Association of Rome**, ✆ 06 687 7348, will recommend something at the cheaper end of the market.

✠ **Peregrinatio Ad Petri Sedem**, Piazza Pio XII 4, ✆ 06 6988 4896, ✉ 06 6988 5617, in front of St Peter's, is the official Vatican office for the placement of pilgrims in Rome. The **Central Welcoming Committee for Jubilee 2000**, Piazza San Marcello 4, Rome ✉ 00187, ✆ 06 696 221, ✉ 06 699 24853, is another source of useful information (*see* p.26).

By far the best-value accommodation in the Rome are those convents which take in paying guests (most convents accept single women, single men, married couples and families with children). Some convents, but not all, require that you eat one meal a day and abide by a nightly curfew. Expect a supplemental fee for single rooms, and don't be surprised if you have to pay a miscellaneous tax here or there. Many convents, but not all, are located near Vatican City.

Hotels

luxury

★★★★★**Hassler-Villa Medici**, Piazza Trinità dei Monti 6, ✆ 06 699 340, ✉ 06 678 9991, is one of Rome's best hotels, with a fine location at the top of the Spanish Steps and wonderful views over the city for those who book far enough in advance. Around for over a century, it has regained its position as the élite hotel of Rome, with a beautiful courtyard, deferential service and large wood-panelled rooms. ★★★★★**Excelsior**, Via V. Veneto 125, ✆ 06 47081, ✉ 06 482 6205, is also located in a choice area, though lacking the aura it had in the 1950s. The reception areas have thicker carpets, bigger chandeliers and more gilded plaster than anywhere in Italy, and most of the rooms are just as good—don't let them give you a modernized one. There are saunas, a famous bar and as much personal attention as you could ask for.

very expensive

★★★★**D'Inghilterra**, Via Bocca di Leone 14, ✆ 06 69981, ✉ 06 6992 2243, is another favourite near Piazza di Spagna. Parts of this building date from the 15th century, when it served as a prince's guest house; in its career as a hotel, since 1850, it has played host to most of the literati and artists of Europe and America. ★★★★**Forum**, Via Tor de' Conti 25, ✆ 06 679 2446, ✉ 06 678 6479, is the only fancy establishment near the ancient Forum; it's somewhat worn, but has unbeatable views from the roof terrace.

expensive

★★★★**Cardinal**, Via Giulia 62, ✆ 06 6880 2719, ✉ 06 678 6376, in the heart of the *centro storico*, is perhaps the best place to experience Renaissance Rome—in a building attributed to Bramante and completely restored, without spoiling the atmosphere. ★★★**Carriage**, Via delle Carrozze 36, ✆ 06 699 0124, ✉ 06 678 8279, almost at the foot of the Spanish Steps, is a sleepy but well-run place with air-conditioning. ★★★**Columbus**, Via della Conciliazione 33, ✆ 06 686 5435, ✉ 06 686 4874, is staid but reliable with nice rooms, some with views over St Peter's; prices are a bit high. ★★★**Fontana**, Piazza di Trevi 96, ✆ 06 678 6113, ✉ 06 679 0024, would be a good hotel anywhere; it is also right across the street from the Trevi Fountain—something to look at out of your window that will guarantee nice dreams.

★★★**Gregoriana**, Via Gregoriana 18, ✆ 06 679 4269, ✉ 06 678 4258, close to the Spanish Steps but reasonably priced, is small, tasteful and gratifyingly friendly, with a devoted regular clientele—there are only 19 rooms, so book early. ★★★**La Residenza**, Via Emilia 22, ✆ 06 488 0789, ✉ 06 485 721, near the Via Veneto, stands out as a very pleasant base, with beautifully appointed rooms in an old town house, and some luxuries more common to the most expensive hotels.

★★★**Teatro di Pompeo**, Largo del Pallaro 8, ✆ 06 6830 0170, ✉ 06 6880 5531, is a small hotel built on the Teatro di Pompeo by Campo de' Fiori, perfect for peace and quiet. ★★★**Villa Florence**, Via Nomentana 28, ✆ 06 440 3036, ✉ 06 440 2709, near the Porta Pia, is a very well-run and friendly hotel in a refurbished 19th-century villa with a garden. ★★★**Villa del Parco**, Via Nomentana 110, ✆ 06 4423 7773, ✉ 06 4423 7572, is similar, but slightly more expensive.

moderate

★★★**Hotel Sant'Anselmo**, Piazza Sant'Anselmo 2, ✆ 06 578 3214, ✉ 06 578 3604, up on Monte Aventino, is a very peaceful hotel with a garden and comfortable rooms. ★★★**Villa San Pio**, Via Sant'Anselmo 19, ✆ 06 574 5232, ✉ 06 574 3547, run by the same management, is just as peaceful. Prices are reasonable. ★★**Campo de' Fiori**, Via del Biscione 6, ✆ 06 6880 6865, ✉ 06 687 6003, has small comfortable rooms and a roof terrace overlooking Campo de' Fiori.

★★**Margutta**, Via Laurina 34, ✆ 06 322 3674, ✉ 06 320 0395, in a quiet street off Via del Babuino, has simple accommodation. ★★**Sole**, Via del Biscione 76, ✆ 06 6880 6873, ✉ 06 689 3787, is a large old hotel with lots of character, just off the Campo de' Fiori market. ★★**Abruzzi**, Piazza della Rotonda 69, ✆ 06 679 2021, has views over the Pantheon, but none of the rooms have private bath. ★**Primavera**, Via San Pantaleo 3, ✆ 06 6880 3109, ✉ 06 6880 3109, is a slightly cheaper hotel just west of Piazza Navona.

cheap

★**Campo Marzio**, Piazza Campo Marzio 7, ✆ 06 6880 1486, is just north of the Pantheon; none of the rooms have private baths. ★**Fiorella**, Via del Babuino 196, ✆ 06 361 0597, in a good location just off Piazza del Popolo, has simple rooms none with private bath. The area around Stazione Termini offers a wide choice of inexpensive hotels, ranging from plain, family-run establishments—often quite comfortable and friendly—to bizarre dives with exposed plumbing run by Sudanese and Sri Lankans for the benefit of visiting countrymen. Via Principe Amedeo is also a good place to look, particularly at No.76, a big building with a pretty courtyard that houses about eight old *pensioni*, and nos.62, 82 and 79. ★**Tony**, Via Principe Amedeo 79, ✆ 06 446 6887, ✉ 06 485 721, is a friendly above-average quality budget hotel. ★**Katty**, Via Palestro 35, ✆ 06 444 1216, ✉ 06 444 1261, is simple and clean, on a street on the east side of the station which has a number of other cheap hotels.

Convents

Suore Teatine, Salita Monte del Gallo 25, ✉ 00165, ✆ 06 637 4084, or ✆ 06 637 4653, 🕿 06 3937 9050 (*L65,000 per person bed and breakfast; each extra meal L20,000*); not all rooms have private bath; curfew 11pm. **The Franciscan Sisters of the Atonement**, Via Monte del Gallo 105, ✉ 00165, ✆ 06 630 782, 🕿 06 638 6149 (*L50,000 per person for bed and breakfast; each extra meal L22,000*), an American order of nuns; spacious pine-shaded garden and parking; curfew 11pm; English spoken. **Suore Dorotee**, Via del Gianicolo 4/a, ✉ 00165, ✆ 06 6880 3349, 🕿 06 6880 3311 (*full board L95,000 per person; half board L85,000*), halfway up the Gianicolo, a 15-min walk from St Peter's, in a quiet spot with a pretty garden; curfew 11pm.

Suore Orsoline, Via Aurelia 218, ✉ 00165, ✆ 06 636 784, 🕿 06 3937 6480 (*single room L70,000, double room L110,000; breakfast extra*); curfew 11.30pm. **Suore Pallottine**, Viale delle Mure Aurelie 7/b, ✉ 00165, ✆ 06 635 697, 🕿 06 3936 6943 (*single room with breakfast L60,000, double room without private bath L100,000, with private bath L150,000*); curfew for one night 10pm, key given out on additional nights. **Istituto Ravasco**, Via Pio VIII 28, ✉ 00165, ✆ 06 3937 5805, 🕿 06 636 721, (*full board L80,000 per person, half board L70,000, bed and breakfast L50,000*).

Suore Sacra Famiglia, Viale Vaticano 92, ✆ 06 3972 3797, 🕿 06 3972 3844 (*double room L80,000, single room L50,000*); no breakfast or other meals. **Figlie Della Carità di S. Vincenzo Dè Paoli**, Via Ezio 28, ✆ 06 321 6686, 🕿 06 323 0261, near ⓜ Lepanto (*full board L80,000 per person, half board L70,000, bed and breakfast L50,000*). **Maestre Pie Filippini**, Via Missori 19, ✉ 00165, ✆ 06 635 201, 🕿 06 636 437 (*bed and breakfast L60,000 per person*); no other meals; curfew 10.30pm.

Padri Trinitari, Piazza S. Maria delle Fornaci, ✆ 06 6383 888, or ✆ 06 3936 7632, 🕿 06 3936 6795 (*bed and breakfast L75,000 per person, double room L130,000, room with 3 beds L160,000*); no other meals. **Domus Pacis**, Via di Torre Rossa 94, ✉ 00165, ✆ 06 638 3888, or ✆ 06 3936 7632, 🕿 06 3936 6795 (*bed and breakfast L70,000 per person, bed, breakfast and supper L85,000*). **Istituto Sacro Cuore**, Via S. Francesco di Sales 18, ✆ 06 6880 6032, 🕿 06 689 3848 (*bed and breakfast L55,000 per person; additional meal L66,000; full board L77,000*).

Centro Diffusione Spiritualità, Via dei Riari 44, ✆ 06 686 1296, 🕿 06 6830 775 (*bed and breakfast L55,000 per person*); rooms with basin, separate bathrooms; curfew 11pm. **Villa Bassi**, Via G. Carini 24, ✉ 00132, ✆ 06 3088 0272 (*L90,000 per person*); no breakfast or other meals. **Fraterna Domus**, Via del Monte Brianza 62, ✉ 00186, ✆ 06 6880 2727, 🕿 06 683 2691 (*full board L75,000 per person, double room L120,000*), between the Tiber and the Piazza Navona; curfew 11pm.

Le Suore di Lourdes, Via Sistina 113, ✉ 00187, ✆ 06 474 5324, 🕿 06 4741 422 (*single room without bath L50,000, with bath L60,000; double room with*

bath L55,000 per person; breakfast included); no other meals; curfew 10.30pm.
Suore di S. Anna della Provvidenza, Via Giusti 5, ✉ 00185, ✆ 06 704 53711,
🖳 06 7045 3513 (*bed and breakfast L70,000 per person; double room L65,000
per person*), midway between San Giovanni and Santa Maria Maggiore; no other
meals; curfew 10pm. **Villa Rosa** (Dominican Sisters), Via Terme Deciane 5,
✉ 00153, ✆ 06 5717 091, 🖳 06 5745 275 (*bed and breakfast L80,000 for a
single room; L120,000 for a double room; L55,000 for a room for three or four*),
between Ⓜ Pyramid and Ⓜ Circus Maximus; no other meals; English spoken.

Eating Out

Unlike many other Italians, the Romans aren't afraid to try something
new. Chinese restaurants have appeared in droves, not to mention
Arab, Korean and macrobiotic places. This should not be taken as a
reflection on local cooking. Rome attracts talented chefs from all
over Italy, and every region is represented by a restaurant
somewhere in town, giving a microcosm of Italian cuisine
you'll find nowhere else.

The grand old tradition of Roman cooking has specialities such as *saltimbocca*
(literally 'jump in the mouth'), tender veal *scalope* cooked with ham, *stracciatella*
(a soup with eggs, parmesan cheese and parsley), fried artichokes called *carciofi
alla giudia* and veal *involtini*. In the less expensive places you are likely to
encounter such favourites as *baccalà* (salt cod), *bucatini all'amatriciana* (in a
tomato and bacon sauce) or *alla carbonara* (with egg and bacon), tripe and
gnocchi. Unless you ask for something different, the wine will probably come from
the Castelli Romani—light, fruity whites, of which the best come from Frascati
and Velletri.

Though you can drop as much as L170,000 (without wine) if you follow the politicians and the TV crowd, prices somehow manage to keep close to the Italian
average. Watch out for tourist traps—places near a major sight with a 'tourist
menu', for example. Rome also has some expensive joints that could best be
described as parodies of old, famous establishments; they advertise heavily and
aren't hard to smell out. Hotel restaurants, those in the de luxe class, can often be
quite good but ridiculously expensive.

very expensive

Perched high above the city, **La Pergola dell'Hotel Hilton**, Via Cadlolo 4, ✆ 06
3509 2211, is one of Rome's most celebrated restaurant for *alta cucina* served in
elegant surroundings with all of Rome at your feet. *Closed Sun and Mon; open for
dinner only; reserve well ahead.* For fish, head to **La Rosetta**, Via della Rosetta 8,
✆ 06 686 1002, near the Pantheon, Rome's best fish-only restaurant; even if you
are't dining, step in to admire the heap of shiny fish, oysters and sea-urchins
arranged on the marble slab in the hall. *Closed Sun; reserve well ahead.*

There is no better place to try *carciofi alla giudia* than right on the edge of the old ghetto at **Piperno**, Via Monte de' Cenci 9, ℭ 06 6880 6629, Rome's most famous purveyor of Roman-Jewish cooking—simple dishes on the whole, but prepared and served with refinement. *Closed Sun eve and Mon.*

Across the river, Trastevere, with its attractive piazzas and tables outside, has long been one of the most popular corners of the city for dining. Many of its restaurants specialize in fish, most notably **Alberto Ciarla**, Piazza San Cosimato 40, ℭ 06 581 8668, some way south of Santa Maria in Trastevere. The French-trained owner, proud enough to put his name on the sign, sees to it that everything is delicately and perfectly done, and graciously served: oysters, seafood ravioli and quite a few adventurous styles of *pesce crudo* (raw fish) are among the most asked for. *Open for dinner only; closed Sun.* Not far away, **Sabatini**, Piazza Santa Maria in Trastevere 13, ℭ 06 581 2026, has been a Roman institution for many a year, as much for the cuisine (again, lots of seafood) as for the tables outside, which face the lovely piazza and its church. *Closed Tues in winter, Wed in summer.* Off Piazza Venezia, **Vecchia Roma**, Piazza Campitelli 18, ℭ 06 686 4604, provides good food, an imaginative seasonal menu and a lovely quiet setting with tables outdoors. *Closed Wed.*

If you find yourself anywhere around Porta San Paolo and the Testaccio district at dinnertime, don't pass up a chance to dine at the acknowledged temple of old Roman cooking, **Checchino dal 1887**, Via di Monte Testaccio 30, ℭ 06 574 6318, which has been owned by the same family for 107 years—the longest known in Rome. Both the fancy and humble sides of Roman food are well represented, with plenty of the powerful offal dishes that Romans have been eating since ancient times, and the setting is unique—on the edge of Monte Testaccio, with one of Rome's best cellars excavated underneath the hill. *Closed Sun eve and Mon.*

moderate

Dal Toscano, Via Germanico 58, ℭ 06 397 25717, is perhaps your best option in the tourist-trap Vatican area: family-run and very popular with Roman families, offering well-prepared Tuscan specialities like *pici* (rough, fresh spaghetti rolled by hand) in game sauce, and *fiorentina* steak—and homemade desserts. *Closed Mon. Reserve.* Another Tuscan place off the Via Veneto, also family-run but slightly fancier and more expensive, is **Papà Baccus**, Via Toscana 33, ℭ 06 4274 2808, which has remarkably good *prosciutto*, delicious potato ravioli and, in winter, baked fish with artichokes, along with regional soups and *fiorentina*. *Closed Sat lunch and Sun. Reserve.*

Only in Rome would you find a good French restaurant run by a Catholic lay missionary society: at **L'Eau Vive**, Via Monterone 85, ℭ 06 6880 1095, not far from the Pantheon, you can have a nourishing meal—*sole meunière* and onion soup—at a modest price; the fixed lunch menu at *L25,000* is a great bargain. *Closed Sun.* Also near the Pantheon, **Myosotis**, Vicolo della Vaccarella 3, ℭ 06

686 5554, is a great family-run restaurant with an ample menu of traditional and creative meat and fish dishes. *Closed Sun.*

The Piazza di Spagna area is not as promising for restaurants, but there are a few, of which the best, perhaps, is **Nino**, Via Borgognona 11, © 06 678 6752, with a flask full of cannellini beans simmering in the window, the signpost for true, well-prepared Tuscan cuisine. *Closed Sun.* In the vicinity, a few steps from the Trevi Fountain, one safe option is **Al Presidente**, Via in Arcione 95, © 06 679 7342, offering fish in all manners. **Dal Bolognese**, Piazza del Popolo 1, © 06 361 11426, with tables outside on the grand piazza and a view of the Pincio, is the place to go to sample Emilian specialities—don't miss the tortellini or any other fresh pasta dish, and finish with *fruttini*, a selection of real fruit shells each filled with its own sorbet flavour. *Closed Mon.*

Paris, Piazza San Calisto 7/a, © 06 581 5378, just beyond Piazza Santa Maria in Trastevere, serves classic Roman-Jewish cuisine; particularly good is the *minestra di arzilla* (skate soup). *Closed Sun eve and Mon.* **Antico Arco**, Piazzale Aurelio 7, © 06 581 5274, is well worth the climb up the Monte Gianicolo; it is a reliable, informal restaurant for no-nonsense creative Italian cuisine. *Closed Mon. Reserve.*

The quarters just outside the Aurelian Wall and north and east of the Villa Borghese are more good places to look for restaurants. **Le Coppedè**, Via Taro 28/a, between Via Nomentana and Villa Ada, © 06 841 1772, is a neighbourhood restaurant totally devoted to Pugliese cuisine, which is lighter than typical Roman fare. **Semidivino**, Via Alessandria 230, © 06 4425 0795, is a classy and intimate wine bar—also good for a first-rate meal based on excellent salads, an interesting selection of cheese and pork-cured meat and comforting soups at reasonable prices. *Closed Sat lunch and Sun.*

cheap

Cheaper places are not hard to find in the *centro storico*, although chances to eat anything different from Roman cuisine are pretty low. One exception is the **Roman Lounge de l'Hotel d'Inghilterra**, Via Bocca di Leone 14, © 06 699 81500, an elegant retreat in the heart of the shopping district at the foot of the Spanish Steps, which at lunchtime offers an interesting *piatto unico* (one-dish menu) for *L35,000*; if you like their style you can return for a very expensive dinner.

The **Grappolo d'Oro**, Piazza della Cancelleria 80, © 06 686 4118, near Campo de' Fiori, offers exceptionally good-value traditional Roman cooking. *Closed Sun.* **Il Collegio**, Via Pie' di Marmo 36, © 06 679 2570, not far from the Pantheon, has tables outside and a few Roman first courses along with more imaginative dishes and a good chocolate soufflé. *Closed Sat lunch and Sun.* Nearby, **Armando al Pantheon**, Salita de' Crescenzi 31, © 06 6880 3034, is an authentic Roman trattoria famous for spaghetti *cacio e pepe* (with pecorino cheese and black pepper) or *all'amatriciana*, *saltimbocca*, and a delicious ricotta tart. *Closed Sat eve and Sun.*

In Trastevere there's a small family trattoria, **Da Lucia**, Vicolo del Mattonato, © 06 580 3601, two streets north of Piazza Santa Maria, that offers local cooking in a typical setting. If you are near the Vatican, an area of forgettable tourist restaurants, venture a little way north to the **Antico Falcone**, Via Trionfale 60, ✆ 06 3974 3385, a simple place housed in what's left of a 15th-century farmhouse, for tasty *rigatoni alla nasona* (pasta with melted cheese and tomato sauce), *melanzane* (aubergines) *alla parmigiana* and, in season, *carciofi alla giudia. Closed Tues.* An excellent budget trattoria in the centre is **Gino in Vicolo Rosini**, Vicolo Rosini 4, off Piazza del Parlamento, ✆ 06 687 3434, near the parliament, and often crammed with civil servants and the occasional deputy. *Closed Sun.*

If the thought of a full meal sandwiched between Roman antiquities and Baroque treasures seems a bit much, consider lunch in a wine bar, which offer good selections of cured meat and cheese, soups, salads and occasional quiches and flans, and desserts (usually) made in house. Choose from about 20 wines *in mescita* (by the glass) and hundreds by the bottle: **Trimani Winebar**, Via Cernaia 37/b, not far from Termini, ✆ 06 446 9661 (*closed Sun*); **La Bottega del Vino di Anacleto Bleve**, Via Santa Maria del Pianto 9/11, in the ghetto, ✆ 06 686 5970 (*closed Sun, open for lunch only Mon, Tues and Sat, open for lunch and dinner Wed–Fri*); **Cavour 313**, Via Cavour 313, ✆ 06 678 5496 (*closed Sun in summer, Sat eve the rest of the year*).

Among the vast array of unexciting restaurants that cram the streets around Termini there are also several African places. **Africa**, Via Gaeta 46, ✆ 06 494 1077, is an Ethiopian/Eritrean restaurant that offers spicy meals at very low prices. *Open for breakfast; closed Mon.* Also try the student area of San Lorenzo, east of the station, where there is a much better assortment of trattorias. **Tram Tram**, Via dei Reti 44, ✆ 06 446 3635, is crowded and trendy. *Closed Mon.* There are also lots of pizzerias; try **Formula 1**, Via degli Equi 13. *Closed Sun; open eves only.*

pizzerias

Roman pizza is crisp and thin, although the softer, thicker Neapolitan-style pizza has recently won a fat slice of the market. Most pizzerias have tables outside and are open only for dinner, often until 2am. **Da Baffetto**, Via del Governo Vecchio 11, ✆ 06 686 1617, is a beloved institution not far from Piazza Navona, or try the large, crowded **Ivo**, Via San Francesco a Ripa 158, in Trastevere, ✆ 06 581 7082. *Closed Tues.*

Panattoni, Viale Trastevere 53, ✆ 06 580 0919, is perhaps the best place to see *pizzaioli* at work. *Closed Wed.* Nearby **Dar Poeta**, Vicolo del Bologna 45, ✆ 06 588 0516, is more on the verge of Neapolitan pizza, and perhaps the only one in town with a pizza dessert, *calzone di ricotta* (filled with ricotta and chocolate) and a non-smoking room. *Closed Mon.*

For strictly Neapolitan pizza, head to the pricy **Al Forno della Soffitta**, Via dei Villini 1/e, off the Via Nomentana, ✆ 06 440 4692, where they also have delicious pastry delivered daily from Naples. *Closed Sun.*

The best entertainment in Rome is often in the passing cosmopolitan spectacle of its streets; as nightlife goes, it can be a real snoozer compared with other European cities, though if you don't expect too much you'll have a good time. Like all Italians, many Romans have most of their fun with their families and a close-knit circle of friends, and teenagers will spend hours simply hanging out in or outside bars, before heading off to a club or back home. The back-streets around Piazza Navona or Campo de' Fiori swarm with people in the evenings; these are the places to come to plan your night ahead, as leaflets and free tickets are always being handed out. Often these are to new places that have opened, offering a long-awaited alternative to the ultra-chic posturing in the 'in' spots of the hour. Another source is *Romac'e'* (from news-stands), with comprehensive listings and a small section in English, or the weekly *Time Out*, with listings and articles (in Italian).

Rome can be uncomfortably sticky in August, but there's plenty going on. The *Estate Romana* (Roman Summer) is a three-month long festival of outdoor events, music, theatre and film (shown on outdoor screens around the city), and most museums run longer hours. Ask at the tourist office for information, check *Romac'e'*, and keep an eye out for posters.

A far older Roman party is the traditional **Festa de' Noantri** in Trastevere (16–31 July), where you may find a gust of old Roman spontaneity along with music from across the spectrum, acrobats, dancing and stall upon stall extending down Viale Trastevere and into the piazzas.

special exhibitions for the Jubilee

Museo Nazionale di Palazzo Venezia: *Pilgrims and Jubilees in the Middle Ages—the Medieval Pilgrimage to the Tomb of St Peter 350–1350*; pilgrimage as a meeting of diverse peoples and cultures (*21 Oct 1999–26 Feb 2000*).

Museo Nazionale di Palazzo Venezia: *Anno 1300: The First Jubilee*; Roman art in the late 13th century, including Giotto, Arnolfo di Cambio and Pietro Cavallini; related exhibitions to take place in various towns of Lazio (*26 Mar–10 July 2000*).

Biblioteca Vallicelliana: *'To Open and Close the Holy Door...' Jubilees, Rome, Popes and Pilgrims*; documents and devotional literature relating to Jubilees (*throughout the year*).

Villa Medici/Académie Française de Rome: *Dreams of a Cardinal: the collections of Ferdinando de' Medici*; the collections of one of the great patrons of the 1500s, displayed in the newly restored Villa Medici, one of the grand palaces of Rome that few people ever get to see (*Nov 1999–Mar 2000*)

Site to be announced: *Women of the Jubilee*; account of famous women pilgrims, including Queen Christina of Sweden, Lucrezia Borgia and others (*Mar 2000*).

Centre for Contemporary Art (a new museum in the former Montello Barracks): *Contemporary Artists for the Millennium*; works of 20 Italian and 20 foreign artists commissioned for the millennium (*Mar 2000*).

Sant'Andrea al Quirinale—Pontificia Università Gregoriana: *The Road and the Holy City: Music and Art in an Interfaith Dialogue*; exhibits and concerts on the theme of pilgrimage in Christianity, Islam, Buddhism, Judaism and Hinduism (*throughout the year*).

Crypt of the Basilica of Santa Maria Maggiore: *Christiana Loca*; art and objects related to the growth of early Christianity in Rome (*April 2000*).

Museo Nazionale di Castel Sant'Angelo: *God: An Idea, A History*; films, sacred music and multimedia on the theme of the sacred (*May–July 2000*).

Palazzo delle Esposizioni: *The Light of the Spirit in 20th-Century Art*; the concept of the sacred in modern art, from Matisse and Picasso through Brancusi to the artists of today (*dates to be announced*).

Palazzo delle Esposizioni: *Roma Christiana*; art and architecture demonstrating the transition of Rome to Christianity in the 3rd–6th centuries; also tours of sites (*Oct 2000*).

Museo delle Arti e Tradizioni Popolari: *Sanctuaries and Cult Centres of Lazio*; including exhibits in architectural sites throughout Lazio (*dates to be announced*).

opera, classical music, theatre and film

If you want to go to any events or concerts in Rome, try to get tickets as soon as possible to avoid disappointment. **Orbis**, Piazza Esquilino 37, ✆ 06 474 4776, is a reliable concert and theatre ticket agency (*open Mon–Sat 9.30–1 and 4–7.30*).

From November until May you can take in a performance at the **Teatro dell'Opera di Roma**, Via Firenze 72 (box office, ✆ 06 4816 0255; information, ✆ 06 481 601). Other concerts are performed at and by the **Accademia Nazionale di Santa Cecilia**, in the auditorium on Via della Conciliazione 4 (box office, ✆ 06 6880 1044; information, ✆ 06 361 1064), and by the **Accademia Filarmonica** at the **Teatro Olimpico**, Piazza Gentile da Fabriano 17 (box office, ✆ 06 323 4936; information, ✆ 06 323 4890). Medieval, Baroque, chamber and choral music are frequently performed at the **Oratorio del Gonfalone**, Via del Gonfalone 32/a, ✆ 06 687 5952.

The long-awaited opening of the **Città della Musica** (City of Music), Rome's new music hall, will be inaugurated with a concert on New Year's Day 2000. 34 programmes of symphonic music are planned for a total of 87 concerts. The season will cover major symphonic and choral works of religious music from the 18th century to the present. Throughout the year, concerts will be held in many of Rome's churches. Check with the tourist information office or *Romac'e'* for details.

The Italians tend to dub foreign films, but you can find films in *versione originale* at the **Alcazar**, Via Cardinal Merry del Val 14 (*Mon*); **Nuovo Sacher**, Largo

Ascianghi 1 (*Mon and Tues*); **Majestic**, Via SS. Apostoli 20 (*Tues*); and **Pasquino**, on Piazza Sant'Egidio, near Santa Maria in Trastevere, ✆ 06 580 3622 (*daily*).

cafés and bars

When you're tired of window-shopping you can rest your legs at Rome's oldest café (1760), the **Antico Caffé Greco**, Via Condotti 86, and sit where Keats and Casanova sipped their java—an institution that offers the cheapest chance for a 20-minute dose of *ancien régime* luxury in Rome.

Another of the city's *grand cafés* is the **Caffé Rosati**, in Piazza del Popolo, an elegant place founded in 1922, and popular with the Roman intelligentsia, no doubt attracted by its extravagant ice-creams. The 150-year-old **Babington's Tea Rooms**, on Piazza di Spagna, is the place for scones and tea or a full lunch in the proper Victorian atmosphere. Trendy **Sant'Eustachio**, Piazza Sant'Eustachio, near Piazza Navona, serves Rome's most famous coffee.

Another kind of Roman bar is represented by the ultra-hip **Bar della Pace**, Via della Pace 3, frequented by celebrities and a place for serious posing. A more funky and friendly atmosphere can be found most evenings at **La Vineria**, Campo de' Fiori 15, a relaxed traditional wine bar/shop with tables outside.

It's not hard to find *gelato* on every corner in Rome, but hold out for the best the city has to offer, at the celebrated **Il Gelato di San Crispino**, Via della Panetteria 42, near the Trevi Fountain. Another novelty are sweets from **Il Forno del Ghetto** (*closed Sat*), the Jewish bakery at the west end of Via del Portico d'Ottavia (note the incredible building—covered in reliefs and inscriptions).

rock, jazz and clubs

Rome has a select band of clubs with live music—*Romac'e'* will have details of current programmes at the **folk**-oriented Folkstudio, Via Frangipane 42, ✆ 06 487 1063; the mainly-**rock** venues such as Big Mama, Vicolo San Francesco a Ripa 18, in Trastevere, ✆ 06 581 2551; a **blues** club, Alpheus, Via del Commercio 36–38, in Ostiense, ✆ 06 574 9826; and Palladium, Piazza B. Romano 8, in Garbatella, ✆ 06 511 0203 (well outside the usual tourist round).

Also for **jazz**—which has a strong local following—there are venues like Alexanderplatz, Via Ostia 9, in Prati, ✆ 06 3974 2971, and the New Mississippi Jazz Club, Borgo Angelico 18/a, near San Pietro, ✆ 06 6880 6348. All feature foreign as well as Italian performers.

For serious **dancing** try Alien, Via Velletri 13, near Piazza Fiume, ✆ 06 841 2212, Alpheus, Via del Commercio 36, off Via Ostiense, ✆ 06 574 7826, or the less juvenile (jacket required) Gilda, Via Mario de' Fiori 97, close to the Spanish Steps, ✆ 06 678 4838. All are what Italians call *di tendenza*, meaning they keep up with current UK and US trends. Most indoor clubs and music venues close down completely in late-July and August. This is the time, though, when **beach discos** along the coast at Ostia, Fregene and points further afield are hugely popular.

Shopping

Rome isn't as exciting for big-game shoppers as Milan, though when it comes to clothing you will find all the major designers and labels well represented. There is no shortage of shops selling **antiques,** a great number of them clustered together between the Tiber and Piazza Navona; look especially off Via Monserrato, Via dei Coronari and Via dell'Anima. For **old prints,** generally inexpensive, try Casali, Piazza Rotonda 81/a; Alinari, Via Alibert 16/a is a good address for artistic **black and white pictures** of old Rome. **L'Art Nouveau,** Via dei Coronari 221, offers just what its name implies. **Antiques** also show up in the celebrated Sunday morning flea market at Porta Portese, as well as anything else you can imagine, all lumped together in often surreal displays (*open just after dawn–around 12 noon*). Beware the pickpockets.

The most **fashionable shopping** is on the streets between Piazza di Spagna and the Corso. Some special items: Massoni, Largo Goldoni 48, near Via Condotti, much frequented by film stars, sells some of Rome's finest **jewellery;** for **menswear,** Testa, Via Borgognona 13, and Via Frattina 42, or Valentino Uomo, Via Condotti 13, or for **custom tailoring,** Battistoni, Via Condotti 61/a. For **women's clothes** try the outlets of the big designers in the same area: Missoni, Via del Babuino 96, Giorgio Armani, Via Condotti 77, and Via del Babuino 102, Mila Schöen, Via Condotti 51, or the Rome-based Fendi, Via Borgognona nos.8, 10, 12 and 39. For **leather,** the Gucci outlet is at Via Condotti 8, and do not miss Fausto Santini, Via Frattina 120.

Discounted designer fashion may be had at Il Discount dell'Alta Moda, Via Gesù e Maria 16/a; for **high-fashion shoes,** try Barrilà, Via Condotti 29, and Via del Babuino 33; and for **Borsalino hats,** Troncarelli, Via della Cuccagna 15, near Piazza Navona.

For a special bottle of **wine,** try Enoteca Costantini, Piazza Cavour 16, for a wide selection. If you wish to stock up on Italian **coffee,** Tazza d'Oro, Via degli Orfani 84, has special bags of the city's best, the 'Aroma di Roma'. If you need a good **book,** try the Anglo-American Book Co., Via della Vite 57, the Lion Bookshop, Via dei Greci 36, or the Economy Book Center, Via Torino 136, near Via Nazionale.

For an amazing selection of **fancy kitchen gear,** there's C.U.C.I.N.A., Via del Babuino 118/a, while for serious, **professional pans, pots and tools** head to Zucchi, Via Sant'Antonio all'Esquilino 15, near Santa Maria Maggiore. Try Image, Via della Scrofa 67, for **alternative posters, postcards and photographs**; and De Ritis, Via de' Cestari 1, for the latest **ecclesiastical fashions,** along with Madonnas, crucifixes and chalices.

Padua

Although only half an hour from Venice, Padua (Padova) has always refused to be overshadowed by Lagoon land and can rightly claim its own place among Italy's most interesting and historic cities. Nicknamed *La Dotta*, 'The Learned', it is the brain of the Veneto, once home of the great Roman historian Livy and, since 1221, to one of Europe's most celebrated universities, which counts Petrarch, Dante and Galileo among its alumni.

Padua's churches, under the brushes of Giotto, Guariento, Altichiero, Giusto de' Menabuoi and Mantegna, were virtually laboratories in the evolution of fresco. But what Padua attracts most of all is pilgrims; it is the last resting place of St Anthony, and his exotic, seven-domed mosque of a basilica is the city's most striking landmark.

History

According to Virgil, ancient Patavium was founded in 1185 BC by Antenor, a hero of the Trojan War, giving it a pedigree nearly as hallowed as Rome's. Unfortunately the archaeological record won't have it: Patavium was a simple Paleoveneto village on a branch of the Brenta River until the 4th century BC, when it became one of the Veneti's capitals. It sided with Rome against the Gauls in 45 BC, and grew into a prosperous Roman *municipium*. In 602 the Lombards burned it to the ground.

From the rubble Padua rose, a slow phoenix, to become an important *comune* by the 12th century. In the 13th century, it hosted one of the best characters of the day, St Anthony, and one of the worst, Ezzelino III da Romano, who robbed Padua of its independence while bleeding it dry. In 1259 local *signori*, most importantly the Da Carrara, picked up where Ezzelino left off and fought over the pieces, then lost the city to the Scaligers of Verona in 1328. Doge Francesco Dandolo (after a deal reportedly made *under* his dining table) returned it to the Da Carrara in 1337, and as a bonus admitted them into Venice's Golden Book.

For all the troubles, the 13th and 14th centuries were a golden age for Padua, in art, architecture and technology; it was the time of the famous Latin lecturer Vergerius, who made the university and Padua itself one of the earliest centres of Latin letters, and Giovanni Dondi (1320–89), who built Europe's first astronomical clocks (and whose descendants, after six centuries, still live just north of the cathedral).

The Da Carrara, however, had ambitions beyond an entry in the *Libro d'Oro*. Francesco da Carrara allied himself with the King of Hungary and raised himself against Venice; in 1373 the Paduans proudly hung the banner of St Mark as a war trophy in the Basilica of Sant'Antonio. After three more decades of the usual betrayals, scheming and conspiring on both sides, Venice besieged Padua, then raging with plague, in 1405; the last of the Da

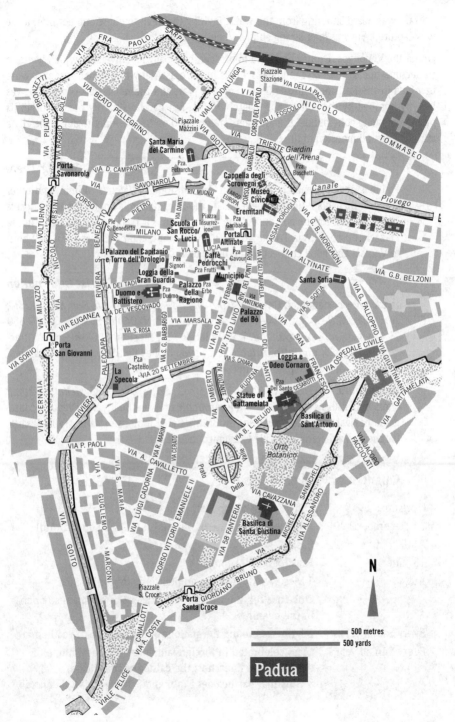

Padua

500 metres
500 yards

N

Carrara was heard shouting from the walls, inviting the devil to come and get him, as he was captured. He was later strangled in a Venetian prison.

Under the Venetians, Padua continued to prosper, especially its university, which went on to become one of the chief medical schools in Europe. Many of Padua's students were involved in the Resistance in the Second World War, and the north part of the city was heavily bombed by the Americans (March 1944). But Padua is hardly one to forget its past—even long-gone buildings and streets are outlined on the pavement, giving the city a curious fourth dimension of time.

Getting There

Padua is easily reached by **train** from Venice (40min), Vicenza (45min) and other cities on the Milan–Venice line. Outside the train station, a booth dispenses tickets and directions for the city buses. The **bus station** is a 10-minute walk away in the Piazzale Boschetti, Via Trieste 40, ✆ 049 820 6844, and has buses every half-hour to Venice, and good connections to other towns in the area.

Tourist Information

In the railway station, ✆ 049 875 2077 (*open Mon–Sat 9–7.30, Sun 8.30–12.30; Nov–Mar 9.20–5.45, Sun 9–12*); Riviera Mugnai 8, ✆ 049 875 0655, ✆ 049 650 794, e-mail *apt@padovanet.it*. If you plan to visit most or all of the main attractions in Padua, a ***biglietto unico*** will save you money on admissions; you can buy it from any one of the participating sites.

Delta Tours, Via Toscana 2, ✆ 049 870 0232, ✆ 049 976 0833, *deltatour@tin.it* offers mini-cruises on *La Padovanella* around Padua on the River Piovego, recently made navigable again. They also run Brenta Canal tours, stopping at Villa Pisana, Barchessa Valmarana and Villa Gradenigo in Oriago.

✠ Calendar of Jubilee Events

Christmas 1999	Official start of the Holy Year
31 December 1999	All-night vigil in the Basilica (also in Assisi and Loreto)
April	Easter
13 June	Feast of Sant'Antonio
Aug	Twice weekly evening guided tours in the Basilica.
	Once a week the cloister and Museo Antoniano also open in the evening
Every Sat all year	Pilgrimage around the stations of the cross in the cathedral
Every Sun all year	Mass celebrated in foreign languages at 11am in one of the following churches: the cathedral, Basilica di S Giustina, Basilica del Santo and Santuario di S. Leopoldo

St Anthony: the Hammer of Heretics, and Much Much More

The sea obeys and fetters break
And lifeless limbs thou dost restore
While treasures lost are found again
When young or old thine aid implore.

13th-century Responsory of St Anthony

One of the busiest and most beloved of heavenly intercessors, Patron Saint of the Poor and a Doctor of the Church, Anthony of Padua was born in Portugal in 1195 (making him 13 years younger than St Francis). The son of a prominent family, he was baptised with the name Fernando Bulhom, and joined the Augustinians in Lisbon at the age of 15. Two years later he was sent to the monastery at Coimbra, where he studied theology for nine years.

In 1221 a band of Franciscan friars arrived in Portugal with the bodies of five of their comrades martyred in Morocco. This made a tremendous impression on the young monk; he at once went to the Franciscans and offered to join up if they would send him to Africa to evangelize and earn a martyr's crown. They accepted him, gave him the name Anthony and, as promised, took him back to Africa with them.

His dreams of martyrdom, however, were never to be. Anthony fell ill almost immediately and was sent home, although he never made it; his ship was blown wildly off course and wrecked on the coast of Sicily. He eventually found his way north to Padua, where he hoped to live a life of quiet contemplation. But his fate was in other hands, and took him to an ordination of Dominican and Franciscan priests in Forlì (although whether or not he himself was ordained as well is unclear). As the new priests dined together, it was suggested that someone give a sermon. Everyone turned shy and ducked, until Anthony, whom everyone presumed was uneducated, was coaxed into saying a few simple words. He began humbly enough, but as he spoke, his voice took on such tremendous power that the friars were convinced that the Holy Spirit had inspired his words.

Now revealed as a talented and well-educated preacher, Anthony was encouraged to abandon his hermit's existence. He became celebrated, not only for his words and conviction, but for practising what he preached. Not everyone was impressed; one day, when his listeners walked away bored, he preached to the fish in the river, who poked their heads out to hear his words. People, according to the chronicles, paid more attention after that.

Anthony travelled extensively to the towns of Northern Italy and France where the Albigensian heresy was the strongest; rather than condemning the heretics, he preached persuasively about Christian goodness, gentleness and justice. He was so successful in bringing the stray sheep back to the fold that he became known as 'the Hammer of Heretics', although 'Coaxer' might seem more apt. His miracles multiplied. To convince one doubter who challenged him, he had a mule kneel down before the Sacrament. He reattached a foot severed from a leg, and on a couple of occasions was even said to bring the dead back to life. Once when someone absconded with his favourite psalter, Anthony prayed that he would find the book again, and the thief at once brought it back. To this day he is famous for finding things; devotees who feel close to him often pray: 'Tony, Tony, turn around. Something's lost and must be found.'

Although at first cautious about his highly educated follower, fearing the pride of the sophisticated theologian, St Francis asked Anthony in 1224 to travel to his communities to instruct his friars in the gospel 'provided that in such studies they do not destroy the spirit of holy prayer and devotedness, as contained in the Rule'. He became the first Franciscan teacher, and chief superior of the order in Northern Italy. He met Pope Gregory IX in 1228 and preached, memorably; it was 'as if the miracle of the Pentecost was repeated.'

Back in Padua in 1230, the saint preached his last and most famous Lenten sermons. The crowds were so great—as many as 30,000 would show up to hear him—that Anthony would preach in the piazzas or the open fields, or even from the boughs of a walnut tree. A bodyguard was required to protect him from the people who wanted to snip or tear off a piece of his habit as a holy relic. He spent days fasting and hearing confessions, and died, exhausted, on June 13 1231. He was only 36.

Anthony was buried in a small Franciscan chapel, where his tomb at once became a centre of pilgrimages and miracles. The bishop of Padua petitioned the Holy See to canonize him, and it happened on May 30 1232—an ecclesiastical speed record, which soon led to his nickname: in Padua Anthony isn't merely *a* saint, he is *The* Saint, Il Santo.

Basilica di Sant'Antonio

Open daily 6.30am–7pm.

Within a year of St Anthony's death, a suitably unique basilica to shelter his remains was begun, according to legend, on a design by a friar who accompanied St Francis to Egypt. For pure fantasy it is comparable only to St Mark's in Venice: a cluster of seven domes around a lofty, conical cupola, two octagonal *campanili* and two smaller minarets— perhaps not what a monk vowed to poverty might have ordered, but certainly a sign of the esteem in which his devotees held and continue to hold him. In an average year 341,810 masses are celebrated in the basilica, with many more expected for the Millennium; even the 50 priests on duty are often hard pressed to keep up with demand to hear confessions.

Inside pilgrims queue patiently in the **Cappella del Santo** to pray, press a palm against his tomb and study the massive array of votive testimonials and photos. With all of the activity surrounding the tomb, no one pays much attention to the 16th-century marble reliefs lining St Anthony's chapel, although they are exquisite works of the Venetian Renaissance: the fourth and fifth are by Sansovino, the sixth and seventh by Tullio Lombardo, and the last by

Antonio Lombardo. Behind the saint's chapel, the **Cappella di Conti** has richly coloured frescoes on the life of SS. Philip and James by Florentine Giusto de'Menabuoi (1382).

The **high altar**, unfortunately dismantled and rearranged over the centuries, is mostly the work of Donatello (1443–50), crowned by his stone *Deposition*, over bronze statues of the Madonna and six patron saints of Padua and dramatic reliefs of the miracles of St Anthony below, each intricately crowded with figures in architectural perspectives that were to be a strong influence on Mantegna. The bronze **Paschal Candelabrum** (1519) is the masterpiece of Il Riccio, who spent nine years on the project; although it was designed for Easter, Christianity takes a backseat to the myriad satyrs, nymphs and other mythological creatures in relief, immersed in imaginative decorative motifs. Earlier in his career, Il Riccio helped his master Belluno (one of Donatello's assistants) cast the 12 **bronze reliefs of Old Testament scenes** on the choir walls. Behind the high altar, in the ambulatory, don't miss the **treasury** where one of a hundred glittering gold reliquaries holds St Anthony's tongue and larynx, found perfectly intact when his tomb was opened in 1981, on the 750th anniversary of his death. In the right transept, the **Cappella di San Felice** contains more beautiful frescoes and a remarkable *Crucifixion*, painted in the 1380s by Altichiero, the leading Giottoesque artist of the day.

The basilica complex, big enough to require its own information office, includes several other exhibitions in its cloisters, including one sponsored by the century-old magazine, the *St Anthony Messenger* which appears in a dozen languages (on-line in English at *www.americancatholic.org/messenger*). There's a free audio-visual (in Italian) on the saint's life, while the **Museo Antoniano** (*open 9–1 and 2–5; closed Mon; adm*) contains art made for the basilica over the centuries, including a lunette frescoed by Mantegna and a delightful 15th-century German reliquary in the shape of a ship.

Sharing the large piazza in front of the basilica, a bit lost among the pigeons and exuberant souvenir stands, is one of the key works of the Renaissance, Donatello's **Statue of Gattamelata** (1453), the first large equestrian bronze since antiquity and Padua's answer to Rome's Marcus Aurelius. The cool 'Honeyed Cat' was a *condottiere* who served Venice so well and honestly that the republic, in a rare moment of generosity, paid for this monument, which Donatello infused with a serene humanistic spirit, in marked contrast to Verrocchio's Colleoni statue in Venice. As a yardstick of taste, it is interesting to note that only 50 years after its completion the horse was being criticized for its too realistic detail.

Flanking the piazza opposite Gattamelata, the **Oratorio di San Giorgio** (*closed for restoration*) was built in 1377, and beautifully frescoed by one of the leading heirs of Giotto, Altichiero of Verona, with help from Jacopo Avanzi. Until it reopens you can, however, visit the adjacent **Scuoletta del Santo**, an old confraternity with paintings on the *Life of St Anthony* by a variety of artists, some of which are winningly absurd; four, certainly not the best, are attributed to a teenage Titian (*open summer 9–1 and 2.30–6.30; winter 10–1 and 2–5; closed Mon; adm*).

Behind the basilica, on Via Cesarotti, the **Loggia and Odeo Cornaro** (1524 and 1530) are two Renaissance gems designed by Giovanni Maria Falconetto of Verona, whose refined use of ancient architectural orders exerted a major influence on Palladio. Built in the gardens of the humanist Alvise Cornaro, the Odeo was used for concerts and is decorated inside with exquisite stuccoes, while the Loggia saw performances of the plays of Ruzante (Angelo Beolco; *c.* 1496–1542), the Paduan dramatist who invented and played the role of Ruzante, 'the Joker', a satirically-minded peasant faced with one catastrophe after another; some of his works prefigure the *commedia dell'arte*.

Around the City

Cappella degli Scrovegni and the Museo Civico Eremitani

Open 9–6, until 7 in summer, closed Mon; same ticket, adm exp.

Padua's artistic gem is Giotto's extraordinary, recently restored series of frescoes in the Cappella degli Scrovegni (or *Madonna dell'Arena*), a pearl sheltered by the crusty shell of Padua's Roman amphitheatre. It is lucky to be there; bombs shattered the surrounding neighbourhood in the last war. In another close call, the Paduans, in a 19th-century fit of 'progress', knocked down the Palazzo Scrovegni and were about to demolish the chapel too, until an opportune campaign by *The Times* of London saved Giotto's masterpiece.

Cappella degli Scrovegni

1   St Joachim chased from the temple
2   St Joachim takes refuge among the shepherds
3   The angel appears to St Anne and informs her of her imminent motherhood
4   The angel appears to St Joachim and tells him his prayer will be answered
5   St Joachim's dream
6   The meeting of SS Joachim and Anne by Jerusalem's Golden Gate
7   The birth of Mary
8   The Presentation of Mary at the Temple
9   Handing over the rod to St Simeone
10 The prayer for the blossoming of the rods
11 The wedding of Mary and Joseph
12 The Wedding Procession
13 God giving the Archangel Gabriel his orders
14 The Annunciation
15 The Visitation
16 The Nativity
17 The Adoration of the Magi

18 Presentation of Jesus at the Temple
19 The Flight into Egypt
20 The Massacre of the Innocents
21 Jesus among the Doctors of the Temple
22 The Baptism of Jesus
23 The Marriage at Cana

24 The Resurrection of Lazarus
25 The Entry of Jesus into Jerusalem
26 Chasing the Merchants from the Temple
27 Judas receiving the Thirty Pieces of Silver
28 The Last Supper
29 The Washing of the Feet

30 The Kiss of Judas
31 Jesus before Caiaphas
32 Jesus crowned with the Crown of Thorns
33 Calvary
34 The Crucifixion
35 The Deposition
36 The Resurrection
37 The Ascension
38 Pentecost

151

The Cappella degli Scrovegni

We owe the Arena Chapel to Enrico Scrovegni, who built it in 1303 in expiation for the sins of his father, Reginaldo the usurer, who died shrieking for the keys to his safe to keep anyone from touching his money. Fortunately he left enough of his filthy lucre behind for Enrico to build a chapel and commission Giotto, then at the height of his career, to fresco the interior with a New Testament cycle (1304–07), on the lives of the Virgin and her Son. In sheer power and inspiration these frescoes are the medieval equivalent of the Sistine Chapel, as revolutionary for the 14th century as Michelangelo's would be for the 16th. Giotto's fresh, natural narrative composition, solidly anchoring three-dimensional figures in their setting, derives its power not from divine trappings but sheer moral authority; his gift of portraying meaning and emotion in a glance or gesture conveys the story directly to the heart.

Giotto's sons worked at his side and, like their father, were remarkably ugly. Their fellow Florentine Dante visited them while they worked, and couldn't help asking Giotto, 'How is it that you make painted figures so well, and real ones so badly?' Giotto returned at once, 'Because I make the former by day and the latter by night.' Dante laughed and, as a compliment to the artist, placed Reginaldo in the seventh ring of the *Inferno* (Canto XVII). Giotto, however, had no doubt where he was going; you'll find him fourth from the left in the front row of the elect in the powerful *Last Judgement* on the west wall. A delegation from heaven accepts Enrico's offering of the chapel, while on the far left a singularly harrowing pre-Dantesque Inferno is ruled by a big blue Satan munching and excreting sinners. Along the bottom of the frescoes note the monochrome *Vices and Virtues,* painted by Giotto in imitation of stone reliefs—history's first *grisailles*—while the frescoes in the apse, depicting the later career of the Virgin, are a slightly later work by Giotto's followers.

Museo Civico

The same ticket gets you into the Museo Civico, installed in the adjacent Augustine convent of the Eremitani, with its noteworthy **archaeological collection**: coins, vases and 14 funerary stelae from the 6th to 1st centuries BC, inscribed in bastard Etruscan. Padua is the only place in northern Italy where such stelae were discovered; apparently the local aristocracy wanted to put on airs by using the Greek alphabet. Other highlights are furnishings from the 8th-century BC tomb, and Roman busts of Augustus and a Silenus.

The **painting section** houses literally acres of art, not always in chronological order, but a gold mine for connoisseurs of lesser-known painters, mingled among the greats— including Giotto, whose *Crucifixion* was designed for the altar of the Cappella degli Scrovegni. In the next rooms are works by his follower Guariento, founder of the Paduan school, who painted the lovely but rather odd series of *Angels,* weighing souls and fighting the devil, each slightly different, as if they were frames from a film. The International Gothic style is represented by Lorenzo Veneziano, Jacopo Bellini (*Christ in Limbo*) and a charming but anonymous *millefleurs* Madonna (1408). The link in Padua from Giotto to the Renaissance was Francesco Squarcione, at least according to old art historians; a rather dry polyptych, one of only two documented works by his hand, is here.

This is followed by a charming *Expedition of the Argonauts* by Lorenzo Costa of Ferrara, and then a number of 16th-century Paduan paintings showing the influence of Andrea Mantegna (including Bartolomeo Veneto's all-dwarfing *Madonna*, and Pietro Paolo Agabiti's *Madonna with SS. Peter and Sebastian*, with the face of a Hollywood starlet— Sebastian, that is). Lombard painters check in with Madonnas by Da Vinci's follower Bernardo Luino and Andrea Previtali. In Italy, a bride brought her trousseau in an ornate wedding chest or *cassione*; Titian as a youth decorated two with mythological scenes, and other works in the room show his later influence. Among the curiosities are three anonymous paintings of the *Influence by the Planets on the Activities of Man*.

In the next rooms you'll find Palma il Giovanni's rather bold *Santa Cristina*; portraits by Padua's leading female artist of the Renaissance, Chiara Varotari (1584–1663); a baroque *David and Goliath* by Pietro Muttoni della Vecchia (David, always so young and dashing in Renaissance paintings, has a grey beard here); and *Portraits of Philosophers* by the prolific Luca Giordano of Naples—his *Job* may be the best portrayal of a bad smell in Italian painting. In the 1600s the nobility in the Veneto began to collect genre scenes and landscapes, bringing in artists from around Europe to cash in: especially represented here are Eismann and Philip Peter Roos, and the local painters they inspired, such as Antonio Marini of Venice, who specialized in battle scenes.

After these, the museum changes gear and returns to the 16th century with paintings by Domenico Campagnolo and Giampiero Silvio, both of whom worked in Padua, luminous Dutch paintings, and an enormous and fantastically detailed Brussels tapestry of *David Ordering Joab to Attack the Ammonites*. Il Romanino of Brescia weighs in with his masterpiece, a huge altarpiece of the *Virgin and Saints* (originally in Santa Giustina), as well as a *Last Supper*, with Judas clutching his money under the table. Other paintings to look for: Tintoretto's *Crucifixion* (with a battle in the background); *Dinner at the House of Simon*; the *Martyrdom of SS. Primo and Feliciano* and a small *Crucifixion* against a black sky by Veronese; and works by 17th-century painter Il Padovinino (Alessandro Varotari) and his followers Pietro della Vecchia, Giulio Carpioni and Francesco Maffei. A portrait of Elena Lucrezia Cornaro Piscopia, painted in 1678 to honour her doctorate from Padua University, shares a room with what must be the campest portrait in all Italy: the 17th-century *Venetian Captain* by Sebastiano Mazzoni, matched only by its frame, carved with cupids, lions and a giant artichoke.

From the same century but from another world are the 'realist' works by Matteo di Pittocchi (Matteo of the Beggars); the paintings of tiny people being chased by snails and attacked by crabs by Faustino Bocchi (1659–1741); and the idyllic landscapes by Francesco Aviani (a Venetian proto-hippy, 1662–1715). There are striking 18th-century *trompe l'œil* by a brother and sister team, Pietro and Caterina Leopoldo della Santa, and G.B. Tiepolo's *St Patrick Bishop of Ireland*, in a very non-Irish setting; also genre scenes by Pietro Longhi, and Rosalba Carrara's *Portrait of a Young Priest*.

Some of the finest paintings are part of the **Quadraria Emo Capodilista**, a private collection donated to the museum in 1864 that includes Giorgione's *Leda and the Swan* and *Country Idyll*; Giovanni Bellini's *A Young Senator* and *Christ's Descent From the Cross*, the latter painted with his father Jacopo; and a *Mythological Scene* by Titian. Another donation, the **Museo Bottacin**, has more from the 18th century, and a fabulous coin collection. The *bronzetti* from the 14th–17th centuries that fill the halls were a speciality of Padua, especially those by Andrea Briosco, better known as Il Riccio ('Curly'). His famous *Drinking Satyr* is here, as well as works by Alessandro Vittoria, Niccolò Roccatagliata and a certain Il Moderno, whose name was probably invented by his agent.

The Eremitani, Santa Sofia and the Carmine

Next to the museum, the church of the **Eremitani** (1306; *open Mon–Sat 8.15–12.15 and 4–6, Sun 9.30–12 and 4–6*) lacked the luck of the Cappella Scrovegni and was shattered in an air raid in 1944. What could be salvaged of the frescoes has been painstakingly pieced together—frescoes by Giusto de'Manabuoi and Guariento (his *Story of SS. Augustine, Philip and James* in the second chapel to the right of the altar), and most importantly the magnificent **Ovetari chapel**, begun by Andrea Mantegna in 1454 at the age of 23. Mantegna was a precocious young man: the pupil and adopted son of Squarcione, he took his master/father to court at age 17 for exploiting him. He also found his unique style at an early age, with its remarkable clarity of line and colour and fascination with antiquity—Squarcione had an archaeological collection, but another influence on Mantegna was Padua itself, with its university and Latin letters. Painted 150 years after Giotto, the *Martyrdom of St Christopher and St James* still astonishes, thanks to Mantegna's wizardly use of scientific perspective to foreshorten the action from below and his use of Roman architecture to depict the power of the state—massive, hard, polished and pitiless, populated by remorseless, indifferent men.

Padua's oldest church, the 9th-century **Santa Sofia**, is to the east, at the corner of Via S. Sofia and Via Altinate; much rebuilt in the 11th century, it has a lovely Veneto-Byzantine apse and a precious polychrome *Pietà* (1430) by Egidio da Wienerneustadt. The quarter to the west of the Eremitani, Borgo Molino, was once an 'island' cut off by the Bacchiglione. Its centrepiece, the **Carmine** church, was rebuilt as the headquarters of a confraternity by Lorenzo da Bologna in 1494 . Although it was heavily damaged in the air raids, the shells somehow missed the sacristy and **Scuola del Carmine** (1377), with its interior covered by elegant *cinquecento* frescoes by Domenico Campagnola and Stefano dall'Arzere. Near here, just off Piazza Petrarca, the **Porta di Ponte Molino** and Torre di Ezzelino are leftovers from the 13th-century walls.

To Caffè Pedrocchi and the University

A short walk south from the Eremitani leads into Piazza Garibaldi, site of Padua's oldest surviving gate, **Porta Altinate**, 'captured from Ezzelino da Romano in 1256' as the plaque boasts. The streets all around, however, were torn up in 1926 to create big squares for big buildings flaunting the might of the Corporate State. A whole neighbourhood, Borgo Santa Lucia, was bulldozed to create **Piazza Insurrezione**, sparing the **Scuola di San Rocco** (1525; *open 9.30–12.30 and 3.30–7.30; closed Mon; adm*) which, like the one in Venice, was built by a confraternity focused on plague prevention. Domenico Campagnola and Gualtiero Padovano frescoed it in 1537, although their work seems stale after Tintoretto's fireworks in Venice. Behind the Scuola, the church of **Santa Lucia** was also spared; founded in the 11th century, it has a fine painting of *San Luca* by G.B. Tiepolo on the left of the high altar. Via Santa Lucia still has a number of medieval houses; a remarkable one built over Via Marsilio da Padova is remembered as the **Casa di Ezzelino**.

South of Piazza Garibaldi and around the corner from another new square, **Piazza Cavour**, you'll find a stylish Egyptian-revival mausoleum with columned stone porches at either end. This is, in fact, the **Caffè Pedrocchi**, built in 1831 by Giuseppe Jappelli, and famous in its day for never closing (it couldn't—it had no doors) and for the intellectuals and students who came here to debate the revolutionary politics of Mazzini. When restorations are completed, you should be able to get a coffee again, as well as visit the upper floor (*open Tues–Sun 9.30–12.30 and 3.30–7; adm*). In Jappelli's adjacent neo-Gothic **Pedrocchino** (built to contain the overflow of clients) students turned words into deeds in 1848, clashing with the Austrian police. Look carefully and you can still see the bullet-scars.

At the far end of the complex, the 16th-century **Municipio** (the former Palazzo Comunale) hides behind an uncomfortable façade of 1904. Opposite is the seat of the **University of Padua**, Andrea Moroni's 16th-century **Palazzo del Bo'** ('of the ox', a nickname derived from the sign of a tavern that stood on this site in 1221; *guided tours Mar–Sept Tues and Thurs 9, 10 and 11, Wed, Tues and Fri 3, 4 and 5; adm*). The façade, attributed to Vincenzo Scamozzi, opens up to a handsome 16th-century courtyard. Galileo delivered his lectures on physics from an old wooden pulpit, still intact, and counted among his students Sweden's Gustavus Adolphus, who went on to mastermind the Protestant victories in the Thirty Years War. The golden Great Hall is covered with the armorial devices of its alumni; the steep claustrophobic **Anatomical Theatre** (1594) was the first permanent one anywhere, designed by Fabricius, tutor of William Harvey who went on to discover the circulation of blood—only one of scores of Renaissance Englishmen who earned degrees at Padua's School of Medicine. Other professors included Vesalius, author of the first original work on anatomy since Galen (1555), and Gabriello Fallopio, discoverer of the Fallopian tubes.

Before continuing to the Palazzo del Ragione, duck around the corner of the university to have a look at **Piazza Antenore**, with a pair of sarcophagi for a centrepiece. The one on columns supposedly contains what remains of Antenor, hero of the Trojan War and founder of ancient *Patavium*; the body was discovered in 1274, although modern scholars have had a peek and say Antenor was really a soldier from the 3rd century AD. The great Roman historian Livy was a son of the nearby Euganaen Hills, and the other sarcophagus commemorates his 2000th birthday. Perhaps he'll get something nicer for his 3000th.

The Medieval Civic Centre: Palazzo della Ragione and Piazza dei Signori

Directly behind the Municipio (*see* above), the delightful medieval **Piazza delle Erbe** and **Piazza della Frutta** still host a bustling market every morning, divided by the massive, arcaded **Palazzo della Ragione** (*open 9–6; closed Mon; adm*). Constructed as Padua's law courts in 1218 and then rebuilt in 1306, its upper story, or *Salone*, is one of the largest medieval halls in existence, measuring 260 by 88ft, with an 85ft ceiling like a 'vaulting over a market square', as Goethe described it. Its great hull-shaped roof was rebuilt after a fire in 1756—an earlier blaze, in 1420, destroyed most of the frescoes by Giotto and his assistants, although some *Virtues* by Menabuoi survived. The rest were replaced with over 300 biblical and astrological scenes by Niccolò Miretto—one of the Renaissance's most important glorifications of astrology, which had had its own renaissance in the 13th century under Ezzelino's chief advisor and uncannily accurate astrologer, Guido Bonatto. Many of the later popes had astrologers; Petrarch roundly condemned them. Exhibitions are frequently staged under the eyes of Mars and Jupiter, but two exhibits never change: the **pietra del vituperio**, a cold stone block where the bankrupt had to sit bare-bottomed during three public meetings to absolve their debts, and a giant **wooden horse**, built for a joust in 1466, its fierce glance complemented by testicles the size of bowling balls.

Just to the west, the stately **Piazza dei Signori** saw many a joust in its day, and can boast Italy's oldest astronomical clock, built by Giovanni Dondi in 1344 and still ticking away, set in the tower of the **Palazzo del Capitaniato**. On the left is the fine Renaissance-style **Loggia della Gran Guardia** (or del Consiglio), completed by Giovanni Maria Falconetto in 1523; while behind Dondi's clock you'll find Padua University's Arts Faculty, the **Liviano**, built in 1939 by Gio Ponti. Ponti incorporated the upper floor of the old Da Carrara palace in the Liviano, with its remarkable **Sala dei Giganti** (*open Sept–June Wed only 9.30–12.30 and 3–6*), named after its huge 14th-century frescoes of ancient Romans and repainted by Domenico Campagnola in the 1530s; Altichiero added the more intimate 14th-century portrait of Petrarch sitting at his desk.

The Duomo and Baptistry

Around the corner from the square stands Padua's rather neglected **duomo**, begun in the 12th century, but tampered with throughout the Renaissance—Michelangelo was only one of several cooks who spoiled the broth here before everyone lost interest and left the façade unfinished. The interior is neoclassical and serene, and the most memorable art is new, along the altar, where the smooth white figures of saints and trees melt into the stairs. In the 1370s Giusto de'Menabuoi frescoed the adjacent Romanesque **baptistry** (*open 9.30–1 and 3–6; adm*) with over a hundred scenes; the dome, with its multitude of saints seated in the circles of paradise, is awesome but chilling.

The 15th-century bishop's palace to the left of the cathedral contains the **Pinacoteca dei Canonici** (entrance at Via Dietro Duomo 15), with portraits of the bishops by Bartolomeo Mantagnana and a portrait of Petrarch (probably from life), transferred here from the house he lived in while he served as a canon (*open only by appointment, © 049 662 814*). Stroll down Via del Vescovado, one of Padua's most characteristic porticoed streets; among the palazzi, No.32, the **Casa degli Specchi** (1502), is especially handsome.

Botanical Gardens, Europe's Biggest Square and La Specola

A few streets south of the Piazza del Santo, next to the river, the **Orto Botanico** (*open April–Sept Mon–Sat 9–1 and 3–6; Oct–Mar 9–1; adm*) is one of Europe's oldest botanical gardens, established in 1545; it retains the original layout, and even a few original specimens. At 'Goethe's palm', planted in 1585 and still flourishing, the great poet-scientist formed his Theory of the Ur-plant: that all plants evolved from one universal specimen.

Beyond, 'the largest piazza on the continent', **Prato della Valle**, was a swampy meadow converted into a square with a moat by the city's Venetian *procuratore* Andrea Memmo in 1775 to give Padua a new commercial centre. Today it does service as municipal car park, flea market, amusement park and 'theatre of acting statues' for 79 illustrious men associated with Padua (and one woman, the Renaissance poet Gaspara Stampa, who gets a bust at the foot of Il Riccio). One statue, of Alberto Azzo II, was erected by an outsider—the brother of King George III, in honour of their illustrious ancestor from Este; the tourist office publishes a booklet in English giving the biography of each worthy.

On one side stands the 393ft **Basilica of Santa Giustina**, the 11th-largest church in all Christendom (*open daily 7.30–12 and 3.30–7.30*), designed by Il Riccio with an exotic cluster of domes echoing St Antony's. But the façade is unfinished and the interior still-born baroque: best bits are an altarpiece by Sebastiano Ricci in the second chapel on the left, the large apse painting of the *Martydom of Santa Giustina* (1575) by Veronese and the 16th-century choir stalls. The left transept has a beautiful 14th-century tomb, the *Arca di S. Luca*, with alabaster reliefs made in Pisa. A door in the right transept leads to the original church, the 5th-century **Sacellum di San Prosdocimo**, burial place of Padua's first bishop, with a marble iconostasis; remains of the other previous churches lie beyond the monastery gate.

West of the basilicas, in Piazza Castello, Ezzelino da Romano rebuilt a castle in the medieval walls, now used as Padua's hoosegow. The tallest and oldest bit, the 144ft Torrelunga (1062) has had a rather more dignified career since 1767, when an astronomical observatory, **La Specola**, was added to the roof (*accessible round the back, off Riviera Tiso da Camposampiero; tickets for guided tours sold at Agenzia Next Tour, Via Bomporti 16, © 049 875 4949; tours Tues, Wed and Fri 9pm–11pm*).

Padua's massive and well-preserved Renaissance **walls**, considered impregnable in their day, were designed by Michele Sammicheli and finished in 1544. The few surviving ornate gates, many in white Istrian stone, are perhaps most easily seen from a bike saddle. The best are the **Porta Portello** (1519) to the northeast; the **Porta San Giovanni** and **Porta Savonarola** (1530, by Falconetto) to the west; and **Porta Santa Croce**, to the south.

Padua ✉ *35100*   **Where to Stay**

The ★★★★**Donatello**, Via del Santo 102, © 049 875 0634, ✉ 049 8675 0829 (*expensive*), by the basilica, has been renovated and is air-conditioned. Also in the historic centre, the newer, more comfortable ★★★★**Majestic Toscanelli**, Via dell'Arco 2, © 049 663 244, ✉ 049 876 0025 (*expensive*) has every luxury, and a popular restaurant, specializing in Brazilian dishes. ★★★★**Grande Italia**, Corso del Popolo 81, © 049 876 111, ✉ 049 875 0850 (*expensive*) is in a beautiful Liberty building, conveniently opposite the railway station.

Small and cosy, ★★★**Leon Bianco**, Piazzetta Pedrocchi 12, © 049 875 0814, 🖅 049 875 6184 (*moderate*) is right in the heart of Padua; from its roof terrace, where breakfast is served in summer, you can look down on the Caffè Pedrocchi. Cheaper and near the station, friendly ★★★**Al Cason**, Via Paolo Scarpi 40, © 049 66236, 🖅 049 875 4217 (*moderate*) will make you feel at home, and fill you up with the classics in its restaurant.

★★**Sant'Antonio**, Via S. Fermo 118, © 049 875 1393, 🖅 049 875 2508 (*cheap*), by the Porta Molino, between the station and the centre, has a friendly, family atmosphere. ★**Pavia**, Via del Papafava 11, © 049 661 558 (*cheap*) is deservedly popular, clean, central and friendly. Near the station but on the wrong side of the tracks, ★★**Arcella**, Via J. D'Avanzo 7, © 049 605 581 (*cheap*) has friendly owners and air conditioning; another 10min walk from the station, the homey ★**Junior**, Via L. Faggin 2, © 049 811 756 (*cheap*) has no en suite baths, but easy parking. The city-run **Ostello Città di Padova**, Via Aleardi 30, © 049 875 2219, 🖅 049 654 210 (*cheap*) is large and pleasant; IYHF cards required. To get there take bus nos.3, 8 or 11 from the station to the Prato della Valle. *Open all year.*

Eating Out

La cucina padovana features what the Italians call 'courtyard meats' (*carni di cortile*)—chicken, duck, turkey, pheasant, capons, goose and pigeon. Pork, rabbit and freshwater fish are other favourites. Try one of the various *risotti* for *primo.*

Not far from the historic centre, **Antico Brolo**, Corso Milano 22, © 049 66455 (*expensive; tourist menu L50,000*) occupies an elegant 15th-century building, with a garden for outdoor dining on its Veneto and Emilian specialities; try the chateaubriand with balsamic vinegar. *Closed Mon and Sun lunch, some of Aug.* There's a good pizzeria down in the old wine cellar where you'll spend a lot less.

In the suburb of Torre, 2km from the Padua-Est *autostrada* exit, **Dotto di Campagna**, Via Randaccio, © 049 625 469 (*moderate; tourist menu L38,000*) serves inventive cookery in elegant surroundings; try their famous *risotti* or *pasta fagioli*. *Closed Sun eve, Mon, Aug.* For classic Paduan home cooking, featuring succulent boiled and roast meats, venture outside the city walls to **Da Giovanni**, Via Maroncelli 22, © 049 772 620 (*moderate*) (bus no.9 from the railway station). *Closed Sat lunch, Sun, Aug.*

For 150 years **Bertolini**, Via Antichiero 162, © 049 600 357 (*cheap*), just north of the station, has been a favourite; go for the hearty vegetarian and seasonal dishes and homemade desserts. *Closed Sat.* Just outside Padua's western walls (take Corso Milano from the centre), **Bastioni del Moro**, Via Bronzetti 18, © 049 871 006 (*cheap*) serves up a delicious gnocchi with scallops and porcini mushrooms, indoors or in the summer garden. (*Tourist menu L25,000, although prices soar if you order fish.*) *Closed Sun.*

Where to Stay within Easy Reach of Padua

Lovely **Venice**, only a half hour by train from Padua, hardly needs an introduction. Although famous as the city of St Mark, the Apostle's basilica is only the most spectacular of a string of churches and religious foundations filled with works of art that rank among the finest in Christendom: SS. Giovanni e Paolo, the Scuola di San Rocco, and the Frari head the list.

Vicenza, 'the city of Palladio', is an architectural pilgrimage shrine. Palladio's great basilica in the Piazza dei Signori was the first major work of his career; his other masterpieces include the Palazzo Chiericati, the mathematically perfect Villa La Rotonda, and his swansong, the Teatro Olimpico, one of the most original works of the Italian Renaissance, and the oldest operational indoor theatre in the world (*open April–Oct*). Vicenza's holy hill, Monte Bérico, just to the south of the city, is crowned by a basilica which commemorates two apparitions of the Virgin in 1428.

The gorgeous rosy-pink city of **Verona** has far more to offer than Romeo and Juliet and the Arena (the best-preserved amphitheatre in Italy after the Colosseum, seating 25,000): there are evocative streets and romantic piazzas, sublime art, magnificent architecture, and all the gnocchi you can eat.

Getting Around

The train from Padua to **Venice** takes just 30mins, or you can spend a day travelling down the villa-lined Brenta in a motorized version of the original public canalboat, the ***Burchiello***, or on the simpler craft of ***I Battelli del Brenta*** (*Mar–early Nov from Padua Wed, Fri and Sun; from Venice Tues, Thurs and Sat*). Book the *Burchiello* through Siamic Express, Via Trieste 42, ✆ 049 660 944, ✇ 049 662 830, *siamic@tin.it*; or through any travel agent or CIT office abroad. Book the *Battelli* at Via Pellizzo 1, Padua, ✆ 049 807 4340, ✇ 049 807 2830, *intercity.shiny.i/ battellidelbrenta*.

Landomas, ✆ 049 860 1426, has direct bus connections to Marco Polo (**Venice**) or **Treviso** airports from Padua—they'll pick you up at your door if you book a day in advance. **Verona**'s airport Valerio Catullo, to the southwest at Villafranca, has direct flights to Rome. For information, call ✆ 045 809 5666. Every 20 minutes buses link the airport to Verona's Porta Nuova train station. Verona is on a direct rail line to Padua. **Vicenza** is also on the main rail line to Padua (45mins).

Tourist Information

Venice: Ascensione 71/c, corner of Piazza San Marco, ✆ 041 522 6356. **Verona**: in the side of Palazzo Barbiera, Via Leoncino 61, ✆ 045 806 8680 (next to the Arena), and Porta Nuova railway station, ✆ 045 800 861 (*both open daily; closed Sun in winter*). *veronapt@mbox.vol.it, www.verona-apt.net*. **Vicenza**: Piazza Matteotti, 12; also Piazza Duomo 5, ✆ 0444 320 854, ✇ 0444 325 001.

Dolo (on the Brenta Canal) ✉ 30031

Sleep in an antique bed under the frescoes at the ★★★**Villa Ducale**, Riviera Martiri della Libertà 75, ✆/✉ 041 420 094 (*expensive*), with garden and fountains. **Locanda alla Posta**, Via Cà Tron 33, ✆ 041 410 740 (*expensive*) has been around a long time, and now has a wonderful new chef: great fish, delicately prepared.

Mira (on the Brenta Canal) ✉ 30030

★★★★**Villa Margherita**, Via Nazionale 416, ✆ 041 426 5800, ✉ 041 426 5838 (*expensive*) offers another chance to live like a patrician; some of its charming rooms have terraces, and breakfast is served on the garden patio. The restaurant, **Margherita**, in a Liberty villa down the road, specializes in seafood and is also one of the best in the area. A less elaborate, 17th-century villa, ★★★**Riviera dei Dogi**, Via Don Minzoi 33, ✆ 041 424 466, ✉ 041 424 428 (*expensive–moderate*) has comfortable modernized rooms near the canal. One of the traditional places to round off a Brenta Canal excursion is the lovely poplar-shaded veranda at **Nalin**, Via Nuovissimo 29, ✆ 041 420 083 (*expensive–moderate*), which serves Venetian seafood, finely grilled, and good Veneto wines.

Venice ✉ 30100

One thing to remember is that whatever class of hotel you stay in, expect it to cost around a third more than it would on the mainland, even before the often outrageous charge for breakfast is added to the bill.

★★★★★**Cipriani**, Giudecca 10, ✆ 041 520 7744 (*luxury*) is one of Italy's most luxurious hotels, a villa isolated in a lush garden at one end of the Giudecca, just a few minutes away from Venice by the hotel's 24-hour private launch service. ★★★★★**Danieli**, Riva degli Schiavoni 4196, ✆ 041 522 6480, ✉ 041 520 0208 (*luxury*) is the largest and most famous hotel in Venice, in what must be the most glorious location, overlooking the Lagoon and rubbing shoulders with the Palazzo Ducale. Each room is beautifully adorned with silken walls, Gothic staircases, gilt mirrors and oriental

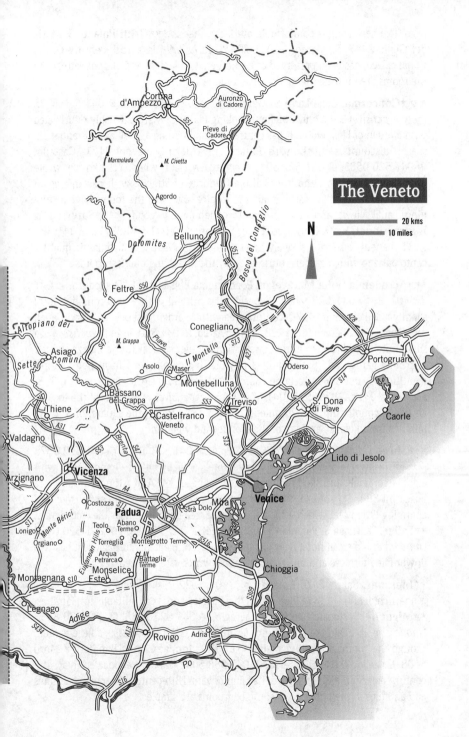

The Veneto

N

20 kms
10 miles

Cortina d'Ampezzo
Auronzo di Cadore
Pieve di Cadore
Marmolada
M. Civetta
Agordo
S51
Dolomites
Belluno
Bosco del Consiglio
S55
Feltre
S50
A27
Altopiano dei
Conegliano
S13
A28
Asiago
Sette Comuni
S47
M. Grappa
Piave
Il Montello
A27
Oderso
Portogruaro
Asolo
Maser
Montebelluna
A4
S14
Thiene
Bassano
del Grappa
S53
Treviso
S. Dona
di Piave
Caorle
Valdagno
A31
Castelfranco
Veneto
Brenta
S47
S13
Lido di Jesolo
Arzignano
S53
Vicenza
Costozza
S11
PADUA
Stra Dolo
Mira
Venice
A4
Lonigo
S11
Monte Bérici
Teolo
Abano Terme
Orgiano
Torreglia
Montegrotto Terme
S516
Euganean Hills
Arqua
Petrarca
Battaglia
Terme
Chioggia
Montagnana
S10
Monselice
Este
Legnago
S434
Adige
A13
Rovigo
Adria
S309
Po
S16

rugs. The new wing is comfortable but lacks charm. ★★★**Gritti Palace**, S. Maria del Giglio 2467, S. Marco, ✆ 041 794 611 (*luxury*), in a 15th-century Grand Canal palace, has been preserved as a true Venetian fantasy and elegant retreat. All the rooms are furnished with Venetian antiques.

★★★★**Concordia**, Calle Larga S. Marco 367, ✆ 041 520 6866, ✇ 041 520 6775 (*very expensive*) is the only hotel overlooking Piazza S. Marco. Swishly refurbished with a touch of Hollywood, it has central air-conditioning as well as substantial off-season discounts. ★★★★**Londra Palace**, Riva degli Schiavoni 4171, Castello, ✆ 041 520 0533, ✇ 041 522 5032 (*very expensive*) is where Tchaikovsky wrote his *Fourth Symphony*, and it was also a favourite of Stravinsky. It has an elegant interior and one of the cosiest lobbies in Venice, over half the rooms have a stunning canal view, and the service is exceptionally good. ★★★★**Saturnia & International**, Via XXII Marzo 2398, S. Marco, ✆ 041 520 8377, ✇ 041 520 7131 (*very expensive*) is a lovely hotel very near S. Marco, in a romantic quattrocento palazzo with a garden court, faced by the nicest and quietest rooms.

★★★**Accademia 'Villa Maravege'**, Fondamenta Bollani 1058, Dorsoduro, ✆ 041 521 0188, ✇ 041 523 9152 (*expensive*) is a hotel with a generous dollop of slightly faded charm in a 17th-century villa with a garden, just off the Grand Canal. ★★★**Flora**, Calle Bergamaschi 2283/a, S. Marco, ✆ 041 520 5844 (*expensive*) is a small hotel on a little street that's remarkably quiet so near to the Piazza, with a charming garden and patio, spilling flowers. It's comfortably furnished and air-conditioned, but ask for a large room. ★★★**Do Pozzi**, Corte do Pozzi 2373, S. Marco, ✆ 041 520 7855, ✇ 041 522 9413 (*expensive*), with a bit of the look of an Italian country inn, has 29 quiet rooms on a charming little square, only a few minutes from Piazza San Marco. It's friendly and well run.

★★★**Sturion**, Calle del Sturion 679, San Polo, ✆ 041 523 6243, ✇ 041 522 8378 (*expensive*) is one of the least expensive hotels actually on the Grand Canal, with eight large, finely furnished rooms. Book well ahead. ★★★**Agli Alboretti**, Rio Terrà Foscarini 884, Dorsoduro, ✆ 041 523 0058, ✇ 041 520 4048 (*expensive*) is a charming little hotel with 19 rooms, on a rare tree-lined lane near the Accademia. ★★**Falier**, Salizzada S. Pantalon 130, S. Croce, ✆ 041 710 882, ✇ 041 520 6554 (*moderate*) is a small hotel near Campo San Rocco. Elegantly furnished, it has two flower-filled terraces and one room with its own private terrace.

★★**Messner**, Salute 216, Dorsoduro, ✆ 041 522 7443 (*moderate*) is a nicely modernized hotel only a hop from the Salute, and very suitable for families. ★★**Mignon**, SS. Apostoli 4535, Cannaregio, ✆ 041 523 7388, ✇ 041 520 8658 (*moderate*), in a fairly quiet area not far from the Ca' d'Oro, boasts a little garden, though the rooms are rather plain. ★★**La Residenza**, Campo Bandiera e Moro 3608, Castello, ✆ 041 528 5315, ✇ 041 588 5042 (*moderate*), located in a 14th-century palace in a quiet square, has flamboyant 18th-century frescoes, paintings and antiques in the public rooms; the bedrooms are simpler.

★Casa Carettoni, Lista di Spagna 130, Cannaregio, ℰ 041 716 231 (*cheap*) is the most comfortable cheap hotel near the station. **★Casa Petrarca**, Calle delle Fuseri 4393, S. Marco, ℰ 041 520 0430 (*cheap*) has six friendly rooms near the Piazza. **★Casa Verardo**, Ruga Giuffa 4765, Castello, ℰ 041 528 6127, ✆ 041 523 2765 (*cheap*) is a classy, 9-room *locanda* with friendly owners. **★Sant'Anna**, Corte Bianco 269, Castello, ℰ 041 528 6466 (*cheap*) is a fine little hotel just north of the Giardini Pubblici. **★Silva**, Fondamenta Rimedio 4423, Castello, ℰ 041 522 7643 (*cheap*) is on one of the most photographed little canals in Venice, between the S. Zaccaria *vaporetto* stop and S. Maria Formosa. The rooms are fairly basic, but quiet, and the staff are friendly.

Ostello Venezia, Fondamenta delle Zitelle 86, Giudecca, ℰ 041 523 8211, is Venice's official youth hostel, with views across the Giudecca canal to San Marco. Reserve in writing well in advance. If you try your luck at the last minute, the office opens at 6pm (doors open at noon for waiting). IYHF cards required (available there) and there's an 11.30pm curfew. **Foresteria Valdese**, Calle della Madonnetta 5170, Castello, ℰ 041 528 6797, is an old palazzo converted into a dormitory/*pensione* by the Waldensians. (*Check-in 9–1 and 6–8*). **Domus Cavanis**, Rio Terrà Foscarini 912, Dorsoduro, ℰ 041 528 7374, is a Catholic-run hostel (*open June–Sept only*).

Antico Martini, Campo S. Fantin 1983, S. Marco, ℰ 041 522 4121 (*luxury*) is a Venetian classic, which started out as a Turkish coffeehouse in the early 18th century, but nowadays is better known for seafood, a superb wine list and the best *pennette al pomodoro* in Venice. The intimate piano bar-restaurant stays open until 2am. **Danieli Terrace**, in the Danieli Hotel, Riva degli Schiavoni 4196, Castello, ℰ 041 522 6480 (*luxury*) has a rooftop restaurant renowned for classic cuisine (try the *spaghetti alla Danieli*, prepared at your table) and perfect service in an incomparable setting overlooking Bacino San Marco.

La Caravella, Calle Larga XXII Marzo 2397, S. Marco, ℰ 041 520 8901 (*very expensive*) is in an annexe to the Saturnia Hotel (*see* above), serving an amazing variety of seasonal and local dishes. Try gilt head with thyme and fennel. Despite the décor, the atmosphere is fairly formal. **Do Forni**, Calle dei Specchieri 468, S. Marco, ℰ 041 523 2148 (*very expensive*) is *the* place to eat in Venice. There are two dining rooms, one 'Orient Express'-style and the other rustic, serving excellent seafood *antipasti*, polenta and seafood.

Harry's Bar, Calle Vallaresso 1323, S. Marco, ℰ 041 523 6797, in a class by itself—a favourite of Hemingway and assorted other luminaries—is as much a Venetian institution as the Doges' Palace. Best to avoid the formal restaurant upstairs and just flit in for a quick hobnob while sampling a sandwich or the justly famous house cocktails at a table downstairs near the bar.

Dall'Amelia, Via Miranese 113, Mestre, ℰ 041 913 951 (*expensive*) is on the mainland across the big bridge. The oysters are delicious and the *tortelli di* *bronzino* (sea bass) divine; it also has one of Italy's most renowned wine cellars. **Antica Besseta**, Salizada da Ca'Zusto (at the end of Calle Savio), S. Croce, ✆ 041 524 0428 (*expensive*) is a family-run citadel of Venetian homecooking, with the family's own wine. **Trattoria Vini da Arturo**, Calle degli Assassini 3656, S. Marco, ✆ 041 528 6974 (*expensive*) is a tiny trattoria with not a speck of seafood on the menu. Instead, try the *papardelle al radicchio* or Venice's best steaks; its *tiramisù* is famous. **A La Vecia Cavana**, Rio Terrà dei SS. Apostoli 4624, ✆ 041 523 8644 (*expensive*) is Cannaregio's smartest restaurant, where you can dine on Adriatic specialities.

Altanella, Calle della Erbe 268, Giudecca, ✆ 041 522 7780 (*moderate*) is a delightful old seafood restaurant: any of the grilled fish will be superb, and the *risotto di pesce* and *fritto* are worth the trip in themselves. **Antica Mola**, Fondamenta degli Ormesini 2800, Cannaregio (no ✆) (*moderate*), near the Ghetto, has all the old favourites, and tables by the canal. **Antico Giardinetto da Erasmo**, S. Croce 2315, ✆ 041 721 301 (*moderate*) serves delicious seafood cooked in a variety of styles and a little garden. **Alla Madonna**, Calle della Madonna 594, S. Polo (off Fond. del Vin, Rialto), ✆ 041 523 3824 (*moderate*) is a large, popular and very Venetian fish restaurant.

Da Remigio, Salizzada dei Greci 3416, Castello, ✆ 041 523 0089 (*moderate*) is a neighbourhood favourite, with solid Venetian cooking. **Tre Spiedi**, Salizzada S. Canciano 5906, Cannaregio, ✆ 041 528 0035 (*moderate*), near the Campiello F. Corner and the central post office, has a cosy atmosphere to go with local specialities like *spaghetti alla veneziana* and *braciola bruno* (pork chops).

Aciughetta, Campo SS. Filippo e Giacomo, Castello, ✆ 041 522 4292 (*cheap*) is one of the best cheap restaurants and bars near the Piazza San Marco, with good pizzas and atmosphere to boot. **Rosticceria San Bartolomeo**, Calle della Bissa 5424, San Marco, ✆ 041 522 3569 (*cheap*) serves honest cooking at honest prices. **San Tomà**, Campo San Tomà 2864, San Polo, ✆ 041 523 8819 (*cheap*) is a good trattoria-cum-pizzeria with convivial outdoor tables. **Da Crecola**, S. Giacomo dell'Orio 1459, S. Croce, ✆ 041 524 1496 (*cheap*), set in a quiet corner by a canal, has outdoor tables, and good pasta dishes, like *tagliatelle alla gorgonzola*, 50 different kinds of pizza, and a delightfully *pétillant* house wine.

Casa Mia, Calle dell'Oca 4430, Cannaregio, ✆ 041 528 5590, near Campo SS. Apostoli (*cheap*) is a lively pizzeria full of locals, with courtyard tables. **Vino Vino**, Campo S. Fantin 1983, S. Marco, ✆ 041 522 4121 (*cheap*) is a trendy offspring of the élite Antico Martini, where you can eat a well-cooked, filling dish (cooked by the same chefs!) with a glass of good wine at prices even students can afford.

Vicenza ✉ 36100

Near the railway station, ★★★★**Campo Marzo**, Viale Roma 21, ✆ 0444 545 700, ✆ 0444 320 495 (*expensive*) has modern, comfortable rooms, with air-conditioning, and a garage. ★★★**Cristina**, Corso B. Felice 32, ✆ 0444 323 751, ✉ 0444 543 656 (*moderate*) is central and comfortable, with parking. Up on the slopes of Monte Bérico, ★★**Casa Raffaele**, Viale X Giugno 10, ✆ 0444 545 767, ✉ 0444 542 2597 (*cheap*) offers good-value, as well as tranquillity and great views. On a quiet street in the historic district are ★★**Due Mori**, Contrà da Rode 26 (near the Piazza dei Signori), ✆ 0444 321 888, ✉ 0444 326 127 (*cheap*), and the more basic ★**Vicenza**, a few doors down, ✆/✉ 0444 321 512.

Nuovo Cinzia & Valerio, Piazzetta Porta Padova, ✆ 0444 505 213 (*expensive*) serves perfectly prepared seafood: tagliatelle with salmon, cuttlefish risotto or grilled sole, followed by homemade ice cream and crisp biscuits. The **Antica Trattoria Tre Visi**, Corso Palladio 25, ✆ 0444 324 868, (*moderate*), a 15th-century palace that was converted into an inn some 200 years ago, is a charming place to enjoy good, basic Veneto cooking and homemade pasta dishes. Just west of the city walls, at the family-run **Trattoria Framarin**, Via Battista Framarin 48, ✆ 0444 570 407 (*moderate*) you'll find delicious homemade pasta and a warm welcome. *Cheaper* choices include **Vecchia Guardia**, Contrà Pescherie Vecchie 11, ✆ 0444 321 231, near Piazza dell'Erbe, for pizza and straightforward meals, and the basic, lively and very popular **Antica Casa della Malvasia**, Contrà delle Morette 5, near Piazza dei Signori, ✆ 0444 543 704, for real home cooking. A popular stop for a cheap lunch, **Righetti**'s bustling self-service canteen has seats spilling on to Piazza Duomo.

Verona ✉ 37100

Goethe and Mozart slept at the ★★★★**Due Torri Baglioni**, Piazza Sant'Anastasia 4, ✆ 045 595 044, ✉ 045 800 4130 (*very expensive*), and would feel just as at home there today, at least in the rooms appointed with 18th-century antiques. The public rooms are equally resplendent, the ceilings adorned with 17th-century frescoes, the banquet rooms with circus scenes. In a quiet, traffic-free street near the Arena, ★★★★**Colomba d'Oro**, Via C. Cattaneo 10, ✆ 045 595 300, ✉ 045 594 974 (*very expensive*) offers very comfortable air-conditioned rooms behind its old stone façade, and secure parking, but no restaurant. A restored 16th-century palace houses the ★★★★**Accademia**, Via Scala 12, ✆/✉ 045 596 222 (*very expensive*), another excellent, atmospheric choice smack in the centre.

Centrally located near the Arena, the ★★★**Giulietta e Romeo**, Vicolo Tre Marchetti 3, ✆ 045 800 3554, ✉ 045 801 0862 (*expensive*) is on a quiet street and offers fine rooms (and parking), but no restaurant. Another good choice in the historic centre, ★★★**De' Capuleti**, Via del Pontiere, ✆ 045 800 0154 (*expensive*) has air-conditioning and satellite TV. If you're arriving by train, ★★★**Novo Hotel Rossi**, Via delle Coste 2, ✆ 045 569 022, ✉ 045 578 297 (*expensive–moderate*) is very convenient and *simpatico*. For tranquil rooms on the other side of the Adige, try ★★★**Italia**, Via Mameli 58, ✆ 045 918 088, ✉ 045 834 8028 (*expensive*); rooms are modern and comfortable and priced right.

About 150 yards from the Arena, **Sammicheli, Via Valverde 2, © 045 800 3749, ✆ 045 800 4508 (*moderate*) is convenient for opera-goers, with easy parking, and TVs in each room. In the same area, the welcoming **Torcolo, Vicolo Listone 3, © 045 800 7512, ✆ 045 800 4058 (*moderate*) is convenient and not too noisy, on its quiet little square. Just south of the Castelvecchio, family-run **Scalzi, Via Scalzi 5, © 045 590 422, ✆ 045 590 069 (*moderate*) has similar amenities in a fairly quiet spot.

For cheaper rooms with or without bath in the centre, try *Catullo, Via Valerio Catullo 1, © 045 800 2786 (*cheap*); some even have balconies. If you have an IYHF card, however, you can't beat the **Ostello Verona**, a 16th-century villa with frescoes in Via Fontana del Ferro 15, © 045 590 360 (*cheap*), just beyond the Castel di San Pietro (take bus no.72 to the first stop across the river). Beds are up in the newer wing. The reception stays open year-round, 24 hours a day, but you won't be allowed in until 5pm; get there early in summer.

The king of the Veronese restaurant scene is **Il Desco**, Via dietro San Sebastiano 7, © 045 595 358 (*very expensive*), in a 15th-century palace. Expect exquisite dishes based on seasonal ingredients: gnocchi with ewe's milk cheese, red mullet with black olives and rosemary, goose liver in a sauce of sweet wine and grapes. Run by the same family for over a hundred years, **Arche**, Via delle Arche Scaligere 6, © 045 800 7415 (*very expensive*) has long been the place to go for a special meal in an aristocratic setting. The freshest of fish is brought in daily from Chioggia and imaginatively prepared.

An even older favourite, **I Dodici Apostoli**, Corticella San Marco 3, © 045 596 999 (*expensive*) offers a traditional Renaissance setting—complete with frescoes of Romeo and Juliet. Some of the delicacies served today are even adapted from Renaissance recipes; the *salmone in crosta* (marinated salmon in pastry) is famous. For a glamorous, gourmet experience, sit outside in Piazza dei Signori at **Nuovo Marconi**, Via Fogge 4, © 045 591910 (*expensive*). The food is as rooted in tradition as the surroundings: tagliolini with crab, gnocchi with pumpkin, and fine scampi and duck. The century-old **Bottega del Vino**, Via Scudo di Francia 3 (off Via Mazzini), © 045 800 4535 (*expensive*) uses organically grown ingredients and pasta made on the premises; the wine list is enormous. **Greppia**, Vicolo Samaritana 3, © 045 800 4577 (*moderate*) serves up traditional and Veronese favourites in a quiet little square.

Assisi

Visible for miles around, Assisi (pop. 25,000) sweeps the flanks of Monte Subasio in a broad curve like a pink ship sailing over the green sea of the valley below. This is Umbria's most famous town, and one of its loveliest, and there's more to it than St Francis. A wealthy Roman *municipium* that survived the invasions intact, the city came into prominence again in the Middle Ages as another of Umbria's battling *comuni*, mostly saving its bile for incessant wars with arch-rival Perugia. The 13th century, the century of St Francis and the great religious revival he began, was also the time of Assisi's greatest power and prosperity, leaving behind a collection of beautiful buildings any Italian city could be proud of.

Nevertheless, it was Francis who made all the difference to Assisi. Five million pilgrims and tourists crowded its narrow streets for Francis' 800th birthday in 1982, and on any day in summer you'll see (besides an overflow of tourists and souvenir stands peddling ceramic friars and plastic medieval torture instruments) flocks of serene Franciscans and enthusiastic, almost bouncy nuns from Africa or Missouri or Bavaria, having the time of their lives visiting a place that, much more than Rome, is the symbol of a living faith. And it's true that something simple and good has survived in Assisi, something that would edify the soul of any cynic who cares to linger—the great joyousness Francis bequeathed Assisi along with his sincere, humane, back-to-basics faith. In recent years the city has hosted some unusual demonstrations of that faith that could never have happened in Rome, or anywhere else—in 1986, when the Pope hosted his inter-faith World Day of Prayer here, complete with Tibetan lamas, Zoroastrians and American Indian medicine-men, and in the 1988 Umbria Jazz Festival, when gospel choirs from New Orleans sang in the upper church of San Francesco. The friars in charge would only let them sing for 15 minutes at a time, fearing that the rhythm might bring down the roof and Giotto's frescoes along with it. Providence saw that the building came to no harm, and by the end the Franciscans were clapping and stomping along with everyone else. Tragically, as everyone knows, where the gospel singing failed, the September 1997 earthquake succeeded, bringing the roof down and killing two friars and two journalists who were examining the damage caused by the first shock of the day. Apparently, the medieval builders, knowing the seismic nature of the land, had given the basilica the flexibility to withstand earthquakes, but the restorers in the 1950s had taken it away. The lower church reopened in late November 1997, and the upper church will hopefully be ready by 2000—the Franciscans have their fingers crossed—in time for the great Jubilee, when Assisi expects several million extra pilgrims.

St Francis of Assisi

 The man who started all the palaver was born in 1182 to a merchant, Pietro Bernardone, and his Provençal wife, Madonna Pica. Some say Pietro was the richest man in Assisi; he travelled often through the south of France, buying and selling fine cloth, and although he named his son Giovanni he called him Francesco after the country he loved. His wealth financed a merry and dissipated youth for Francesco; according to his first biographer, an early Franciscan convert named Celano, he was 'the first instigator of every evil, and behind none in foolishness'. He was also a poet, a troubadour, his French upbringing giving him an early introduction into the cult of chivalry and mystic love, imported from Provence and at that time immensely popular among the young Italians. His conversion to saintliness did not happen overnight; a long, severe illness, and a year spent as a prisoner of war in Perugia, were two of the events that made him stop and think.

Francis began to spend his time alone in the woods and meadows around Assisi, reflecting on the world's vanity. A revelation came to him while attending mass one Sunday in 1209, as the priest read the words of the Gospel: '... and as ye go, preach, saying, the kingdom of Heaven is at hand. Heal the sick, cleanse the lepers, raise the dead, cast out devils: freely have ye received, freely give.' Much to his father's fury, he publicly stripped off his rich clothes and fat purse and did just that, preaching a message of poverty, humility and joy in this world as well as the next, attracting a band of followers who lived with him in the Porziuncola, a little chapel on the plain below the city. His visit to Pope Innocent III is part of Franciscan legend. At first that very worldly pope and his court scoffed at the shabby Umbrian holy man, but that night Innocent dreamt that his Church of St John Lateran—then the seat of the popes—was collapsing, and that this same Francis came along to hold up its walls.

The pope gave his permission for the founding of an order, and attempted on many occasions to impose on it a monastic rule, like that of the Benedictines. Francis resisted this, and in fact never even took holy orders himself. From 1209 onwards, he spent his time travelling and preaching, mostly in Umbria, but also as far as Spain—attempting to reach Morocco—and the Holy Land and Egypt, accompanying the Crusaders. At Damietta, on the Nile, he preached to Sultan Malik el Kamil and was warmly received. Later writers claimed Francis was trying to convert the infidels, but it's just as likely he went to learn from them, and to meet kindred souls. Francis' connections with Islamic Sufi mystics are a fascinating subject, not too surprising for a former troubadour, immersed in ideas of divine love from the east. Intriguingly, there was a new Sufi order in the Middle East at that time, founded some sixty years before Francis' birth by a holy man named Najmuddin Kubra, another wandering preacher with an uncanny influence over birds and animals.

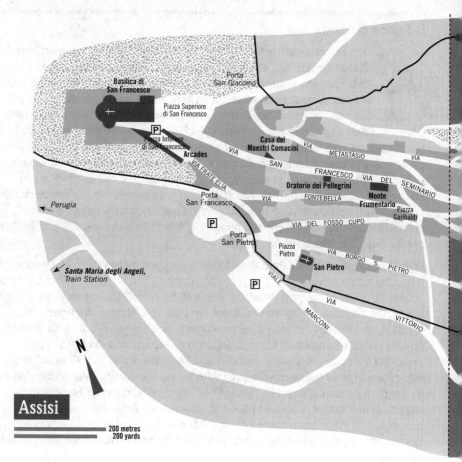

Assisi

200 metres
200 yards

Drawing on his troubadour days, Francis composed some of the first and finest vernacular verse in Italy, including the famous 'Canticle of the Sun' in the Fioretti. It was the foundation of a literary movement, combining the new poetry with Christian devotion. By 1221 the Franciscan movement had spread across Italy and beyond. In that year the Franciscan rule of poverty, chastity and obedience was sanctioned by Pope Honorius III. In his later years, Francis spent much of his time at the sanctuary of La Verna in Tuscany, where he received the stigmata. Increasingly frail in health, he returned to the Porziuncola in Assisi to die in 1226, aged 44.

Getting Around

 Assisi is a 23km/30mins train ride from Perugia or Foligno, where you'll have to change from Rome (77km/2½hrs) or Terni. The station is down on the plain, only a block from the suburban Basilica

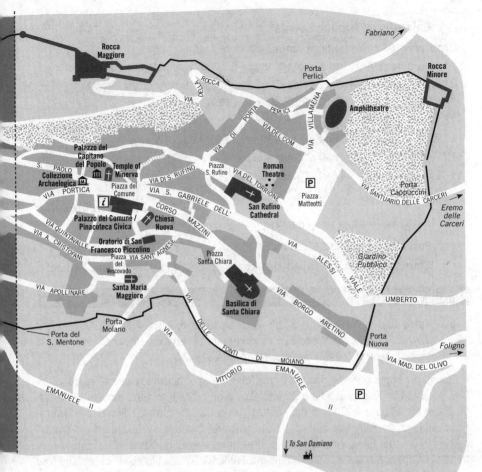

of Santa Maria degli Angeli, and there are
regular connecting buses to Piazza Unità d'Italia.
There are also convenient direct buses from Perugia,
Bettona, Foligno, Gubbio and Gualdo Tadino (APM, ✆ 075 573
1707), Rome and Florence (SULGA, ✆ 075 500 9641); Siena and San
Benedetto del Tronto and Porto San Giorgio in the Marches (LAZZI and
CONTRAM, ✆ 0737 632 402); one a day from Norcia and Cascia (SIT, ✆ 0743
212 211) and a few from Bevagna, Montefalco, Foligno and Spello (APM or SIT):
stops are in Piazza Matteotti, Largo Properzio and Piazzale Unità d'Italia.

If you're driving, use one of the three car parks on the fringes of town: in the
Piazza Unità d'Italia, below the Basilica of San Francesco, at the Porta Nuova at
the eastern end of town, and in a vast underground lot in the walls at Piazza
Matteotti, by the duomo.

✛ Calendar of Jubilee Events

Christmas 1999	Official start of the Holy Year
31 December 1999	All-night vigil in the Basilica (also in Padua and Loreto)
21 April	Good Friday; Procession and Stations of the Cross
first Thurs in May	Calendimaggio (*see* p.179)
22 June	Feast of the Vow
11 Aug	Feast of San Rufino (patron saint of Assisi)
12 Aug	Feast of Santa Chiara
3–4 Oct	Feast of San Francesco

Tourist Information

Piazza del Comune 12, ✆ 075 812 534, ✉ 075 813 727

Post office: Piazza del Comune.

Churches: Unless otherwise stated, churches are open daily 7–12 and 2–sunset.

Basilica di San Francesco

Open Easter–Nov daily 6.30am–7pm, festivals 6.30am–7.30pm; Nov–Easter daily 6.30am–6pm; closed Sun morning during services. Upper Church due to reopen December 1999. Information ✆ 075 819 001.

Although the popes were originally mistrustful of the spontaneous, personal approach to faith preached by Francis and his followers, they soon realized that this movement would be better off within the Church than outside it. In transforming the Franciscans into a respectable, doctrinally safe arm of the Church, they had the invaluable aid of Francis' successor, Brother Elias, Vicar-General of the Order, a worldly, businesslike man, something of an epicurean and a friend of Emperor Frederick II. Elias' methods caused the first split within the Franciscans, between those who enjoyed the growing opulence of the new dispensation and those who tried to keep to the original simplicity and poverty of St Francis. This monumental building complex, begun the day after Francis' canonization in 1228, was one of the biggest causes of contention. Nothing could have been further removed from the philosophy and intentions of Francis himself; on the other hand, nothing could have been more successful in perpetuating the memory of Francis and his teaching. And with its remarkable frescoes, by Giotto or his school and many other trecento masters, the basilica is one of the greatest monuments of Italian art.

From the beginning, the popes were entirely behind the effort. They paid for it by promoting a great sale of special indulgences across Europe. There's a story that Brother Elias himself supplied the design—maybe he did, for the building does have an amateurish, clumsy form, one of the less successful attempts to transplant the Gothic style on Italian soil. As in many Assisi churches, the façade projects above the roofline like a shop-front in a Wild West town, to make the building look more imposing. The usual approach to the basilica is from the Piazza Inferiore, lined with arcades where medieval pilgrims bought their souvenirs before returning home. The grandest entrance is the one to the Lower Church, with a Renaissance portico of 1487 covering a fine Gothic portal.

The Lower Church

With its low dark vaults, it seems at first to be a simple crypt, although once your eyes adjust to the dim light you can see that they are covered with magnificent 13th- and 14th-century frescoes (bring plenty of coins and a torch to illuminate them). The first chapel to the left of the nave contains magnificent frescoes, stained glass, and other decorations on the *Life of St Martin* by Simone Martini (*c.* 1322) while the third chapel on the right contains frescoes on the *Life of Mary Magdalene*, attributed to Giotto (1314). All of the frescoes attributed to Giotto in Assisi (from 1295), constitute one of the longest-raging controversies in art history. Italians are convinced that the frescoes in the lower and upper churches are the climax of Giotto's early career, while most foreign scholars believe Giotto didn't paint them at all. Whatever the case, Martini's 'International Gothic-style' poses are a serious artistic challenge to the great precursor of the Renaissance. This master of line and colour creates a wonderful narrative of St Martin's life; the Gaulish soldier and wastrel who ended up as a bishop and split his cloak to give half to a beggar seems a perfect foreshadowing of St Francis.

Giotto is also credited with the four beautiful allegorical frescoes over the high altar, depicting Poverty, Chastity, Obedience and the Glory of St Francis. Note the *Marriage of St Francis with Lady Poverty*, one of the most striking images ever to come out of the 13th-century religious revival. In the left transept are frescoes by Pietro Lorenzetti of Siena, among the best in the basilica, especially the lovely *Madonna della Tramontana* ('of the sunset') *with St Francis and St John*, a *Crucifixion* and a *Descent from the Cross*. In the right transept is a work considered Cimabue's masterpiece, the *Madonna and Saints*, with a famous portrait of St Francis (1280), believed to be an accurate likeness; a serious-looking female saint nearby, by Simone Martini, is believed to be St Clare.

In the **crypt** lie the bones of St Francis and four of his closest followers, discovered only in 1818. Brother Elias, worried that the Perugians would come to steal the saint's body, hid it with exceeding care, behind tons of stone. His fears were not unfounded; when Francis was coming back from La Verna to die, the Perugians (who never listened when Francis came to preach) were waiting to kidnap him along the road; Brother Elias had the foresight to direct Francis on a longer route. From the transepts, stairs lead up to a terrace and the **Museo-Tesoro della Basilica** (*open 9.30–12 and 2–6; closed Sun Nov–Mar; adm*), containing what wasn't pillaged or pinched from the treasury through the centuries—a beautiful Venetian cross, a French ivory Madonna from the 13th century, a Flemish tapestry with St Francis, and more. In 1995 the contents of the former 'secret sacristy' were put on display as well, in another room: Pope Honorius III's Bull approving the Order's Rule (1223), the saint's tunic, cowl, girdle and sandals, an ivory horn given to Francis by the Sultan of Egypt which he would blow to assemble his followers, the Laud to the Creator and Benediction of Brother Leone on parchment, in the saint's own hand, and a chalice and paten used by Francis and his followers.

The Upper Church

The Upper Church is due to be reopened in December 1999, with the Pope plan-
ning to officiate at Christmas Mass. The painstaking restoration of the painted
vault will be finished; the areas which could not be reconstructed have been left
bare, but a special system has been devised to project the 'missing' images on to
these areas, giving the viewer a sense of the original whole.

In comparison with the lower church, the Upper Church on its emerald-green lawn is
strikingly bright and airy and vibrant with colour. The earthquake left its two major series
of medieval frescoes cracked and broken in places, but more or less intact. The lower set
of 28 panels on the *Life of St Francis* is by Giotto or his school, while the upper, with *Old
and New Testament Scenes*, is usually attributed to Cimabue's followers and Roman
painters Pietro Cavallini and Jacopo Torriti.

What makes most Italian scholars attribute the St Francis frescoes at least partially to
Giotto is the artist's mastery of composition; Giotto amazed his contemporaries with his
ability to illustrate the physical and spiritual essentials of a scene with simplicity and
drama, cutting directly to the core of the matter. The scenes begin with the young *St
Francis Honoured by the Simple Man*, who lays down his cloak and foretells the saint's
destiny (note Assisi's Temple of Minerva in the background); Francis returns his clothes to
his father who, in his anger and disappointment, has to be restrained; Pope Innocent III
has a dream of Francis supporting the falling Church; the demons are expelled from
Arezzo by Brother Sylvester; Francis meets the Sultan of Egypt; he creates the first
Christmas crib, or *presepio*, at Greccio; he preaches to the attentive birds, and then to
Pope Honorius III; he appears in two places at the same time and, next, receives the stigmata from a six-winged cherub; he dies, bewailed by the Poor Clares, and is canonized.

The **transepts** were painted with a famous cycle of frescoes by Giotto's master, Cimabue,
though the works had oxidized into mere shadows, or negatives of their former selves
even before the earthquake turned them to crumbs; what can be salvaged will, and by
hook or by crook some kind of Cimabue clones will eventually refill the rebuilt transepts,
good enough to give most of us non-experts a feeling for what was lost, perhaps even of
the *Crucifixion*, a faded masterpiece of 1277 that still radiated some of its original drama
and feeling. Behind the basilica, propped up on huge arches, the enormous convent is now
used as a missionary college.

Around the City

To the Piazza del Comune

On entering Assisi, through the main road from the car park, you may have noticed the
excellent Romanesque façade of **San Pietro** (*closed for restoration; due to reopen Easter
2000; information © 075 812 311*) just inside the gate of the same name (down Via Frate
Elia from the piazza of the lower basilica). This recently restored Benedictine church was

built in
the 1200s, though
Assisi's chroniclers date the
original building back to the 2nd
century; relics of Assisi's first bishop, San Vittoriano, are kept inside.

From the upper basilica, Via San Francesco, the main street of Assisi, leads past a rather unexpected **Museo degli Indios dell'Amazzonia** (*open Mon–Sat 8–12 and 3–6, Sun 10–1 and 3–7; donation*), with ethnographic items collected by missionaries in the Amazon, while Amazonian fish and plants are on show at the **Mostra Ittioligica**, No.19/c Via San Francesco (*same hours as above*). There are also some fine medieval houses. At No.14 stands the Masons' Guild, or **Casa dei Maestri Comacini** (most of the basilica-builders came from Como); at No.11, the **Oratorio dei Pellegrini**, a 15th-century gem surviving from a pilgrims' hospice, frescoed in part by Matteo da Gualdo. At No.3, the **Monte Frumentario** began as a 13th-century hospital, and was later converted into a granary; its 16th-century fountain still bears the warning that the penalty for washing clothes here is one *scudo* and confiscation of laundry.

Near the entrance of the Piazza del Comune, the **Collezione Archeologica**, Via Portica 1 (*open April–Sept Tues–Sun 10–1 and 3–7; Oct–Mar Tues–Sun 10–1 and 2–5; adm*) is located in the crypt of the now-vanished church of San Nicolò, with a small collection of Etruscan urns. A passage from the museum leads into the ancient **Roman forum**, recently excavated, and directly under the modern square.

The Temple of Minerva

The long, attractive Piazza del Comune, the medieval centre of Assisi, is embellished with 13th-century buildings of the old *comune*: the **Torre and Palazzo del Comune**, the **Palazzo del Capitano del Popolo**, and what at first looks like a decrepit bank building but is in reality a Roman **Temple of Minerva**, its Corinthian columns and travertine steps incorporated into what is now the church of Santa Maria. When Goethe, a muddle-headed classicist who felt a national embarrassment whenever he heard the word 'Gothic', came to Assisi it was to see this—and nothing else. It is the best surviving Roman temple front on the Italian peninsula, sitting on its square in the exact position it had in the ancient forum, as good as any ruin in Rome for helping your imagination conjure up the classical world. Only the façade with its Corinthian columns remains; inside you'll be treated to some eccentric Baroque.

The Palazzo del Comune contains the **Pinacoteca Civica** (*closed indefinitely*), with some 13th-century secular knightly frescoes from the Palazzo del Capitano del Popolo and a sleepy collection of Umbrian Renaissance art. To the left of the palazzo, the **Chiesa Nuova** was built by Philip III of Spain on property owned by St Francis' father; the **Oratorio di San Francesco Piccolino** (*closed indefinitely*), of 'Little baby St Francis', is believed to mark the saint's birthplace.

Upper Assisi: the Cathedral and Castle

Most visitors labour under the impression that the Basilica of St Francis is Assisi's cathedral, and never find their way up Via di San Rufino from the Piazza del Comune to the real **Cattedrale di San Rufino**. This has a huge campanile and a beautiful Romanesque façade, the finest in Assisi, designed by Giovanni da Gubbio in 1140 and adorned with fine rose windows and the kind of robust medieval carvings of animals and saints that Goethe so disdained. Inside, it houses the porphyry font where Saints Francis and Clare were baptized, as well as Emperor Frederick II, who was born nearby in Jesi, in the Marches. It is an amazing coincidence that these two leading figures of the 13th century should have been baptized in the same place; the holy water must have had a special Muslim essence in it, to connect these two figures so influenced by the East. They also had poetry in common: both were among the first to write verses in Italian, rather than Latin.

The rest of the interior was restored in the 16th century, when the beautiful carved wooden choir was added; it still waits for an 'unrestoration' to clear all the clutter and bring it back to its original state. Off the right nave, there's a small **Museo Capitolare** (*open daily exc Sun morning mid-Mar–mid-Oct and Christmas 10–12 and 2–6; adm*) with Romanesque capitals and other bits from the building: codices, detached frescoes, paintings by Matteo da Gualdo and a beautiful tryptych by L'Alunno (1470); you can explore the ancient **crypt**, dating from an earlier, 11th-century San Rufino, with some surviving frescoes and a 3rd-century Roman sarcophagus (*open same hours as church; adm; combined ticket available*). Don't miss the Roman cistern directly under the cathedral's campanile.

From the cathedral, it's a bracing walk up to the **Rocca Maggiore** (*open 10–sunset; adm*), Assisi's well-preserved castle, built in 1174 and used by Conrad von Luetzen (who cared for the little orphan Emperor Frederick II), and then destroyed and rebuilt on several occasions; it offers excellent views of Assisi, the Valle Umbra and the surrounding countryside.

East of the cathedral you can visit more of Roman *Assisium*—the **theatre** in Via del Torrione, flanking the cathedral, and the remains of the **amphitheatre**, off Piazza Matteotti and Via Villamena. The **Porta Perlici** near the amphitheatre dates from 1199, and there are some well-preserved 13th-century houses on the Via del Comune Vecchio. The **Giardino Pubblico**, with its pavilions and goldfish ponds, is an exquisite city park, a fine place to have a picnic after a hard day's sightseeing. Roman Assisi had up-to-date plumbing; you might be able to pick out parts of the Roman drain between the amphitheatre and the Giardino Pubblico, built to carry off water after the amphitheatre was flooded for mock sea battles.

Basilica di Santa Chiara

When Santa Chiara (St Clare) was 17 she ran away from her wealthy and noble family to become a disciple of St Francis, and later became head of the Franciscan order for women, the Poor Clares. Whatever the later Church mythology, gratifying rumours were never lacking that there was more to her relationship with Francis than practical piety. Gentle, humble and well loved by everyone, she once had a vision of a Christmas service in the Basilica of St Francis while at the monastery of San Damiano, over a kilometre away, a feat that brought Pope Pius XII in 1958 to declare her the Patron Saint of Television.

Her basilica, built in 1265 below the Piazza del Comune by way of Corso Mazzini, is a pink-and-white-striped beauty with a lovely rose window, supported by huge flying buttresses added a century later that not only keep it from falling over but create a memorable architectural space below. The basilica was built on the site of old San Giorgio, where Francis attended school and where his body lay for two years awaiting the completion of his own basilica. The interior of Santa Chiara was frescoed by followers of Giotto, although they only survive in fragments. The main chapel on the right contains the famous *Crucifix of San Damiano* (*see* below), while the adjacent chapel of the Holy Sacrament has fine Sienese frescoes; these two chapels survive from the original church of San Giorgio and contain some of St Clare's garments and golden curls. The nearby portrait of St Clare, with scenes from her life, is by the Byzantinish, 13th-century Maestro di Santa Chiara, while Clare's body, rediscovered in 1850 under the high altar, shrivelled and darkened with age, lies in a crystal coffin in the neo-Gothic crypt.

From Santa Chiara, Via Sant'Agnese leads to the very simple 1163 church of **Santa Maria Maggiore**, Assisi's first cathedral, built on the site of the Roman Temple of Apollo, traces of which are still visible in the crypt. Near here the house of Sextus Propertius, the Roman poet of love (46 BC–AD14), was discovered, complete with wall paintings (*now awaiting funds to have it kitted out for public access*). Between here and the Piazza Unità d'Italia, stroll along Via Cristofani and Via Fontebella, the latter adorned with wrought-iron dragons and another old fountain.

On the Outskirts of Assisi

The seminal events of Francis' life all took place in the countryside around Assisi, all easily visited by car, although **San Damiano** (*open 10–6*) is a pleasant 2km walk down from Santa Chiara. It was here in this simple, lovely, asymmetrical little church that the Christ on the Cross (now in the Basilica di Santa Chiara) bowed and spoke to Francis, commanding him to 'Rebuild my church.' Francis took the injunction literally, and sold his father's cloth to raise the money—which the priest at San Damiano refused to take. He brought Clare to San Damiano in 1212, and here she and her sisters passed their frugal, contemplative lives; while sitting in her garden during one of his visits, Francis composed his superb *Cantico della creature*, the 'Canticle of All Things Created'.

Another Franciscan shrine more true to the spirit of the saint than the great art-filled basilicas, is the peaceful **Eremo delle Carceri**, located in the woods along the road up Monte Subasio, a spectacular walk or drive 4km east of Assisi (*leave by way of the Porta dei Cappuccini; open 6.30–5; summer till 7*). This was Francis' forest hermitage, where he would retreat to walk through the woods and meditate; here you can see his humble bed hollowed from the rock. St Bernardino of Siena founded the small convent here in 1426, where a handful of Franciscans live a traditional existence on the alms they receive.

The real centre of early Franciscanism, however, was the chapel called the **Porziuncola** ('the little portion'), where angels were wont to appear, down on the plain near the train station. Francis, in return for the use of the chapel, owed a yearly basket of carp from the river Tescio to the Benedictines, still faithfully paid by the Franciscans. In 1569 a monumental basilica, **Santa Maria degli Angeli** (*open Nov–Feb daily 7–12 and 2–sunset; March–Oct daily 7am–7pm*) was built over the Porziuncola. The building, not completed until 1684, is an excellent piece of nostalgic Baroque—most of it rebuilt after an 1832 earthquake, and the surprisingly elegant façade not added until 1927.

In the austere interior, the Porziuncola stands out, dolled up with frescoes tarted up in the 19th century. The rugged stone of the original chapel can be seen inside (it may be as old as the 6th century), along with some darkened 1393 frescoes of St Francis' life by Ilario da Viterbo, this artist's only known work. Remains of the original Franciscan monastery have been partially excavated under the high altar; here St Clare took her vows of poverty as the spiritual daughter of Francis; here Francis died 'naked on the bare earth' in the convent's infirmary, now the **Cappella del Transito**, with some unusual frescoes by the Umbrian painter Lo Spagna, along with a statue of St Francis by Andrea della Robbia.

The garden contains the roses that Francis is said to have thrown himself on while wrestling with severe temptation, staining their leaves red with blood, only to find that they lost their thorns on contact with his body. Still thornless, they bloom every May. Francis' cell has been covered with the frescoed **Cappella del Roseto**; and there's an old pharmacy and, in the refectory of the old convent, a **museum** (*open same hours as church*) with a portrait of St Francis by an unknown 13th-century master, another attributed to Cimabue, and a *Crucifix* (1236) by Giunta Pisano; there's also a **Museo Etnografico Universale**, in Piazza Porziuncola, with items relating to Franciscan missionary work (*open Mon–Fri 8–2 and 3.30–6.30, Sat 9–1 and 3.30–6.30, Sun 9–1*).

Activities

Assisi is both Umbria's spiritual and shopping centre, overflowing with little ceramic friars, crossbows, local ceramics and glass, textiles and serious art galleries. Besides the many special events planned for the Holy Year, annual festivals in

Assisi include the medieval May Day celebrations of *Calendimaggio* during the first 10 days of May, commemorating St Francis' troubadour past with song, dance, torchlit parades, competitions between Lower and Upper Assisi and beautiful costumes. Easter week is busy with activities—on Holy Thursday there's a mystery play on the Deposition from the Cross, followed by processions on Good Friday and Easter Sunday; 1–2 August sees the *Festa del Perdona* ('Feast of Pardon') at the Porziuncola, initiated by St Francis, who once had a vision of Christ asking him what would be most helpful for the soul. Francis replied forgiveness for anyone who crossed the threshold of the chapel; indulgences are still given out on the day. In July and early August the *Festa Musica Pro* sponsors concerts throughout the city, often including early Italian music.

Assisi ✉ 06081   **Where to Stay**

Tourists have been coming to Assisi for longer than to any town in Umbria, and it does its best to please. There are plenty of rooms, but it's advisable to book in advance.

Long Assisi's top hotel, the traditional, formal ★★★★**Subasio**, Via Frate Elia 2, ✆ 075 812 206, 🖷 075 816 691 (*expensive*) is linked to the Basilica of St Francis by a portico. Many of the rooms have views over the famous mystical countryside from vine-shaded terraces, and it has a private garage and an attractive medieval-vaulted restaurant. St Francis never slept here, but the King of Belgium and Charlie Chaplin did.

★★★**Fontebella**, Via Fontebella 25, ✆ 075 812 883, 🖷 075 812 941 (*expensive*) is a bit nearer the centre, housed in a 17th-century *palazzo*. Rooms are comfortable, public rooms elegant and a garden and garage are added attractions. ★★★★**Giotto**, Via Fontebella 41, ✆ 075 812 209, 🖷 075 816 479 (*expensive*) has very pleasant modern rooms near the basilica, as well as a garage and garden terraces.

At Armenzano, 10km from the centre on Monte Subasio, the 10th-century hostel ★★★★**Le Silve**, ✆ 075 901 9000, 🖷 075 801 9005 (*expensive*) has been prettily fixed up for 20th-century guests, with antique furnishings and a pool and sauna. *Open Mar–Oct.*

For longer stays, a 16th-century farmhouse on a working farm has recently been converted into the three self-catering **Brigolante Guest Apartments**, 6km from the centre of Assisi at the foot of Mount Subasio at Via Costa di Trex 31, ✆ 075 802 250 (*expensive*); each houses 4–6 people and has fine views over Subasio, as well as a chance to experience rural life and purchase fresh meat, vegetables, eggs and cheese from the premises.

The ★★★**San Francesco**, Via San Francesco 48, ✆ 075 812 281, 🖷 075 816 237 (*moderate*) has modern rooms—all with air conditioning—several looking out on to the façade of the Basilica. ★★★**Umbra**, Via degli Archi 6, ✆ 075 812 240, 🖷 075 813 653 (*expensive–moderate*), near Piazza del Comune at the end of a narrow alley, is a real charmer, a little family-run inn; quiet, sunny and friendly with a little walled garden in front. Rooms can be a bit small but serendipitous, and many have balconies overlooking the countryside. The Umbra's restaurant is one of the most attractive in Assisi, with the best of regional cuisine like risotto with white truffles from Gubbio and a cellar full of excellent wine; in good weather meals are served in the garden. Parking can be a minor problem, however—the nearest car park is by S Chiara.

★★★**Hotel dei Priori**, Corso Mazzini 15, ✆ 075 812 237, 🖷 075 816 804 (*expensive–moderate*) is housed in a gracious 18th-century palazzo, well-restored and very conveniently placed, just off Assisi's main piazza. ★★★**Hermitage**, Via G. Degli Aromatari 1, ✆ 075 8127 64, 🖷 075 816 691 (*moderate*) is a comfortable, reasonably priced hotel in a central position, a short walk from the basilica. In the historic centre, ★★**San Giacomo**, Via S Giacomo 6, ✆ 075 816 778, 🖷 075 816 779 (*moderate*) is reliable and welcoming.

Nearly a kilometre away and a bit hard to find—a 10-min walk to the west gate of Assisi—in a pretty country setting, the old stone ★★**Country House**, S Pietro Campagna 168, ✆/🖷 075 816 363 (*moderate*) has lovely rooms, furnished with items from the owner's antique shop on the ground floor (no restaurant, but the *signora* prepares a substantial, reasonably priced evening meal for guests in her kitchen; ask in the morning).

★★**Ideale per Turisti**, Piazza Matteotti 1, ✆ 075 813 570, 🖷 075 813 020 (*moderate*), near the amphitheatre, has a name that says it all: a fine, small hotel with a garden and views. Twelve km northwest of Assisi, ★★★**Castel San Gregorio**, Via S. Gregorio 16, ✆ 075 803 8009, 🖷 075 803 8904, at San Gregorio ✉ 06086 (*moderate*) offers only 12 rooms in a romantic, restored 13th-century castle, set in a pretty garden.

★**Anfiteatro Romano**, Via Anfiteatro 4, ✆ 075 813 025, 🖷 075 815 110 (*cheap*) is a good quiet choice near Piazza Matteotti, with only seven rooms, some with private bath. Other good central choices include ★**Italia**, Vicolo della Fortezza, ✆ 075 812 625, 🖷 075 804 3749 (*cheap*), near Piazza del Comune; ★★**Sole**, Corso Mazzini 35, ✆ 075 812 373, 🖷 075 813 706 (*cheap*), a large place with a good restaurant, the **Ceppo della Catena**; or the much smaller ★★**Pallotta**, Via S Rufina 4, ✆/🖷 075 812 307 (*cheap*), also attatched to a good, traditional eatery.

Three budget hotels down the hill, near the Basilica of Santa Maria degli Angeli, are ★★**Franco Antonelli**, Via Los Angeles 25, ✆ 075 804 3690, 🖷 075 804 1549; ★★**Cristallo**, Via Los Angeles, ✆ 075 804 3535, 🖷 075 804 3538; and ★★**Dal Moro**, Via Santarelli, ✆ 075 804 3688, 🖷 075 804 1666.

If everything is full, try the large pilgrimage houses in Santa Maria degli Angeli, especially the ★★**Cenacolo Francescano**, Via Piazza d'Italia 70, ✆ 075 804 1083, 🖷 075 804 0552 (*cheap*), with 130 basic rooms, all with private bath, a short walk from the train station; or go to the tourist office for a list of smaller religious houses and rooms in private houses, of which there are dozens in Assisi.

American sisters run one of the nicest, **Sant'Antonio's Guest House**, Via G. Alessi 10, ✆ 075 812 542, ✉ 075 813 723 (*cheap*), in a 12th-century villa, with pleasant rooms. Guests can also have a good cheap lunch here, but no dinner. Beware the early curfew. There are three youth hostels, all outside the centre: **Victor**, Via Sacro Tugurio 116, ✆ 075 806 5562, at Rivotorto, 3km south of Assisi; the new dormitory **Della Pace**, at Via San Pietro Campagna, ✆/✉ 075 916 767, 1km out of Porta San Pietro; and **Fontemaggio**, 3km east on Via Eremo della Carceri, ✆ 075 813 636.

Eating Out

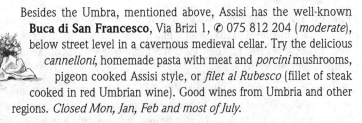

Besides the Umbra, mentioned above, Assisi has the well-known **Buca di San Francesco**, Via Brizi 1, ✆ 075 812 204 (*moderate*), below street level in a cavernous medieval cellar. Try the delicious *cannelloni*, homemade pasta with meat and *porcini* mushrooms, pigeon cooked Assisi style, or *filet al Rubesco* (fillet of steak cooked in red Umbrian wine). Good wines from Umbria and other regions. *Closed Mon, Jan, Feb and most of July.*

Another venerable choice, **Il Medio Evo**, Via dell' Arco dei Priori 4, ✆ 075 813 068 (*moderate*) has an elegant medieval atmosphere and tasty *antipasti* with Umbrian *prosciutto*, pasta with truffles, and *faraone all'uva* (woodcock cooked with grapes). *Closed Wed, Sun eve, most of Jan and the mid two weeks of July.*

San Francesco, Via S. Francesco 52, ✆ 075 812 329 (*moderate*), with a veranda beautifully overlooking the basilica, serves good Umbrian cuisine accompanied by an *enoteca* wine list. *Closed Wed and some of Aug.* **La Fortezza**, Via della Fortezza (near the Piazza del Comune), ✆ 075 812 418 (*moderate*) has delicious truffle- or mushroom-filled pasta caps (*cappelletti al tartufo nero o funghi*), roast guinea hen (*faraona alla Fortezza*), or rabbit in asparagus sauce. *Closed Thurs and in Feb.*

Near the temple of Minerva, **Piazzetta dell'Erba**, Via S. Gabriele dell'Addolorata 15b, ✆ 075 815 352 (*cheap*) features delicious daily specials at kind prices. *Closed Mon.* A lovely stop on the road up to the breathtaking sanctuary of Eremo delle Carceri is **La Stalla**, Via Eremo delle Carceri, at Fontemaggio, ✆ 075 812 317 (*cheap*), a typical country trattoria, converted from an old barn. Good hearty fare is served here at very reasonable prices, washed down with flagons of local wine. *Closed Mon.*

In town, leave room for one of the rich strudels or chocolate-and-nut breads in the speciality **bakery** in Piazza del Comune, near the Temple of Minerva, or at **La Bottega del Pasticcera**, Via Portica 9.

Where to Stay within Easy Reach of Assisi

Perugia, a university town of hillside terraced gardens, is famous for art and chocolate. As the capital and largest city of Umbria, it offers the widest choice of accommodation when nearby Assisi is full up. Perugia is also well worth a detour, with the finest collection of Umbrian painting, in its Galleria Nazionale dell'Umbria, a fascinating medieval centre, and walls and gates that date back to the Romans and Etruscans.

Spello could be Assisi's little sister, a beautiful medieval town lounging on the same sort of gentle hillside, done in the same prevailing pink and cream Umbrian stone. The church of Santa Maria Maggiore houses Spello's treasure, the Cappella Baglioni with its brilliant frescoes by Pinturicchio. A circumnavigation of the city's walls will reveal the Roman gates and the amphitheatre.

Foligno is one of the most distinctive Umbrian towns, not as archaic or as cute as Assisi, but a minor medieval capital with a pinch of grandeur and an air of genteel dilapidation that the terrible earthquake of 1997 has aggravated; its monuments are gradually being restored and reopened.

Spoleto is a medieval hill town with its share of lovely monuments, full of exhibitions and art workshops all year round. Below its citadel is one of the greatest engineering works of the trecento, the Ponte delle Torri, a bridge and aqueduct linking Spoleto with the slopes of Monteluco, its holy mountain, a serene spot overlooking the surrounding countryside. And of course Spoleto is famous for its Festival of Two Worlds (information from the Associazione Festival dei Due Mondi, Piazza del Duomo 9, ✆ 0743 45028, ✉ 0743 220 321), which takes place for around three weeks every summer.

Getting Around

One of the FS's main lines runs from Rome through **Foligno**, **Spello**, **Assisi** and **Perugia.** All of these towns are also connected by frequent bus links. Rome–Perugia trains continue northwards to Florence, while Foligno, 158km/2½hrs from Rome, is one of the principal rail junctions for eastern Umbria. A new FS bus service connects Foligno to Assisi, Perugia and Siena three times a day. The Rome–Ancona railway follows the Via Flaminia to **Spoleto**. During the Spoleto Festival, there are special trains and buses between Rome and Spoleto (130km/2hrs) to accommodate the crowds of festival-goers from the capital. SSIT, ✆ 0743 212 211, has connections from Piazza Garibaldi on the western edge of town to Assisi.

Tourist Information

Perugia: Piazza IV Novembre, and at the main rail station, ✆ 075 572 3327. **Spello**: Piazza Matteotti 3, ✆ 0742 301 009. **Foligno**: Porta Romana, ✆ 0742 354 459, ✉ 0742 340 545, or Corso Cavour 51, ✆ 0742 355 722. **Spoleto**: Piazza della Libertà 7, ✆ 0743 220 311, ✉ 0743 46241.

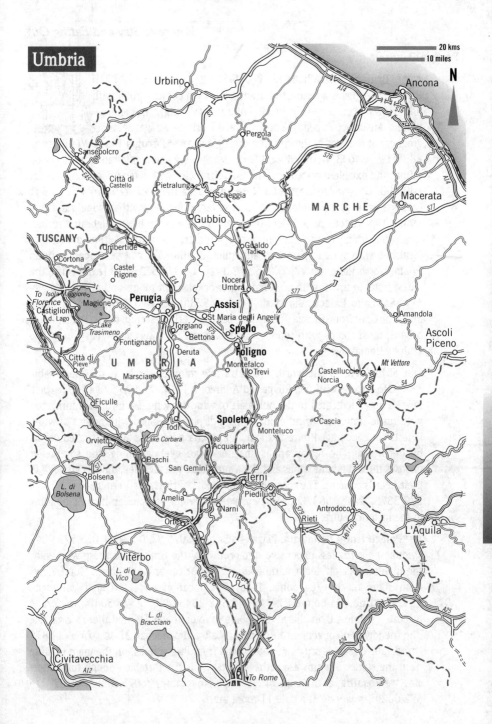

Perugia ✉ 06100

*****Brufani, Piazza Italia 12, ✆ 075 573 2541, 🖨 075 572 0210 (*very expensive*) is a renovated, traditional 19th-century hotel with fine views over the countryside, luxurious fittings, air-conditioning, an attractive central courtyard and a private garage. Set in greenery at the foot of the city, the prestigious ******Perugia Plaza**, Via Palermo 88, ✆ 075 34643, 🖨 075 30863 (*expensive*) is big and comfortable, with a pool, sauna, and excellent restaurant, the **Fortebraccio**, with fixed-price menus under L40,000. *Closed Mon.* ******La Rosetta**, Piazza Italia 19, ✆/🖨 075 572 0841 (*expensive*) is another older hotel, deservedly popular, with a wide variety of rooms from various periods and remodellings. The hotel has a celebrated restaurant, and dining in the garden in the summer; the rooms, either modern or furnished with antiques, are cosy and quiet. Goethe slept at ******Locanda della Posta**, Corso Vannucci 97, ✆ 075 572 8925, 🖨 075 572 2413 (*expensive*), the oldest hotel in town, with an ornate exterior, pleasant rooms and private garage. ******Sangallo Palace**, Via Masi 9, ✆ 075 573 0202, 🖨 075 573 0068 (*expensive*), not far from Piazza Italia, has been soberly restored to its Renaissance origins, most rooms with reproductions of great paintings and tapestries, a few with hydromassage.

Out of the centre, but worth the extra few minutes' drive, is the memorable ******Giò Arte e Vini**, Via Ruggero d'Andreotto 19, ✆/🖨 075 573 1100 (*expensive*), a hotel dedicated to the noble art of wine-drinking. Each room is furnished with rustic Umbrian furniture, including a display case filled with bottles of wine. Guests are encouraged to taste them and purchase from the amply stocked cellars on departure. The restaurant is another treat: every evening, the sommelier chooses three different wines and, for a surprisingly modest fee, diners can quaff to their heart's content. The recently refurbished ****Priori**, Via Vermiglioli 3, ✆ 075 572 3378, 🖨 075 583 3213 (*expensive–moderate*) occupies an historic building in the historic centre.

***Palace Hotel Bellavista, Piazza Italia 12, ✆ 075 5720 741, 🖨 075 572 9092 (*moderate*) is the less expensive step-brother of the Brufani, for those who enjoy the high-style salon décor without the 5-star prices and amenities. Good views from some of the 70 rooms. In a good location just off Corso Vannucci, ******Fortuna**, Via Bonazzi 19, ✆ 075 572 2845, 🖨 075 573 5040 (*moderate*) has more comfort than charm; all rooms have bath and TV, and there's a garage. The friendly and convenient ****Aurora**, Viale Indipendenza 21, ✆ 075 572 4819 (*moderate–cheap*) is only a minute's walk from Piazza Italia, on the main road up from the station. Rooms are rather spartan, but comfortable enough for a short stay. ****Rosalba**, at the edge of Piazza IV Novembre, ✆ 075 572 8285, 🖨 075 572 0626 (*moderate*) is a cute 11-room inn.

Etruria, Via della Luna 21, ✆ 075 572 3730 (*cheap*) is a simple place just off Corso Vannucci (only a few en suite rooms). Similar and just as central are **Piccolo**, Via Bonazzi 25, ✆ 075 572 2987, **Anna**, Via dei Priori 48, ✆ 075 573 6304, or **Paola**, Via della Canapina 5, ✆ 075 572 3816 (*all cheap*). Even without a youth hostel card, you can check in at the **Centro Internazionale Accoglienza per la Gioventù**, Via Bontempi 13, ✆/ 🖷 075 572 2880, by the Duomo, with bunk-beds. The tourist office has a list of rooms to rent.

There are a number of comfortable hotels in Perugia's environs for motorists, including two special choices: the Neo-Renaissance ★★★★**Castello dell'Oscano**, in a large park at Cenerente, ✉ 06070, 9km northwest of Perugia, ✆ 075 690 125, 🖷 075 690 666 (*expensive*), with 20 lovely, antique-furnished rooms, satellite TV and pool; and at Bosco, ✉ 06080, 10km east on the road to Gubbio, the larger ★★★★**Relais San Clemente**, ✆ 075 591 5100, 🖷 075 591 5001 (*expensive*), occupying a 14th-century Benedictine abbey, has a pool and tennis on its lovely grounds, luxurious, stylish rooms and a choice restaurant.

Some of the best restaurants are in the aforementioned hotels, especially La Rosetta and Brufani. For a taste of old Umbria, try the **Osteria del Bartolo**, Via Bartolo 30, ✆ 075 573 1561 (*expensive*), where beautifully prepared dishes have been re-created from ancient recipes. *Closed Sun*. The *enoteca* **Aladino**, Via della Prome 11 (the extension of Via del Sole) ✆ 075 572 0938 (*expensive*) is one of the most popular restaurants in the city, specializing in sunny Sardinian and other fresh Mediterranean dishes to go with its fine choice of wines. *Closed Mon*.

La Taverna, Via delle Streghe 8, ✆ 075 572 4128 (*moderate*), in the medieval quarter west of Corso Vannucci, serves simple dishes like succulent roast lamb and game, and a wide variety of pasta with truffles and mushrooms. *Closed Mon*. Another fine old inn is **Falchetto**, Via Bartolo 20, ✆ 075 573 1775 (*moderate*), near the cathedral, featuring Umbrian specialities—salumeria, *crostini*, tagliatelle with truffles, *pasta e fagioli*, grilled lamb and trout, and tasty desserts. *Closed Mon*. **La Lanterna**, Via Ulisse Rocchi 6, ✆ 075 5736 064 (*moderate*) is a pretty trattoria, turning out good game dishes such as *cinghiale al ginepro* (wild boar with juniper berries) and *capriolo ai mirtilli* (venison with bilberries). *Closed Wed*.

At **Ubu Re**, Via Baldeschi 17, ✆ 075 573 5461 (*moderate*), close to the cathedral, there are good variations on the usual Umbrian theme, including an excellent *coscio di agnello alle olive* (leg of lamb cooked with olives). *Closed Mon, Sat, and Sun midday*. **Il Cantinone**, Via Ritorto 6, ✆ 075 573 4430 (*moderate*), nearby, offers *spaghetti all'amatriciana* and *filetto tartufato*—fillet of steak smothered with a black truffle sauce. *Closed Tues*.

In a Renaissance palace, **Paiolo**, Via Augusta 11, ✆ 075 572 5611 (*cheap*) has good-value good food, and delicious pizzas. *Closed Wed and part of Aug*. If you watch the prices, you can dine very well for around L25,000 at **Osteria Il Gufo**, Via della Viola 18 (by San Fiorenzo), ✆ 075 573 4126 (*cheap*), which serves seasonal dishes with a flair. *Evenings only, closed Sun and Mon.* **Cambio**, Corso Vannucci 29, ✆ 075 572 4165 (*cheap*) serves reasonable meals and simple lunches. *Closed Wed.*

Spello ✉ 06038

The elegant, frescoed 17th-century ★★★★**Palazzo Bocci**, Via Cavour 17, ✆ 0742 301 021, ✇ 0742 301 464 (*moderate*) has been beautifully fitted out as a hotel with everything you need, plus a hanging garden; dining is *bello* and mellow in its restaurant, **Il Molino**, ✆ 0742 651 305, just opposite in Piazza Matteotti—home-made pasta or traditional Umbrian meats cooked over the flames. *Closed Tues.*

★★★**La Bastiglia**, in a charmingly restored mill on Via dei Molini, ✆ 0742 651 277, ✇ 0742 301 1559 (*expensive–moderate*) stands out for its pleasant rooms, beautiful terrace, views and good restaurant. ★★★**Altavilla**, Via Mancinelli 2, ✆ 0742 301 515, ✇ 0742 651 258 (*moderate*) also has a pleasant terrace and 24 well-furnished rooms run by the Prioetti family. ★★★**Del Teatro**, Via Giulia 24, ✆ 0742 301 140, ✇ 0742 301 1612 (*moderate*) is a beautifully restored and finely decorated 18th-century palazzo; many rooms have good views.

★★**Il Portonaccio**, Via Centrale Umbra, ✆ 0742 651 313, ✇ 0742 301 615, is a sound, *cheap* choice; rooms at ★★**Il Cacciatore**, Via Giulìa 42, ✆ 0742 651 141, ✇ 0742 301 603 (*moderate*) are a bit more, but will save you a walk to its very popular restaurant, the **Trattoria del Cacciatore** (*moderate*) with beautifully prepared homemade pasta and other dishes at decent prices. *Closed Mon.*

The local **Convent of S Maria Maddalena**, Via Cavour 1, ✆ 0742 651 156, in front of the church of S Maria Maggiore, offers rooms which are tidy and *cheap*.

At **La Cantina**, Via Cavour 2, ✆ 0742 651 775 (*moderate*), the menu changes according to the season; you may be offered *oca al sagrantino e castagne* (goose braised with chestnuts) or *agnello al limone* (lamb with lemon). *Closed Wed.*

Foligno ✉ 06034

The 17th-century ★★★Villa Roncalli, just south of the centre on Viale Roma 25, ✆ 0742 391 091, ✇ 0742 671 001 (*moderate*) is a fashionable villa-hotel with a shady garden and pool, garage and comfortable rooms, and the city's finest restaurant serving Umbrian dishes with a gourmet flair. *Closed Mon and two weeks in Aug.* ★★★**Le Mura**, Via Mentana 25, ✆ 0742 357 344, ✇ 0742 353 327 (*moderate*), next to the church of San Giacomo, has comfortable rooms and a solid restaurant. Near the station, the family-run ★★**Belvedere**, Via Ottaviani 19, ✆ 0742 353 990, ✇ 0742 356 243 (*moderate–cheap*) is more than adequate, with pleasant rooms and breakfast, but no restaurant.

For dinner, try **Da Remo**, Viale C. Battisti 11, ✆ 0742 340 679 (*moderate*) serving tasty *strangozzi* (fat, home-made spaghetti) and roast kid cooked in Sagrantino wine. *Closed Sun evenings and Mon.* Wine-lovers can enjoy their favourite tipple with cheeses and other snacks at cosy **Bacco Felice**, Via Garibaldi 73, ✆ 0742 341 019. East of Foligno, **★Lieta Sosta**, Via Adriatica 228/a, loc. Colfiorito, ✆/✇ 0742 681 321 (*cheap*) has seven rooms and a pool. Its restaurant offers fine country dining.

Spoleto ✉ 06049

The tourist office in Spoleto has a list of private rooms to rent.

The most spectacular hotel is the bijou **★★★★Gattapone**, Via del Ponte 6, ✆ 0743 223 447, ✇ 0743 223 448 (*expensive*), located in a stone house, clinging to the slope near the Rocca and the Ponte delle Torri, with fabulous views. Its eight rooms are spacious and finely furnished; another house next door contains the restaurant. Just outside the historic centre near the Piazza della Libertà, the **★★★★Albornoz Palace**, Viale Matteotti, ✆ 0743 221 221, ✇ 0743 221 600 (*expensive*) is refined and stylish and has a pool. Nearby, **★★★★Dei Duchi**, Viale Matteotti 4, ✆ 0743 44541, ✇ 0743 44543 (*expensive*), an attractive contemporary hotel, is popular among visiting artists and performers.

The beautiful and central 16th-century **Palazzo Dragoni**, Via del Duomo 13, ✆ 0743 222 220, ✇ 0743 222 225 (*expensive*) has kept much of its original atmosphere during its renovation into a *residenza d'epoca*. In the historic centre, **★★★★San Luca**, Via Interna delle Mura 21, ✆ 0743 223 399, ✇ 0743 223 800 (*expensive*) offers a sophisticated 19th-century ambience and a chance for self-indulgence, if you book a room equipped with a hydromassage.

★★★Charleston, Piazza Collicola 10, ✆ 0743 220 052, ✇ 0743 222 010 (*moderate*) is in a pretty 17th-century palazzo, with 18 comfortably furnished rooms in the *centro storico*. **★★★Clarici**, Piazza della Vittoria 32, ✆ 0743 223 311, ✇ 0743 222 010 (*moderate*), in the lower part of town, is more modern, but still decorated with taste and style. **★★★Nuovo Clitunno**, Piazza Sordini 6, ✆ 0743 223 340, ✇ 0743 222 663 (*moderate*) is a good, fairly central hotel. **★★Dell'Angelo**, Via Arco di Druso 25, ✆/✇ 0743 222 385 (*cheap*) has seven good double rooms near the centre. Also try **★★Due Porte**, Piazza della Vittoria 5, ✆/✇ 0743 223 666, or **★★Il Panciolle**, Via Duomo 4, ✆ 0743 45677 (both *cheap*), with a good restaurant (*moderate*) where meat is grilled over an open fire. *Closed Wed.*

There are a few good choices up at Monteluco. **★★★Paradiso**, ✆ 0743 223 082, ✇ 0743 223 427 (*moderate*) has a garden, great views and peace and quiet. Near the top, **★★★Michelangelo**, ✆ 0743 40289, ✇ 0743 47890 (*moderate*) has large rooms and very friendly staff. *Open April–Oct.* **★★Ferretti**, ✆ 0743 49849, ✇ 0743 222344 (*moderate–cheap*) is a *pensione* with plenty of charm; some rooms have balconies looking out on to the pretty tree-shaded piazza.

About 12km from Spoleto, the **Pecoraro**, ✆ 0743 54431, in Strettura, on the scenic SS33 to Terni, is a very pretty and above all welcoming *pensione*, where guests are treated like one of the family by owners Sandro and Illy Montefalchesi. There is also a small outdoor pool, a luxury in these parts. Very good home-cooking and wickedly strong home-made grappas make this a memorable place to stay or eat (*rooms cheap, meals moderate*).

At **Il Tartufo**, Piazza Garibaldi 24, ℂ 0743 40236 (*expensive*), Umbrian truffle dishes are the speciality, utilizing the black truffles of the Valnerina in various combinations of pasta and eggs; other dishes include grilled lamb and kid, and veal. *Closed Wed.*

Sabatini, Corso Mazzini 54, ℂ 0743 221 831 (*moderate*) serves good traditional Umbrian fare, indoors and out. *Closed Mon.* At **Il Panciolle**, Via Duomo 3, ℂ 0743 45598 (*moderate*), diners feast on truffles and meat grilled over the open fire. There are also seven nicely decorated rooms for rent. *Closed Wed.* In the heart of Spoleto, the **Trattoria del Festival**, Via Brignone 8, ℂ 0743 220 993 (*moderate*) has a pretty dining room with arched ceilings, and a blazing fire in winter. The chef has a winning way with truffle dishes and desserts. *Closed Fri.* For a good glass of wine and tasty snacks, try **La Cantina**, Via Filitteria 10/a, ℂ 0743 44475 (*moderate*). *Closed Mon.*

Other Pilgrim Destinations Around Italy

Italy showing important pilgrim destinations

✠ Though the vast majority of the pilgrims descending on Italy in the Jubilee Year will be concentrated in Rome and Assisi, nearly every diocese in Italy has a full schedule of events planned, and a number of sites will also be pilgrimage destinations, largely for Italians: Venice's San Marco, the neighbouring basilica in the ancient Roman city of Aquileia, L'Aquila and other towns in the Abruzzo, among others. Three that will attract pilgrims from outside Italy are Loreto in the Marches, where pilgrims have come for centuries to the house of the Virgin Mary, Pompei, near Naples, and San Giovanni Rotondo in Puglia, home of the Blessed Padre Pio.

Loreto

Getting There

Loreto is in the Marche, on the railway line along the coast between Ancona and Pescara—the station is outside the town, but there is a regular connecting bus.

Tourist Information

Tourist information: Via Solari 3, ✆ 071 970 276, ✉ 071 970 020. *www.imar.net/aptloreto*
Sanctuary of the Holy House: ✆ 071 970 108, ✉ 071 976 837.

The Miracle of the Holy House

The story of Loreto is a mystery of the faith. During the 1200s the Church found itself threatened on all sides by heretical movements and free-thinkers. The popes responded in various subtle ways to assimilate and control them; creating the Franciscan movement was one, and the encouragement of the cult of the Virgin Mary another. Conveniently enough, a legend of a miracle in the Marches gained wide currency. Mary's house in Nazareth—site of the Annunciation, and where the Holy Family lived after their return from Egypt—was transported by a band of angels to a hill in Istria on 10 May 1291, then decided to fly off again on 9 December 1294, this time landing in these laurel woods (*loreti*) south of Ancona. Supposedly the house had bestirred itself in protest over Muslim reoccupation of the Holy Land; the popes were thumping the tub for a new Crusade, and Loreto was just coincidentally located on the route to the Crusader ports on the Adriatic. Among the thousands of devout pilgrims to make their way here were Galileo, Montaigne and Descartes.

Since the 1960s, archaeologists and scholars had a closer look. When they compared the Santa Casa with other buildings that survive in the grotto of Nazareth (now in the Basilica of the Annunciation) they found that the stones of the Holy House are similar to those in the Grotto, and that they date from the same period, and that the Hebrew-Christian graffiti cut in the stones of the Holy House is very similar to that in Nazareth. The Holy House, they also found, has no foundation at all, but sits in the middle of an old road. But it appears that angels had little to do with its removal: a recently discovered document dated September 1294 refers to the dowry given by Nikeforos Angelo, king of Epirus, to his daughter when she wed Philip of Taranto, son of the Angevin King of Naples, Charles II, which included 'the holy stones carried away from the House of Our Lady.' When the Crusaders lost Palestine in 1291, apparently Nikeforos had the house in Nazareth dismantled and took the stones with him, to keep them from falling into Muslim hands, and they ended up here.

The Santuario della Santa Casa

Basilica open daily 6am–7pm (8pm in summer); the Santa Casa between 12.30–2.30.

Beginning in 1468, the simple church that originally housed the *Santa Casa* was re-constructed and embellished in a massive building programme that took well over a century to complete. Corso Boccalini, lined with souvenir stands, leads from the town centre up to the Sanctuary—a surprise, when you turn the corner and enter the enclosed **Piazza della Madonna**, with the church, a great fountain by Carlo Maderno, one of the architects of St Peter's, the **Palazzo Apostolico** and its elegant **loggia** by Bramante. This being a papal production, a big bronze statue of Sixtus V, in front of the church doors, dominates the piazza—many of the most important figures in the Roman art world had a hand in the work. In the summer this space is often filled up with the 'white train' loads of sick people, in the hopes that Loreto's Madonna may succeed where modern medicine has fallen short.

The sanctuary's understated façade is typical early Roman Baroque, though a little ahead of its time (1587); no one is perfectly sure to whom to ascribe it, since so many architects had a hand in the work. Giuliano da Sangallo built the cupola, almost a copy of Brunelleschi's great dome in Florence, Bramante did the side chapels, and Sansovino and Sangallo the Younger also contributed. One of the best features is the series of reliefs on the bronze doors, by the Lombardis and other artists; another is the circle of radiating brick **apses** on the east end, turreted like a Renaissance castle; be sure to walk around for a look. Apparently the original architects really did intend the back of the church, overlooking the town walls, to function as part of the fortifications, a bookend to Antonio da Sangallo the

Younger's round bastion supporting under Piazza Garibaldi, at the far end of town. The only unfortunate element in the ensemble is the ungainly neoclassical **campanile**, topped with a bronze-plated garlic bulb. Luigi Vanvitelli designed it in the 1750s. Don't blame the architect for the proportions; the tower had to be squat and strong to hold the 15-ton bell, one that has little trouble making itself heard once it gets going.

Chapels line the walls inside, embellished by the faithful from around the world, including recent ones from the United States (with an aeroplane) and Mexico. The sedate Spanish chapel is one of the better ones, the Knights of Malta's chapel has one of the goriest crucifixes in all Italy, and the English chapel commemorates the lyric poet Richard Crashaw, a refugee from Protestant intolerance who served as canon here until his death in the 1640s. A good deal of Loreto's art was swiped by Napoleon, and most of the paintings in the interior are from the last two centuries; the two **sacristies** on the right aisle, however, have fine frescoes by Luca Signorelli and Melozzo da Forlì (with 3D angels, and a beautiful *Christ Entering Jerusalem*). Under the dome you'll see the object of the pilgrims' attention.

The **Santa Casa**, a simple brick room with traces of medieval frescoes, contains the venerated black Madonna of Loreto, sculpted out of cedar in 1921, after the original was destroyed in a fire. The house was sheathed in marble by Bramante to become one of the largest and most expensive sculptural ensembles ever attempted—the better to make the flying house stay put. In size and plan it is rather like Michelangelo's original project for the tomb of Pope Julius II; its decoration includes beautiful reliefs by Sansovino, Sangallo, della Porta and others, showing scenes from the *Life of Mary*. The reliefs on the back show the airborne house removal that made Loreto's Virgin the patroness of the airline industry; Charles Lindbergh took her image with him on his historic transatlantic flight.

The **Sala del Tesoro** (1610) off the left nave has a ceiling frescoed with the *Life of Mary* by Pomarancio, who won the (rigged) competition over Caravaggio, only to get his face knifed by a gangster hired by Caravaggio, a great painter but alas, never a good sport. After Napoleon and his troops looted the treasures that once sparkled below, many were eventually returned, only to fall victim to a spectacular robbery in 1974 that still makes Loreto's custodians shudder. The upper floor of the Apostolic palace houses what the crooks missed in the **Museo-Pinacoteca** (*open April–Oct daily exc Mon, 9–1, 4–7, winter by appointment only, © call 071 977 759; adm*), especially the excellent, dramatic late paintings by Lorenzo Lotto, who spent his last gloomy impoverished years in Loreto, took orders, and died in 1556; there are Flemish tapestries from cartoons by Raphael, and a superb collection of ceramics, many from the 16th-century workshop of Orazio Fontana, donated by Duke Guidobaldo II della Rovere of Urbino. Just by the basilica there's a large Polish War cemetery, with over a thousand graves of men who died on the Adriatic front.

The rest of Loreto is devoted to the pilgrim trade, the pastry shops selling almond sweets such as *amaretti di Loreto* and *dolci del Cónero*. From the 1600s until the 1940s, the favourite souvenir of a Loreto pilgrim was either an envelope containing Holy Dust (i.e. the daily sweepings from the Holy House) or a tattoo of the Virgin, but now you'll only find the usual plaster models, holy pictures and plastic catapults.

Calendar of Jubilee Events

31 Dec 1999	Vigil of Prayer
24 March 2000	80th anniversary of the proclamation of the Madonna of Loreto as the patron saint of aviation: opening of festivities
28 March	Pilgrimage of aviation
21 April	The Living Passion: re-enactment of the Passion of Christ
21 May	Mass in Piazza della Madonna
15 June	Evening Rosary and torchlight procession to the Scala Santa
16 June	Afternoon of folklore from the Marche
12–14 Aug	Welcome of young pilgrims on their way to Rome
3–4 Oct	Pilgrimage to Assisi to deliver oil to the Basilica di S. Francesco
14–15 Oct	3rd World Meeting of the Family: coronation of the Madonna di Loreto as the Queen of the Family by the Holy Father
10 Dec	Annual Feast of the patron saint of the airforce: Mass in the Basilica della Santa Casa
22 Dec	Christmas Concert organized by the Italian Red Cross

Loreto ✉ *60025*   ***Where to Stay and Eating Out***

Loreto's helpful Tourist Office will recommend other hotels if the following are full; or you can check their web site (*see* p.191).

At Loreto Archi, just outside the centre, the elegant 19th-century ★★★★**Villa Tetlameya**, Via Villa Constantina 187, ✆ 071 978 863, 📠 071 976 639, has the most comfortable rooms in the area (*expensive*) and one of the best restaurants, **Zì Nene** (*expensive–moderate*), specializing in classic seafood dishes, as well as historical recipes from the Marches. *Closed Mon.*

Nearby ★★**Orlando**, Via Villa Constantina 89, ✆ 071 978 501, 📠 071 978 501 (*moderate*) has simple but pleasant rooms and good game dishes, along with snails or *coniglio con porchetta*. *Closed Wed.*

In the centre of Loreto hotels are invariably clean, quiet and respectable. A good many of them are run by religious orders—Ursulines, Franciscan Sisters, the Holy Family Institute of Piedmont—as accommodation for pilgrims: ★★★**Casa del Clero Madonna di Loreto**, Via Asdrubali 104, ✆ 071 970 298, 📠 071 970 102 (*moderate*) is a typical example. For a slightly more secular atmosphere, try ★★**Centrale** Via Solari 7, ✆ 071 970 173, 📠 071 750 0219. **Adreina**, for donkey's years on Via Buffaloreccia 14, ✆ 071 970 124 (*moderate*) serves wonderful grilled meats and Marchegiano specialities.

San Giovanni Rotondo and Monte Sant'Angelo

The tourists who come to Puglia's beautiful Gargano Peninsula for the beaches probably never notice, but this is holy ground, and has been since the time of the ancient Daunians, whose territory this was before the Romans conquered it. Sanctuaries, ancient and modern, are scattered all over the Gargano, and there are many stories of the apparitions of saints and angels. A thousand years ago, pilgrims from all over Europe came here to visit the shrine of St Michael at Monte Sant'Angelo; now they are more likely to be headed for San Giovanni Rotondo, to honour the memory of the newly-beatified, miracle-working Capuchin Padre Pio.

Getting There

However you are coming to the Gargano, you will probably have to pass through the provincial capital, **Fóggia**. This city is a main stop for all trains from Rome or Naples to Bari, and there is a connecting line to Manfredonia, a town that makes a convenient base for seeing the region (and a good place to look for a resort when the pilgrimage towns are packed). Fóggia's **railway station** is on Piazza Veneto, at the end of the central Viale XXIV Maggio (information ✆ 0881 621015). **Buses** also leave from Piazza Veneto, with frequent connections on the SITA line for Manfredonia, Monte Sant'Angelo and San Giovanni Rotondo (call ✆ 0881 773 117, for information)

Tourist Information

Manfredonia: Corso Manfredi 26, ✆ 0884 581 998.
San Giovanni Rotondo, Piazza Europa 104, ✆ 0882 456 240

San Giovanni Rotondo

San Giovanni Rotondo, a little town on the slopes of Monte Calvo, began as a stop on a pilgrimage path, the *Via Sacra* that took the Lombards to their national shrine at nearby Monte Sant'Angelo. Its name comes from an ancient domed church that started as a baptistry, rebuilt over an ancient temple of Janus. Today, however, San Giovanni has become a pilgrimage site of its own, one that has put the ancient shrine of St Michael in the shade.

Padre Pio was born Francesco Forgione in 1887, son of a poor farm family in Pietralcina, a tiny village of the Abruzzo. A chronically sickly child, he showed a vocation for piety in his early years and was sent off to the small Capuchin monastery in San Giovanni. There, praying before the crucifix of Santa Maria delle Grazie in 1918, he received the stigmata—the bleeding wounds of Christ—on his hands, feet and side, as had St Francis of Assisi 700 years previously. Over the years, miracles associated with Padre Pio multiplied: Once, he appeared before cardinals in Rome while his body was sleeping back in San Giovanni, and during World War II an allied bomber crew had a vision of him up in the clouds, warning them off from bombing the Gargano. Most of the miracles came in curing the sick; though never entirely healthy himself (he once recorded a fever of 130°, said to be a medical record) he managed to do a lot for others—including building a modern hospital in 1947, the first in the Gargano.

Padre Pio's name became known all over the world, and he was consulted by popes, including John Paul II before his accession, but nevertheless he continued to lead a simple life of prayer and devotion in San Giovanni. He died in 1968, and since then the number of pilgrims to San Giovanni has increased steadily, currently reaching over a million people each year. Miracles associated with the holy man have increased apace, including perhaps the earthquake, with its epicenter at San Giovanni, that struck during the mass given for the 30th anniversary of his death; though it reached 6 on the Richter scale, the town suffered no damage whatsoever. Padre Pio was beatified in May 1999.

Pilgrims in San Giovanni visit the **Sanctuary of Santa Maria delle Grazie** and Padre Pio's cell (*open daily 7–1 and 3.30–7.15*), and follow the Stations of the Cross at the **Via Crucis**, laid out on Monte Castellano with bronze statuary by Francesco Messina, an artist personally converted by Padre Pio (*open daily 6—6*). Besides Padre Pio's beatification the big news in San Giovanni is the opening of the **Chiesa Nuova**, a remarkable free-form structure by Italy's most celebrated architect, Renzo Piano. With 27 huge arches curving around a central altar, the church has room for 10,000 worshippers.

Monte Sant'Angelo

Before Padre Pio, the focus of spirituality in the Gargano was always Monte Sant'Angelo, one of the most important pilgrimage towns of medieval Italy. Before Christianity the cavern now dedicated to St Michael was the site of a dream oracle; a 5th-century bishop of Sipontum (an ancient town near Manfredonia, now abandoned) had a vision of the archangel, who left his red cloak as a token and commanded the sanctuary be converted to Christian worship. Early on, the new Monte Sant'Angelo was attracting pilgrims from all over Europe—continuing a tradition that had begun long before the site became Christian. St Michael always had a special attraction for warriors, including the Lombards, who ruled here. Among the foreign pilgrims were the first Normans, in the 9th century. They returned home with tales of a rich and fascinatingly civilized Puglia—inspiring the Hautevilles and their men to come down and conquer two centuries later. All the other sites dedicated to St Michael around the coasts of Europe—including of course Mont-St-Michel in Normandy—are the spiritual descendants of this one, founded as the cult of St Michael spread across Christendom in the early Middle Ages.

That Monte Sant'Angelo is a special place becomes evident even before you arrive. The trip up from Manfredonia passes through an uncanny landscape: chalky cliffs dotted with caves, ancient agricultural terraces, and a strange clarity in the light and air. After much twisting and grinding of gears, you arrive at a quiet, whitewashed city, a maze of steps and tunnels. The medieval centre of town, the **Junno**, is one of the most beautiful old quarters in southern Italy, a nonchalant harmony of colour and form that only a few coast towns in Puglia can achieve. Here you will find the **Santuario di San Michele** (*open Easter–Sept daily 7.30–7; Oct–Easter daily 7.30–12.30 and 2.30–5*), behind an eight-sided tower built by Charles of Anjou that reproduces the proportions (on one level) and much of the decoration of Frederick's Castel del Monte. The exterior of the sanctuary seems to be a normal church, with a Gothic porch and portals (mostly built in the 19th century, although one of the two identical portals is original 12th-century). Above the doors is a Latin inscription: 'Terrible is this place; this is the house of God and the Gate of Heaven.'

Inside, instead of the expected church, there is a long series of steps leading down to the cavern, passing a beautiful pair of bronze doors made in Constantinople in 1076, perhaps by the same artists who did the ones at Amalfi Cathedral. In the darkness most of the scenes are difficult to make out, but Jacob's ladder and the expulsion from Eden stand out clearly. Down in the cave, it is chilly and dark; in the old days pilgrims would come down on their knees, shuffling through the puddles to kiss the image of the archangel. The grotto is laid out like a small chapel. There are plenty of bits of medieval sculptural work around, but the best is a wonderful crazy-medieval bishop's chair, from the 12th century.

The town records give us an almost endless list of celebrity pilgrims: a dozen popes, King Ferdinand of Spain, four Holy Roman Emperors, saints Bernard, Catherine of Siena, and so on; even St Francis, and they can show you the mark he made on the cavern wall. Behind the altar you can see the little well that made this a holy site in the first place. Long before there was a St Michael, indigenous religions of Europe had a great reverence for springs and underground streams; many scholars believe the idea of dragons began with a primeval fascination with buried streams and accompanying lines of telluric forces beneath the earth's surface; the sleepless 'eye' of the dragon is the fountain, where these forces come to the surface. In the icons of Monte Sant'Angelo, as well as in the souvenir figurines hawked outside the sanctuary, Michael is shown dispatching Lucifer in the form of a dragon.

There's more to see in Monte Sant'Angelo, and more oddities. Downhill from the sanctuary, next to the half-ruined church of San Pietro, stands the 12th-century so-called tomb of Rotari (open mornings; if closed see custodian in San Michele). The idea that this was the tomb of 'Rotarus', a Lombard chief, stems from a misreading of one of the inscriptions. It is now believed this was intended to be a baptistry—a very large and unusual baptistry, if so; it is hard to make out the original intention since much of it has been swallowed up into the surrounding buildings. Some of the sculpted detail is extremely odd; note the figure of a woman nursing a serpent (or dragon).

Where to Stay and Eating Out

San Giovanni Rotondo ✉ 71013

Most of the hotels are simple places along the main street that cater to pilgrims and relatives of patients at the hospital, such as the ****S. Maria delle Grazie**, Viale Cappucini 25, ✆ 0882 456 031, ✍ 0882 413 282, and the *****Gaggiano**, Viale Cappuccini 144, ✆ 0882 453 701, ✍ 0882 456 650 (*both moderate–cheap*).

****Masseria Agropolis, Località Sant'Egidio, ✆ 0882 456 599 (*expensive*) is impressive, if a bit sterile, with a pool, cultivated fields, cooking workshops and horse-riding. The best restaurant in San Giovanni is **Da Costanzo**, on Via Santa

Croce, ℂ 0882 452 285, an old local favourite for traditional Pugliese cooking (*moderate*). *Closed Sun eve and Mon.*

Manfredonia ✉ 71043

****Gargano**, Viale Beccarini 2, ℂ 0884 587 621 (*moderate*) is the best hotel in town, with a sea-water pool and views from every room. Its restaurant (*expensive–moderate*) offers a range of fish dishes from soup to mixed fry. *Closed Tues and several weeks in Nov.* A more basic choice is **Sipontum**, Via di Vittorio 229, ℂ 0884 542 916 (*cheap*). **Al Porto**, Piazza Libertá 3, ℂ 0884 581800 (*moderate*), is justifiably proud of its seafood risotto, and the linguine with clam sauce is also a treat. *Closed Mon.* There are more treats to be had in the cool modern surroundings of **Il Baracchio**, Corso Roma 38, ℂ 0884 23874 (*moderate*) where the octopus salad has to be tasted to be believed. *Closed Mon.*

Monte Sant'Angelo ✉ 71037

The only hotel up here is the bizarrely named but comfortable ***Rotary**, 1km from town on Via Pulsano, ℂ 0884 562 146 (*moderate*); there are also three campsites nearby at Frazione Macchia. At **Al Grottino**, Corso Vittorio Emanuele 179, ℂ 0884 561 132 (*cheap*), you can get a dinner worth L50,000 for about half that— roast lamb and kid, truly elegant *antipasti*, sweets and cheeses. *Closed Mon.* Another good choice for lunch is the **Garden Paradise**, Via Basilica 51 (*cheap*), with well-prepared seafood and good *involtini*. *Open Oct—Mar; closed Mon.*

Pompei

Everyone knows the two-i Pompeii, the city destroyed by the eruption of Vesuvius in 79 AD that has become an open musem of the ancient Roman world. Its modern successor, one-i Pompei, has grown up from a tiny hamlet only in the last hundred years, partly because of the famous ruins, but also because of the presence of a miraculous image of the Virgin Mary that has made the village one of the most important pilgrimage sites in Italy. For the Holy Year, Pompei is expecting some four million visitors.

Getting There

Most people visiting Pompei for the Jubilee will be staying in Naples or Sorrento (both about 25km away) or other places around the Bay of Naples. Getting there should be relatively easy, thanks to Naples' modern and usually dependable suburban rail line, the **Circumvesuviana** (ℂ 081 779 2444), which has two lines, one for Sorrento and one for Pompei; they diverge at Torre Annunziata, and anyone travelling from Sorrento to Pompei will have to change there. Both lines run about every half-hour from 5.45am to 10.45pm.

Tourist Information

Pompei town: Via Sacra 1, 80045, ℂ 081 850 7255, ✉ 081 863 2401, with a branch office near the Porta Marina entrance to the old Pompeii site.

For information about the Sanctuary of the Madonna, contact the **Pontificio Santuario di Pompei**, Piazza B. Longol, Pompei 80045, ✆ 081 857 7111, 🖷 081 850 3357, *www.santuario.it*

The Madonna del Rosario

Pompei's story begins with the Blessed Bartolo Longo, a lawyer and former spiritualist adept who was converted by a vision of the Virgin Mary near the village in 1875. Thereafter he devoted himself to prayer, with a particular devotion ot the rosary (as the Virgin had requested), and also to good works, including the building of a parish church for the village. In a shop on Via Toledo in Naples, one of his friends found a worn and dirty old painting of the Madonna for the new church. Longo didn't want it at first; he thought it the most ill-featured Madonna he had ever seen. But nothing better was available for the small amount they had raised, and this rather large painting (a 16th-century work from a follower of Luca Giordano), made its way to Pompei on top of a load of manure.

Longo found a local artist, working on the ruins of Pompeii, to do some cleaning and restoration, and when the painting was finally unveiled, the first of innumerable miracles credited to it occured, the curing of an epileptic young girl. Soon people were coming to see the miraculous icon from all over Italy; the simple church Longo planned ended up a Papal basilica, lined with ex-votos from the faithful commemorating interventions of the Virgin in everything from moral illnesses to shipwrecks. Longo, who died in 1921, continued his charitable works, founding numerous institutions that continue today, including Italy's first home to care for the children of convicts.

The **Santuario della Madonna del Rosario**, begun in 1876 and expanded in 1933, was built in the Neapolitan Baroque style with a 187ft dome, one of the largest in Italy (*open daily 6–2 and 3–6.30*). For a good view over the town and the excavations take the lift up the campaile, added in 1912 (*open Sat–Thurs 9–1 and 3–6; adm*). There is a small musem in the sacristy (open *daily 9–1 and 3–6.30; adm*) with a Neapolitan *presepe* (Christmas crêche) from the 1800s. The Madonna of the church holds a special place in the affections of Neapolitan women. You'll probably see some of them, saying their rosaries, asking for the Madonna's intercession to help sort out their problems. If they have bare feet, this is not poverty, but devotion—usually the fulfilment of a personal pledge to the Madonna in thanks for a favour received. Neapolitans who ask for the Madonna's help often promise to walk there barefoot from Naples (26km) if their prayers are answered.

The **Pompei Museum** is on Via Colle San Bartolomeo (*open Mon–Sat 8–2*), a couple of minutes' walk from Piazza B. Longo in front of the basilica. This was the home of Blessed Bartolo Longo, and it contains exhibits on his life as well as a floor dedicated to Pompei's troublesome neighbour, Mount Vesuvius.

Calendar of Jubilee Events

24 Dec 1999	Beginning of the Jubilee, midnight mass and procession
30 Jan–8 May 2000	Quindici Sabati, the Pompei Sanctuary's particular devotion: fifteen Saturdays of meditations and prayers of the rosary leading up to the Supplica alla Madonna
Fridays in Lent	Via Crucis devotions in Piazzale Giovanni XXIII
8 May	Supplica alla Madonna: Pompei's major biannual event, with the adoration of the image of the Madonna Vigilia; numerous other pilgrimages in this month, including a procession with the Madonna Vigilia on 31 May
15 Aug	Assumption
1 Sept	Second Supplica alla Madonna
5 Oct	Anniversary of the death of the Blessed Bartolo Longo
7 Oct	Feast of the Rosary
13 Nov	Anniversary of the arrival of the sacred image of the Madonna in Pompei
5 Jan 2001	End of the Jubilee

Where to Stay and Eating Out

Pompei ✉ 80045

Thanks to the ruins of Pompeii and all the tourists that come to see them, Pompei has quite a few places to stay. Most of these are mid-range, modern, centrally located establishments, such as the small and comfortable ★★★**Villa Laura**, Via delle Salle 13, ✆ 081 863 1024, 🖷 081 850 4893 (*moderate*); and the larger ★★★**Bristol**, Piazza Vittorio Veneto, ✆ 081 850 3005, 🖷 081 863 1625 (*moderate*). Less expensive is the family run ★**Piccolo Sogno**, close to the basilica at Via Carlo Alberto 1, ✆ 081 863 1279, 🖷 081 863 1279 (*cheap*).

Zi Caterina, Via Roma 20, ✆ 081 850 7447 (*moderate*), with live lobsters in the tank and other noteworthy seafood dishes, is also a good place to try Lacrima Christi wine from the nearby slopes of Vesuvius. At **Al Gamberone**, Via Piave 36, ✆ 081 863 8322 (*moderate*), close to Pompei's main church, you can feast on prawns doused in cognac and other good fish dishes. In summer you may dine outside under the lemons and oranges. If you do not want fish there is an array of other dishes including a good cannelloni. Immediately outside the excavations' exit, next to the amphitheatre, is **Anfiteatro**, Via Plinio 9, ✆ 081 863 1245. Here the seafood is more modest—it's one of the few places in Pompei you'll see *baccalà* (salt cod) on the menu, along with truly good *spaghetti alle vongole*.

The picturesque Sorrentine peninsula, with its excellent selection of hotels, means you would be unwise to base yourself anywhere else. Sorrento itself is only 40 minutes away on the Circumvesuviana railway.

The turn of the century ★★★★**Grand Hotel Excelsior Vittoria**, Piazza T. Tasso 34, ✆ 081 807 1044, ✆ 081 877 1206 (*expensive*) is the place to stay for Grand Tour atmosphere. Owned by the same family for four generations, it's set in a park complete with orange and olive groves, overlooking the sea. Wagner, Alexandre Dumas, Nietzche, Princess Margaret, Sophia Loren and Pavarotti have all stopped by. The ★★★★**Grand Hotel Ambasciatori**, Via Califano 18, ✆ 081 878 2025, ✆ 081 807 1021 (*expensive*), a bit removed from the centre, has a palatial interior, pool, sea-bathing platform and gardens overlooking the sea. In the same area, the beautifully remodelled ★★★★**Grand Hotel Royal**, ✆ 081 807 3434, ✆ 081 877 2905 (*expensive*) has the same owners, and a pool and beach access.

In a more central location, the ★★★★**Imperial Tramontana**, on Via Vittorio Veneto, ✆ 081 878 1940, ✆ 081 807 2344 (*expensive*) has tropical gardens, a lift down to a private beach, and a pool. The ★★★★**Bellevue-Syrene**, on Via Marina Grande, ✆ 081 878 1024, ✆ 081 878 3963 (*expensive*) has beautifully restored rooms, lush gardens and a lift to the beach. If you have a car, follow the coastal road past the Marina Grande, and turn left up SS145, to the ★★★★**President**, Via Nastro Verde, Colle Parise, ✆ 081 878 2262, ✆ 081 878 5411 (*expensive*), set in a park, with lovely views and a pool.

A real bargain, in a villa with a private beach, and a good restaurant, is the ★★**Pensione La Tonnarella**, Via Capo 31, ✆ 081 878 1153, ✆ 081 878 2169 (*moderate*). On the road east out of Sorrento, the ★★★**Minerva**, Via Capo 30, ✆ 081 878 1011, ✆ 081 878 1949 (*moderate*) has 50 nice rooms, some with stunning views over the sea. The *pensione* ★★**Loreley et Londres**, Via Califano 2, ✆ 081 807 3187 (*cheap*) has lovely sea views; the friendly staff make up for the somewhat dreary décor, and there's a lift down to a private sea-bathing platform. The ★**City**, Corso d'Italia 217, ✆ 081 877 221, ✆ 081 877 2210 (*cheap*) is one of the nicest simple hotels—close to the centre but not too noisy. The ★**Nice**, Corso Italia 257, ✆ 081 807 2530, ✆ 081 807 1154 (*cheap*), near the Circumvesuviana station, is also a surprisingly good find, close to the town centre.

If you have a car, stay up on the hill at the *azienda agrituristica* **Il Giardino di Vigliano**, Località Villazzano, Massa Lubrense, ✆ 081 533 9823 (*cheap*); through an olive grove and under a lemon pergola, is the 17th-century building complete with a Saracen tower. Half-board and apartment rental are also available.

The grand and gloriously decorated restaurant, **O' Parrucchiano**, Corso Italia 67, ✆ 081 878 1321 (*very expensive–expensive*) is by tradition one of Italy's best. On Piazza Tasso, **Caruso** ✆ 081 807 3156 (*very expensive–expensive*) has a vast and inventive menu, attentive service and an extensive wine list. Save room for dessert.

La Lanterna, Via S. Cesareo 23–25, ✆ 081 878 1355 (*moderate–cheap*) has outside tables, tasteful décor, friendly and efficient service and impeccable *risotto ai frutti di mare*. The family-run **Trattoria da Emilia**, Via Marina Grande 62, ✆ 081 807 2720 (*moderate–cheap*) has a terrace overlooking the sea, and an excellent-value menu based on fresh local ingredients and classic Sorrento recipes. *Closed Tues.* In the basement of an old Roman villa, the **Taverna Artis Domus**, Via San Nicola 56, ✆ 081 877 2073 (*moderate–cheap*) is a lively place for a snack or a drink in the evening. In summer there is live music every night. For a very cheap meal, or a take-away, try the **Panetteria-Pizzeria Franco**, Corso Italia 265, ✆ 081 877 2066 (*cheap*), where you sit at long wooden tables and watch your pizza prepared in front of you. A popular place with locals.

Turin (Torino)

Getting There

Turin's **Caselle airport** is 15km north of the city; for information call ✆ 011 567 6361. Every 30 minutes an **airport bus**, run by SADEM, stops at Porta Susa Station, the main bus terminal, and outside Porta Nuova Station. Tickets can be bought from a kiosk in the arrivals hall or at the Café Negrita on the corner of Via Sacchi and Corso Vittorio Emanuele II (opposite Porta Nuova).

Turin's massive neoclassical station, **Porta Nuova** (information, ✆ 147 888 088, *open daily 7am–9pm*), is near the centre, with connections to France and Milan (1½ hrs) and Venice (5 hrs).

Tourist Information

The main office, Piazza Castello 161, ✆ 011 535 181/✆ 011 535 901 (*open Mon–Sat 9–7.30*) has a free room-finding service; other offices are at Porta Nuova Station, ✆ 011 531 327; Via Garibaldi 25, ✆ 011 442 3838; and Caselle Airport.

For all information concerning the *Ostensione della Sindone* (especially if you are taking a group), contact the **Segreteria Ostensione Sindone**, Via XX Settembre 87, 10122 Torino, ✆ 0115 215 960, ✉ 0115 215 992, e-mail *sindone @torino.chiesacattolica.it*; *sindone.torino.chiesacattolica.it*

The Turin Shroud

Turin's plain **Duomo di San Giovanni**, on Via XX Settembre, was built by three dry 15th-century Tuscan architects. What it lacks in presence it compensates for with one of the most provocative artefacts of Christendom: the Turin Shroud, brought from the old Savoy capital of Chambéry in the 16th century by Emanuele Filiberto.

To house the relic properly, Guarini designed the striking, black marble **Cappella della Sacra Sindone** (Chapel of the Holy Shroud), crowned by a bold oliaphonous dome-cone zig-zagging to a climax of basketweave arches full of restless energy. The shroud, shown only on special occasions, is kept in a silver casket in an iron box in

The *Ostensione della Sindone*, 'exhibiting of the Shroud', in the Jubilee year will take place from 26 August to 22 October. In the Duomo, Mass will be celebrated for pilgrims every evening at 6.45; at 7.15, after Mass, pilgrims will be allowed to view the Shroud after a preparatory speech and prayer. The Duomo will remain open until 11pm.

a marble coffer in the urn on the chapel altar; an exact replica, however, is displayed along with a multilingual explanation of the results of several scientific investigations, which tried to determine whether it was possible that the shroud was used at Christ's burial. Although forensic scientists and their computers have concluded that it would have been impossible to forge the unique front and back impressions of a crucified man with a wound in his side and bruises from a crown of thorns, the shroud flunked a carbon-dating test in 1989, and is now believed to date from the 12th century.

Besides the shroud, the cathedral contains in its second chapel a fine polyptych of SS. Crispin and Crispinian by Defendante Ferrari, and a copy of Leonardo da Vinci's *Last Supper*, painted when the original began to crumble.

Detroit without the degradation, Turin is the aristocratic capital of the Savoys, an elegantly planned Baroque city of arcades and squares, frequent venue of international bridge tournaments, the home of—as well as the famous shroud—Juventus, Fiat, the Red Brigades and vermouth, and reputedly the centre of black magic in the Mediterranean. Its cuisine is influenced by France; its winters are colder than Copenhagen's; its most renowned museum is Egyptian. Central Turin is laid out in a stately rhythm of porticoed streets and squares. Turin's finest, **Piazza San Carlo**, is a 17th-century confection with a flamboyant centrepiece in its bronze equestrian statue of Duke Emanuele Filiberto. This is a city of elegant cafés; the piazza's 19th-century Caffè Torino, a veritable palace of java with chandeliers and frescoed ceilings, is the most celebrated of them all. The **Museo Egizio (Egyptian Museum)** (*open Tues–Sat 8.30am–10pm, Sun and hols 8.30–8; adm exp*) is rated (except by the directors of the Louvre!) as the second most important in the world, after the museum in Cairo. The first Egyptian museum in the world (founded in 1824), its star is the reconstruction of the 15th-century BC rock-cut Temple of Ellessya.

Turin ✉ *10100*   ***Where to Stay and Eating Out***

The ★★★★**Turin Palace**, Via Sacchi 8, ✆ 011 562 5511, ✉ 011 561 2187 (*very expensive*) is a traditional grand hotel with the deserved reputation for being Turin's top hotel. The public rooms are sumptuous, the restaurant elegant and expensive, and the bedrooms luxurious. ★★★★**Villa Sassi**, Via Traforo del Pino 47, ✆ 011 890 556, ✉ 011 890 095 (*very expensive*), in the hills east of the Po in a lovely park, is converted from a 17th-century patrician villa retaining most of its original features—marble floors, Baroque fireplaces and portraits. It also has one of Turin's finest restaurants, **El Toulà** (*very expensive*) whose menus feature garden-fresh ingredients from the estate; there's a renowned wine cellar containing over 90,000 bottles. You need a car. *Closed Aug; minimum stay three days.*

In a quiet street near the centre, the ★★★★**Grand Hotel Sitea**, Cia Carlo Alberti 35, ✆ 011 517 0171, ✆ 011 548 090 (*very expensive*) has luxurious bedrooms, and an excellent restaurant, **Carignano**, which serves a variety of Piemontese fare. The excellent-value ★★★**Victoria**, Via Nino Costa 4, ✆ 011 561 1909, ✆ 011 561 1806 (*expensive*) is furnished in a delightful hotchpotch of screens, chairs, tables and sofas. The staff are friendly and helpful. The ★★★**Roma & Rocca Cavour**, Piazza Carlo Felice 60, ✆ 011 561 2772, ✆ 011 562 8137 (*moderate*) is a somewhat impersonal choice, but has some lovely rooms.

★★**Sila**, Piazza Carlo Felice, ✆ 011 544 086 (*cheap*) has a great location and views, although it's slightly gloomy. ★**Kariba**, Via San Francesco d'Assisi 4, ✆ 011 534 856 (*cheap*) is clean and comfortable (no ensuite bathrooms). **Ostello Torino**, Via Alby 1, ✆ 011 660 2939 (*cheap*), the youth hostel, is on the other side of the river, near the Piazza Crimea (bus no.52 from the station). *Closed 9–6.*

Turin's temple of fine cuisine, **Vecchia Lanterna**, Corso Re Umberto 21, ✆ 011 537 047 (*very expensive*) is a subdued and classy restaurant whose gourmet delights include quail pâté, ravioli filled with duck in a truffle sauce, shellfish salad, stuffed trout and sea bass in the old Venetian style; and there's a perfect wine list. *Reserve.* **Cambio**, Piazza Carignano 2, ✆ 011 546 690, or ✆ 011 543 760 (*very expensive*) is a nostalgic trip back to the old royal capital: the décor, the chandeliers, gilt mirrors, frescoes, red upholstery, and even the waiters' costumes. The old recipes have been lightened to appeal to modern tastes.

Charming **Due Lampioni**, Via Carlo Alberto 45, ✆ 011 546 721 (*expensive*) serves a delightful array of *antipasti*, many featuring salmon, scampi and lobster. In the spring try the *gnocchi agli'asparagi*, followed by rack of lamb, or tournedos with foie gras. **Montecarlo**, Via San Francesco da Paola 37, ✆ 011 830 815 (*expensive*) is one of Turin's most romantic restaurants, in the atrium of a palazzo, under stone arches, with a delectable variety of *antipasti*, followed by carrot soup with barley and well-prepared *secondi* like baked liver, lamb or duck. Excellent desserts and wines.

Da Giuseppe, Via San Massimo 34, ✆ 011 812 2090 (*moderate*) offers a wide array of Piemontese *antipasti* and other specialities. *Reserve.* **L'Archimboldo**, Via Santa Chiara, ✆ 011 521 1816 (*moderate*) is an excellent choice north of the city centre, with over a hundred sauces to accompany your pasta. **Deligia Ignazia**, Via Urbaro Rattazzi, ✆ 011 534 068 (*moderate*) is a friendly family-run place packed every night with locals and serving various Piemontese specialities. **Arcadia**, Galleria Subalpina 16, ✆ 011 561 3898 (*moderate*) is a popular lunchtime spot, with excellent *antipasti*, pasta and country-style meat dishes. **Lullaby**, Via XX Settembre 6, ✆ 011 531 024 (*cheap*) serves delicious, filling local fare in a still-smart but unpretentious atmosphere.

The fathers of modern Italian were Dante, Manzoni, and television. Each did their part in creating a national language from an infinity of regional and local dialects; the Florentine Dante, the first 'immortal' to write in the vernacular, did much to put the Tuscan dialect in the foreground of Italian literature. Manzoni's revolutionary novel, *I Promessi Sposi* (*The Betrothed*), heightened national consciousness by using an everyday language all could understand in the 19th century. Television in the last few decades is performing an even more spectacular linguistic unification; although the majority of Italians still speak a dialect at home, school, and work, their TV idols insist on proper Italian.

Perhaps because they are so busy learning their own beautiful but grammatically complex language, Italians are not especially apt at learning others. English lessons, however, have been the rage for years, and at most hotels and restaurants there will be someone who speaks some English. In small towns and out of the way places, finding an Anglophone may prove more difficult. The words and phrases below should help you out in most situations, but the ideal way to come to Italy is with some Italian under your belt.

Pronunciation

Italian words are pronounced phonetically. Every vowel and consonant (except 'h') is sounded. Consonants are the same as in English, except the 'c' which, when followed by an 'e' or 'i', is pronounced like the English 'ch' (*cinque* thus becomes 'cheenquay'). Italian 'g' is also soft before 'i' or 'e' as in *gira*, pronounced 'jee-ra'. 'H' is never sounded; 'z' is pronounced like 'ts'. The consonants 'sc' before the vowels 'i' or 'e' become like the English 'sh' as in 'sci', pronounced 'shee'; 'ch' is pronouced like a 'k' as in Chianti, kee-an-tee; 'gn' as 'ny' in English (*bagno*, pronounced 'ban-yo'; while 'gli' is pronounced like the middle of the word 'million' (Castiglione, pronounced 'Ca-steely-oh-nay'). Vowel pronunciation is: 'a' as in English father; 'e' when unstressed is pronounced like 'a' in 'fate' as in *mele*, when stressed can be the same or like the 'e' in 'pet' (*bello*); 'i' is like the 'i' in 'machine'; 'o' like 'e', has two sounds, 'o' as in 'hope' when unstressed (*tacchino*), and usually 'o' as in 'rock' when stressed (*morte*); 'u' is pronounced like the 'u' in 'June'. The accent usually (but not always!) falls on the penultimate syllable. Also note that, in the big northern cities, the informal way of addressing someone as you, *tu*, is widely used; the more formal *lei* or *voi* is commonly used in provincial districts.

Days

Monday	*lunedì*	Friday	*venerdì*
Tuesday	*martedì*	Saturday	*sabato*
Wednesday	*mercoledì*	Sunday	*domenica*
Thursday	*giovedì*		

Language

Time

What time is it?	*Che ore sono?*	today	*oggi*
day/week	*giorno/settimana*	tomorrow	*domani*
month	*mese*	soon	*fra poco*
morning/afternoon	*mattina/pomeriggio*	later	*dopo/più tardi*
evening	*sera*	It is too early	*È troppo presto*
yesterday	*ieri*	It is too late	*È troppo tardi*

Numbers

one	*uno/una*	forty	*quaranta*
two/three/four	*due/tre/quattro*	fifty	*cinquanta*
five/six/seven	*cinque/sei/sette*	sixty	*sessanta*
eight/nine/ten	*otto/nove/dieci*	seventy	*settanta*
eleven/twelve	*undici/dodici*	eighty	*ottanta*
thirteen/fourteen	*tredici/quattordici*	ninety	*novanta*
fifteen/sixteen	*quindici/sedici*	hundred	*cento*
seventeen/eighteen	*diciasette/diciotto*	one hundred & one	*cent'uno*
nineteen	*dicianove*	two hundred	*duecento*
twenty	*venti*	one thousand	*mille*
twenty-one	*ventuno*	two thousand	*duemila*
thirty	*trenta*	million	*milione*

Useful Words and Phrases

yes/no/maybe	*si/no/forse*	Good afternoon/	*Buonasera*
I don't know	*Non lo so*	evening (also formal hello)	
I don't understand	*Non capisco*	Good night	*Buonanotte*
...(Italian)	*...(italiano)*	Goodbye	*Arrivederla* (formal),
Does someone here	*C'è qualcuno qui*		*arrivederci/ciao* (informal)
...speak English?	*...che parla inglese?*	What do you call this	*Come si chiama questo*
Speak slowly	*Parla lentamente*	...in Italian?	*...in italiano?*
Could you assist me?	*Potrebbe aiutarmi?*	What?/Who?/Where?	*Che?/Chi?/Dove?*
Help!	*Aiuto!*	When?/Why?	*Quando?/Perché?*
Please	*Per favore*	How?	*Come?*
Thank you (v. much)	*(Molte) grazie*	How much?	*Quanto?*
You're welcome	*Prego*	I am lost	*Mi sono smarrito*
It doesn't matter	*Non importa*	I am hungry/thirsty	*Ho fame/sete*
All right	*Va bene*	sleepy	*Ho sonno*
Excuse me	*Mi scusi*	I am sorry	*Mi dispiace*
Be careful!	*Attenzione!*	I am tired	*Sono stanco*
Nothing	*Niente*	I am ill	*Mi sento male*
It is urgent!	*È urgente!*	Leave me alone	*Lasciami in pace*
How are you?	*Come sta?*	good	*buono;bravo*
Well, and you?	*Bene, e lei?*	bad	*male;cattivo*
What is your name?	*Come si chiama?*	hot/cold	*caldo/freddo*
Hello	*Salve/ciao* (both	slow/fast	*lento/rapido*
	informal)	up/down	*su/giù*
Good morning	*Buongiorno* (formal	big/small	*grande/piccolo*
	hello)	here/there	*qui/lì*

Transport

airport	*aeroporto*	platform	*binario*
bus stop	*fermata*	taxi	*tassì*
bus/coach	*autobus/pullman*	ticket	*biglietto*
railway station	*stazione ferroviaria*	customs	*dogana*
train	*treno*	seat (reserved)	*posto (prenotato)*

Shopping, Service, Sightseeing

I would like...	*Vorrei...*	money	*soldi*
Where is/are...	*Dov'è/Dove sono...*	newspaper (foreign)	*giornale (straniero)*
How much is it?	*Quanto costa questo?*	pharmacy	*farmacia*
open	*aperto*	police station	*commissariato*
closed	*chiuso*	policeman	*poliziotto*
cheap	*a buon prezzo*	post office	*ufficio postale*
expensive	*caro*	sea	*mare*
bank	*banca*	shop	*negozio*
beach	*spiaggia*	room	*camera*
bed	*letto*	tobacco shop	*tabacchi*
church	*chiesa*	WC	*toilette/bagno*
entrance/exit	*entrata/uscita*	men	*Signori/Uomini*
hospital	*ospedale*	women	*Signore/Donne*

Useful Hotel Vocabulary

I'd like a double room please	*Vorrei una camera doppia, per favore*
I'd like a single room please	*Vorrei una camera singola, per favore*
with bath, without bath	*con bagno, senza bagno*
for two nights	*per due notti*
We are leaving tomorrow morning	*Partiamo domani mattina*
Is there a room with a balcony?	*C'è una camera con balcone?*
There isn't (aren't) any hot water, soap, light, toilet paper, towels	*Manca/Mancano acqua calda, sapone, luce, carta igienica, asciugamani*
May I pay by credit card?	*Posso pagare con carta di credito?*
May I see another room please?	*Per favore potrei vedere un' altra camera?*
Is breakfast included?	*E compresa la prima colazione?*
How do I get to the town centre?	*Come posso raggiungere il centro città?*

Driving

near/far	*vicino/lontano*	garage	*garage*
left/right	*sinistra/destra*	This doesn't work	*Questo non funziona*
straight ahead	*sempre diritto*	mechanic	*meccanico*
forward/backwards	*avanti/indietro*	map/town plan	*carta/pianta*
north/south	*nord/sud*	Where is the road to...?	*Dov'è la strada per...?*
east	*est/oriente*	breakdown	*guasto/panne*
west	*ovest/occidente*	driving licence	*patente di guida*
round the corner	*dietro l'angolo*	driver	*guidatore*
crossroads	*bivio*	speed	*velocità*
street/road	*strada/via*	danger	*pericolo*
square	*piazza*	parking	*parcheggio*
car hire	*noleggio macchina*	no parking	*sosta vietata*
motorbike	*motocicletta*	narrow	*stretto*
scooter	*Vespa*	bridge	*ponte*
bicycle	*bicicletta*	toll	*pedaggio*
petrol/diesel	*benzina/gasolio*	slow down	*rallentare*

Travel Directions

I want to go to...	*Desidero andare a...*
How can I get to...?	*Come posso andare a...?*
Do you stop at...?	*Ferma a...?*
Where is...?	*Dov'è...?*
How far is it to...?	*Quanto siamo lontani da...?*
What is the name of this station?	*Come si chiama questa stazione?*
When does the next ... leave?	*Quando parte il prossimo...?*
From where does it leave?	*Da dove parte?*
How long does the trip take...?	*Quanto tempo dura il viaggio?*
How much is the fare?	*Quant'è il biglietto?*
Have a good trip	*Buon viaggio!*

Italian Menu Vocabulary

Antipasti (Hors d'œuvres)

These before-meal treats can include almost anything; among the most common are:

antipasto misto	mixed antipasto
bruschetta	garlic toast (sometimes with tomatoes)
carciofi (*sott' olio*)	artichokes (in oil)
frutti di mare	seafood
funghi (*trifolati*)	mushrooms (with anchovies, garlic, and lemon)
gamberi ai fagioli	prawns (shrimps) with white beans
mozzarella (*in carrozza*)	cow or buffalo cheese (fried with bread in batter)
prosciutto (*con melone*)	raw ham (with melon)
salsicce	sausages

Minestre (Soups) and Pasta

These dishes are the principal typical first courses (*primi*) served throughout Italy.

agnolotti	ravioli with meat	*pastina in brodo*	tiny pasta in broth
cacciucco	spiced fish soup	*risotto* (*alla milanese*)	Italian rice (with stock, saffron and wine)
cappelletti	small ravioli, often in broth		
crespelle	crêpes	*spaghetti all' amatriciana*	with spicy pork and chilli sauce
frittata	omelette		
gnocchi	potato dumplings	*spaghetti alla carbonara*	with bacon, eggs, and black pepper
orecchiette	ear-shaped pasta, often served with turnip greens		
		spaghetti al sugo/ ragù	with meat sauce
panzerotti	ravioli filled with egg, mozzarella and anchovies	*spaghetti alle vongole*	with clam sauce
		stracciatella	broth with eggs and cheese
pappardelle alla lepre	pasta with hare sauce		

Formaggio (Cheese)

Bel Paese	a soft white cow's cheese	*Parmigiano*	Parmesan cheese
cacio/ caciocavallo	pale yellow, often sharp cheese	*pecorino*	sharp sheep's cheese
		provolone	sharp, tangy cheese
fontina	rich cow's milk cheese	*...dolce*	...less strong
groviera	mild cheese (gruyère)	*stracchino*	soft white cheese
gorgonzola	soft blue cheese		

Carne (Meat)

abbacchio	milk-fed lamb
agnello	lamb
animelle	sweetbreads
anatra	duck
arista	pork loin
arrosto misto	mixed roast meats
bocconcini	fried veal with ham and cheese
bollito misto	stew of boiled meats
braciola	chop
brasato di manzo	braised beef with vegetables
bresaola	dried raw meat (similar to ham)
carne di castrato/ suino	mutton/pork
carpaccio	thin slices of raw beef served with piquant sauce
cassoeula	winter stew with pork and cabbage
cervello	brains
...al burro nero	...in black butter sauce
cervo	venison
cinghiale	boar
coniglio	rabbit
cotoletta	veal cutlet
...alla milanese	...fried in breadcrumbs
...alla bolognese	...with ham and cheese
fagiano	pheasant
faraona	guinea fowl
...alla creta	...in earthenware pot
fegato	liver (usually of veal)
...alla veneziana	...with filling
lombo di maiale	pork loin
lumache	snails

maiale (al latte)	pork (cooked in milk)
manzo	beef
osso buco	braised veal knuckle with herbs
pancetta	rolled pork
pernice	partridge
petto di pollo	boned chicken breast
...sorpresa	...stuffed and deep fried
piccione	pigeon
pizzaiola	beef steak with tomato and oregano sauce
pollo	chicken
...alla cacciatora	...with tomatoes and mushrooms
...alla diavola	...grilled
...alla marengo	...fried with tomatoes, garlic and wine
polpette	meatballs
quaglie	quails
rane	frogs
rognoni	kidneys
saltimbocca	veal scallop with prosciutto, sage, wine and butter
scaloppine	thin slices of veal sautéed in butter
spezzatino	pieces of beef or veal, usually stewed
spiedino	meat on a skewer or stick
stufato	beef braised in white wine with vegetables
tacchino	turkey
vitello	veal

Pesce (Fish)

aciughe or Alici	anchovies
aragosta	lobster
aringa	herring
branzino	sea bass
calamari	squid
cappe sante	scallops
cozze	mussels
fritto misto	mixed fried delicacies
gamberetto	shrimp
gamberi (di fiume)	prawns (crayfish)
insalata di mare	seafood salad
merluzzo	cod
orata	bream

ostriche	oysters
pesce spada	swordfish
pesce di San Pietro	John Dory
rombo	turbot
sarde	sardines
sgombro	mackerel
sogliola	sole
squadro	monkfish
tonno	tuna
trota	trout
trota salmonata	salmon trout
vongole	small clams
zuppa di pesce	mixed fish in sauce/stew

Contorni (Side Dishes, Vegetables)

carciofi (alla giudia)	artichokes (deep fried)	lattuga	lettuce
cetriolo	cucumber	lenticchie	lentils
cipolla	onion	melanzane	aubergine/eggplant
fagioli	white beans	patate (fritte)	potatoes (fried)
fagiolini	French (green) beans	peperonata	stewed peppers, onions, etc.
fave	broad beans	pomodoro (i)	tomato(es)
funghi (porcini)	mushrooms (boletus)	porri	leeks
insalata (mista, verde)	salad (mixed, green)	zucchini	courgettes

Dolci (Desserts)

coppa gelato	assorted ice-cream	sorbetto	sorbet/sherbet
crema caramella	caramel-topped custard	spumone	a soft ice-cream
crostata	fruit flan	torta	cake, tart
gelato	ice-cream	zabaglione	whipped eggs and
granita	flavoured water ice		Marsala wine, served hot
panettone	sponge cake with	zuppa inglese	trifle
	candied fruit and raisins		

Frutta (Fruit)

albicocche	apricots	macedonia di frutta	fruit salad
ananas	pineapple	mele	apples
arance	oranges	melone	melon
banane	bananas	more	blackberries
ciliege	cherries	pera	pear
datteri	dates	pesca	peach
fichi	figs	pesca noce	nectarine
fragole (con panna)	strawberries (with cream)	prugna/susina	prune/plum
lamponi	raspberries	uva	grapes
limone	lemon		

Bevande (Beverages)

acqua minerale	mineral water	latte	milk
con/ senza gas	with/without fizz	limonata	lemon soda
aranciata	orange soda	succo di frutta	fruit juice
birra (alla spina)	beer (draught)	tè	tea
caffè (freddo)	coffee (iced)	vino	wine
cioccolata	chocolate	rosso, bianco, rosato	red, white, rosé

Cooking Terms, Miscellaneous

aceto (balsamico)	vinegar (balsamic)	olio	oil
aglio	garlic	pane (tostato)	bread (toasted)
burro	butter	panini	sandwiches
conto	the bill	panna	cream
forno	oven	sale	salt
fritto	fried	salsa	sauce
ghiaccio	ice	tramezzini	finger sandwiches
griglia	grill	uovo	egg
miele	honey	zucchero	sugar

Barzini, Luigi, *The Italians* (Hamish Hamilton, 1964). A perhaps too clever account of the Italians by an Italian journalist living in London, but one of the classics.

Dante Alighieri, *The Divine Comedy* (plenty of equally good translations). Few poems have ever had such a mythical significance for a nation. Anyone serious about understanding Italy and the Italian world view will need more than a passing acquaintance with Dante.

Hutton, Edward, *Florence, Assisi, and Umbria Revisited*; *Venice and Venetia* and *Rome* (Hollis & Carter).

Morton, H. V., *A Traveller in Rome* and *A Traveller in Southern Italy* (Methuen, 1957, 1969). Among the most readable and delightful accounts of the region in print. Morton is a sincere scholar and a true gentleman. Also a good friend to cats.

Nichols, Peter, *Italia, Italia* (Macmillan, 1973). Account of modern Italy by an old Italy hand.

Petrarch, Francesco, *Canzoniere and Other Works* (Oxford, 1985). The most famous poems by the 'First Modern Man'.

Vasari, Giorgio, *Lives of the Artists* (Penguin, 1985). Readable, anecdotal accounts of the Renaissance greats by the father of art history, also the first professional Philistine.

Belitto, Christopher, *What Every Catholic Should Know About the Millennium* (Liguori Press, 1998). The teachings of the Church on the significance of the millennium and contemporary issues.

Coleman, Simon and Elsner, John, *Pilgrimage: Past and Present in the World Religions* (Harvard University Press, 1997). A comprehensive historical meditation on the meaning of pilgrimage across the globe, in every faith.

Dunlap, Lauren Glen, *And I, Francis: The Life of Francis of Assisi in Word* (Chiron Publications, 1996). A modern recounting of the life of St Francis, with striking illustrations.

Harris, Maria, *Proclaim Jubilee! A Spirituality for the 21st Century* (Westminster/John Knox, 1994). Proposes the millennium as an opportunity for inner and outer renewal of Christian spirituality.

McMichaels, Susan, *Journey Out of the Garden: St. Francis of Assisi and the Process of Individuation* (Paulist Press, 1997). St Francis' spiritual journey interpreted in terms of the Jungian theory of individuation.

Ruffin, Bernard C., *Padre Pio: The True Story* (Our Sunday Visitor, 1991). Account of the life of Padre Pio and the phenomenon that grew up around him in the context of post-war Italian society.

Sumption, Jonathan, *Pilgrimage: An Image of Medieval Religion* (Faber and Faber, 1975). A scholarly and entertaining history of Christian pilgrimages. Probably the best work on the subject.

Turner, Victor, and Turner, Edith L. B., *Image and Pilgrimage in Christian Culture* (Columbia University Press, 1995). Theological concepts and popular beliefs in a history of the idea of Christian pilgrimage.

Further Reading

Ugolino and Heywood, W. (eds.), *The Little Flowers of St Francis of Assisi* (Vintage Spiritual Classics, Vintage Books, 1998) . The classic medieval account of the life of St Francis and his earliest disciples.

CADOGAN

'Humorous, informed...
irresistible'

Italy

Rome, Naples
& Sorrento

Venice, Padua
& Verona

the Italy series

Main page references are in **bold**. Page references to maps are in *italic*

Index

Also Available from Cadogan Guides...